AutoCAD

for Mechanical Engineers
and Designers

AutoCAD

for Mechanical Engineers and Designers

Pete Karaiskos

Nancy Fulton

WILEY

John Wiley & Sons, Inc.

New York ▲ Chichester ▲ Brisbane ▲ Toronto ▲ Singapore

Publisher: Katherine Schowalter
Editor: Tim Ryan
Managing Editor: Micheline Frederick
Text Design & Composition: Impressions, a division of Edwards Brothers, Inc.
Developmental Editor: Nancy Fulton

Library of Congress Cataloging-in-Publication Data:
Karaiskos, Peter, 1952–
    AutoCAD for mechanical engineers and designers / Peter Karaiskos.
    Nancy Fulton.
        p.   cm.
    Includes index.
    ISBN 0-471-01779-5 (paper : acid-free paper)
    1. Engineering design.   2. AutoCAD (Computer file)   I. Fulton,
    Nancy.   II. Title.
    TA174.K375   1995
    620'.0042'02855369—dc20   95-16528
                                                                 CIP

Printed in the United States of America
10 9 8 7 6 5 4 3 2 1

To my parents, Emanuel and Mary,
to my wife Angela, and my children, Nicholas, Christopher, and Alicia.

To my uncle Jim Mills, who builds plances and boats in his garage,
and to my aunt Sue Mills who decorates his spectacular sculpture garden
of mechanical excellence with wild flowers and exotic insects.

About the Authors

Pete Karaiskos is the owner of PK & Company, an independent AutoCAD design, consulting, and software development firm in Newbury Park, California. Pete has been working with AutoCAD for ten years. As a mechanical and electro-mechanical designer with over 25 years of experience, Pete has worked in many disciplines on all types of drawings and has shared his experiences in several published articles about using and customizing AutoCAD.

Nancy Fulton is a co-founder of OpenCAD International, Inc. Nancy has written eight books and over thirty articles about AutoCAD, 3D Studio, and multi-platform CAD networking in the last three years. She is an Education Training Specialist for Autodesk Incorporate, creating courseware and providing instruction and demonstration support of 3D Studio, AutoSURF, and Designer. She currently teaches courses in 3D Studio and AutoCAD for the UCLA Department of Entertainment and Performing Arts. She can be reached at Nancy.Fulton@opencad.cam and you can see her home pages on the World Wide Web on www.opencad.com.

Contents

Introduction

Designers and mechanical engineers use AutoCAD to design and document everything from differential gears to telecommunications satellites. But if you use AutoCAD in a mechanical application, you know how hard it is to find a book that addresses your special needs.

If you are a mechanical engineer or draftsman who plans to use AutoCAD to create mechanical drawings, you need to know how to use AutoCAD commands to construct views of your part. You want to know how to dimension objects, how to create and use layers, and how to keep your file sizes small so drawings don't become unwieldy and difficult to manipulate.

If you are a mechanical designer, you need to know how to construct three-dimensional models using standard AutoCAD commands. You want to know how you can display multiple views of a model on a single plotted page, and how you can independently scale those views. You should also become familiar with Autodesk's new three-dimensional design applications, Designer and AutoSurf. These applications let you construct parametric solid and surface models of your parts, and dramatically reduce the time it takes to bring a part into production.

If you are a CAD manager, you need to know how layering standards, prototype drawings, and custom menus can increase productivity. You want to find out about networking and design to production work groups. You should learn how to configure AutoCAD to work in a networked environment, and how AutoCAD's new licensing policies affect you. You can make AutoCAD a better investment for your company if you know how to select an AutoCAD dealer, how to find third-party applications that meet your needs, and how you can use CAD management applications to make your users more efficient while protecting your drawings against accidental or intentional destruction.

If you use AutoCAD in a mechanical environment, this book is for you.

What You Will Find in This Book

AutoCAD for Mechanical Engineers and Designers features up-to-date information about AutoCAD Release 13 and associated applications, and demonstrates how to use new and old commands to achieve design and production objectives. Chapters 1 through 5 contain a comprehensive introduction to AutoCAD in a mechanical environment. You learn how to control AutoCAD via the mouse, keyboard, pull-down and screen menus, and through the set variables. You learn how and when to create layers, construct prototype drawings, and build symbol libraries. You master AutoCAD's three-dimensional drawing commands and learn how creating three-dimensional models can be easier than drawing a series of two-dimensional views of a part.

Chapters 6 and 7 introduce two Autodesk products designed specifically for mechanical users, Designer and AutoSurf. You learn to create parameter-driven mechanical solid models, and sophisticated NURBs-based surfaces that can be used to generate numerical control code.

Chapters 8, 9, and 10 teach you how to manage AutoCAD in a production environment. These chapters demonstrate customization alternatives, review networking standards, brief you on new Autodesk licensing agreements, and give you tips for selecting dealers, trainers, and consultants.

How to Use This Book

This book is designed for use as a hands-on reference manual. Unlike many books that focus on AutoCAD commands and their options, this book concentrates on the work you do using AutoCAD. You learn AutoCAD in the context of a mechanical environment, and you see AutoCAD commands used to achieve practical objectives.

As you read this book, you will find industry-specific tips and tricks, learn about pitfalls you should avoid, and receive step-by-step instructions for procedures you should follow when constructing AutoCAD drawings.

Read this book from cover to cover if you are new to AutoCAD, need a comprehensive introduction to the new Release 13 commands, or just want to make AutoCAD more productive in your environment. You can also use this book as a reference manual. Use the Index or Contents to locate procedures when you need specific advice to help you solve a problem. Refer to the sections on AutoSurf and Designer when you need to purchase new design tools. Turn to the sections on customization, networking, and management when your network seems to be slowing things down, or productivity is falling off.

AutoCAD

for Mechanical Engineers and Designers

CHAPTER 1

AutoCAD for Mechanical Drafting and Design

Exploring AutoCAD's Mechanical Capabilities

AutoCAD has many features that distinguish it from other CAD systems or other methods of generating mechanical working drawings, and before you start drawing, it is important to know and understand its mechanical capabilities and limitations. In this chapter, you will learn about achieving accuracy in CAD and about the tools for creating accurate drawings. You will get a tour of the AutoCAD drawing editor and the menu areas. You will issue commands, control the system settings, and learn how scale applies to CAD drawings. Finally, you will discover how to separate and control the various elements of your drawings by using *layers* and *linetypes*.

AutoCAD's Design

What most distinguishes AutoCAD from other CAD systems has to do with its design. AutoCAD has an *open architecture,* which means that you have access to almost every aspect of AutoCAD, from the appearance of the screen to the commands themselves.

As you learn to use AutoCAD, your first level of control will be the *system variables*, which you can think of as storage areas for the current settings of the system. By changing the value of a system variable, you are changing the current setting for a particular feature. You can specify an arrowhead or a tick mark or your own symbol at the end of a leader line. You can control the interval for automatic saves of your drawing. You can even tell the system to prevent you from drawing "off the paper." And system variables (there are over 250 in AutoCAD Release 13) represent only the simplest level of control.

The next level of control is the menu system. The menus are available for you to customize; in fact, you should customize the menus for productivity. The menus, as well as many other features in AutoCAD, are accessed through a simple text editor such as the DOS editor. You may discover that you are repeating the same tasks frequently, and it is a fairly simple process to automate repetitive tasks. You could, for example, create a menu selection that displays your company's drawing formats. You might choose a D-Size format from the menu and automatically insert the format into the drawing, at the scale that you specify. It could automatically display a window, called a *dialog box*, in which the information for the title block could be entered.

With a little programming, you can create custom dialog boxes, which are a good way to display hardware or symbol libraries. You could develop a dialog box that shows welding symbols as icons. Then adding a symbol to your drawing would be as easy as pointing to the symbol.

AutoCAD has several internal programming languages, including Script, AutoLISP, and DIESEL. You may also integrate programs written in languages such as C++, Visual C++, and even BASIC. Because it is relatively easy to develop custom programs, there are literally thousands of programs and routines available for AutoCAD.

Indeed, AutoCAD's open architecture has been the key to its success. It is why AutoCAD is used for all types of drawings, from mechanical design to printed circuit boards, schematic capture to architecture, clothing design to mapping.

The Concept of Accuracy

Accuracy is another significant feature of AutoCAD. It provides many ways to control accuracy and precision. One way is by locating points accurately. When you work in two dimensions, points are expressed as X and Y values based on the Cartesian coordinate system. You can use the keyboard to specify the exact point 3.125,1.875, which translates to 3.125 units along the X axis and 1.875 units along the Y axis. For three-dimensional drawings, three sets of coordinates describe a point. The distance along the Z axis is represented by the third coordinate value. Distances are measured in units which can represent inches, millimeters, miles, or any other linear unit of measurement.

Entering Points

In addition to typing Cartesian coordinates, you may also specify the point by selecting it on the screen. But since AutoCAD calculates each point to 14 significant digits, it is impossible to select a point from the screen accurately. Without tools, you cannot be sure if you selected the point 3.125,1.875 or 3.124998237752,1.875178023764. Fortunately, AutoCAD has many tools that can help you select points on the screen while maintaining accuracy.

You can also supply fractional input. You can express the point 3.125,1.875 as 3-1/8,1-7/8, which translates to 3-1/8 units along the X axis and 1-7/8 units along the Y axis. For architectural units, points are expressed as feet and inches. Fractional input represents fractions of an inch.

The coordinate display also helps you control accuracy. It identifies the X and Y coordinates of the cursor when it is in the graphics area, and can display any number of decimal places up to eight.

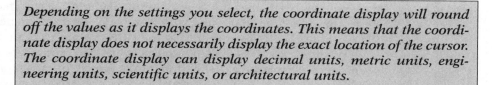

Depending on the settings you select, the coordinate display will round off the values as it displays the coordinates. This means that the coordinate display does not necessarily display the exact location of the cursor. The coordinate display can display decimal units, metric units, engineering units, scientific units, or architectural units.

Keeping It All Straight

Ortho is a tool that makes sure that points you select align with the crosshairs of the cursor. In two-dimensional drafting, that often means perfectly vertical or horizontal. If you don't see the word Ortho on the status line, Ortho mode is off. To turn it on, press the key marked **F8**. The word Ortho should now be visible in the status line. Press **F8** again and it disappears. This is an example of a *toggle*. Toggles turn features or settings on and off.

There are many other tools in AutoCAD to help you draw objects accurately by identifying exact points on the screen or exact points on the objects themselves. Chapter 2 identifies these tools and discusses them in detail.

Snapping to Points

Snap is a tool that allows you to pick points accurately from the graphics screen. It makes sure that points selected on the screen attach to the nearest defined snap increment. Snap also helps you place graphic elements at specified locations without having to type in the exact coordinates of those locations. The toggle key for Snap is F9; the command options are detailed in Chapter 2.

The AutoCAD Environment

The AutoCAD environment consists of many elements working together. Some of these elements are visible as you look at the screen; many more are not immediately apparent, therefore, learning the layout of the screen will help you become comfortable in the drawing editor.

A Tour of the AutoCAD Screen

The way to start exploring the environment is by beginning a drawing. In DOS, AutoCAD starts with a *batch* file. A batch file runs many DOS commands in succession that set up your computer system for AutoCAD. The batch file tells AutoCAD where to look for certain files, sets aside memory, and often loads specific drivers for hardware and software devices that are used with AutoCAD. The batch file may have any name, but DOS restricts file names to eight characters with a three-character extension. Remember this restriction when you begin naming your files. If you don't know the name of the batch file that begins AutoCAD, refer to the Installation and Performance Guide that came with AutoCAD. Type the name of the batch file (without the .BAT extension) at the DOS prompt to begin AutoCAD.

When AutoCAD is loaded and ready, the cursor appears and the word Command is displayed at the bottom of the screen, or on a separate monitor for dual-monitor systems. This is called the Command prompt because, like the DOS C:> prompt, it expects a command. The Command prompt will also prompt you to select the options of a command or the location of a point.

Drawings contain far more than just graphical information, but because the drawings we see are graphic, it is easy to forget there is much more in a drawing file. Think of drawing files as places where information is stored. Before graphics are placed on a new drawing, each drawing file contains all of the system settings for the drawing, and references to many drawing elements. When AutoCAD begins, it loads a blank prototype drawing which may have settings and other information predefined. For now, begin a new drawing without a prototype to set AutoCAD up with the default settings.

To begin a new drawing without a prototype:

1. From the File menu, choose **New.**
2. Select **No Prototype** to indicate that you don't want to use another drawing as a template for the new drawing. An X appears in the checkbox when it is selected.
3. Select **OK** to exit the Create New Drawing dialog box.

This is a good opportunity to look at the layout of the AutoCAD screen (Figure 1.1).

Save a blank drawing with all your favorite settings as a template or prototype *drawing. A typical engineering firm may have many prototype
drawings. Because AutoCAD gives you complete control over your system, there are many settings and system variables to master. Each time
AutoCAD loads, it opens either an existing drawing or a new drawing.
When a new drawing is loaded, AutoCAD uses a prototype drawing as
the template for the new drawing. When No Prototype is selected, Auto-
CAD uses the default settings.*

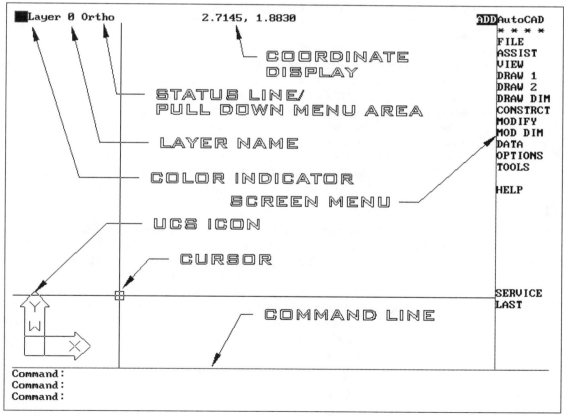

Figure 1.1 The AutoCAD screen.

The Status Line

At the top of the screen is the *status line*. It consists of two parts, the status display and the coordinate display. At the leftmost part of the status line is the color indicator. This is often a small square that indicates the current drawing color although some graphics cards don't use a square; instead, they display the layer name in the current drawing color. As you learn about layers and colors, you will discover that layer colors and object colors are not necessarily related.

Moving from left to right along the status line, next is the Layer, followed by the name of the current layer. (Layers are described in detail at the end of this chapter.) After the layer name are two indicators that display the current conditions or status of the Snap and Ortho tools.

To the right of the status display is the coordinate display, which normally reports the position of the cursor, depending on your settings. You can set it to display only the last cursor selection point or relative distances and polar coordinates during certain activities.

Move the cursor using your pointing device. If the coordinates don't seem to change, press the **F6** key to toggle the coordinate display mode. The command line should read <COORDS ON>. If the coordinate display still doesn't change, issue the command COORDS by typing it at the Command prompt. In AutoCAD, default values and current settings are enclosed by carets (<>). If the default value is 0, enter 1 to display the position of the cursor only; enter 2 to display the cursor position as well as relative and polar distances during commands that require distance input. If you entered a value of 1 or 2, the coordinate display should change as you move your cursor. For mechanical drawings, it is helpful to see relative linear distances and polar direction for linear commands. Set COORDS to a value of 2 to enable this feature.

The Pull-Down Menu Area

On some CAD systems, placing your cursor on the status line reveals the pull-down menu area. On other systems, the pull-down menu area is directly below the status line. If you don't see the pull-down menus on your screen, move your cursor up to the status line to display them.

The pull-down menus permit access to many of the most frequently used commands (Figure 1.2). Pull-down menus logically group commands. Use them to help you identify a command when you don't know the actual name of the command. Note that the labels on the pull-down submenus are not necessarily the name of the command they issue.

The pull-down menus and their primary functions are:

File   File utilities for beginning, opening, saving, and printing drawings. Also external references, importing, exporting, and file management.

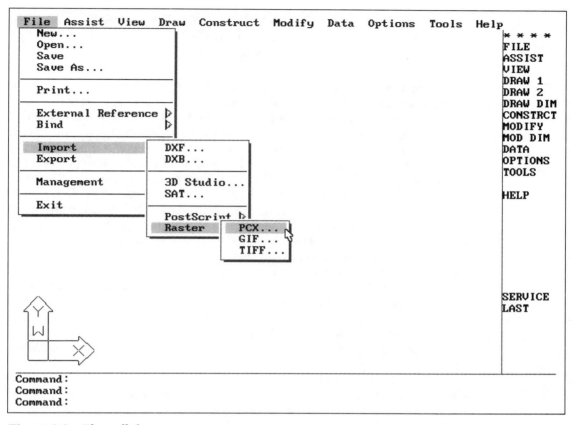

Figure 1.2 The pull-down menus.

Assist	Commands that assist in selecting or manipulating objects or groups of objects, point filters, Undo/Redo, Snap, Grid, and Ortho toggles.
View	Commands that control the display and coordinate system.
Draw	Drawing primitives for creating new objects, lines, circles, arcs, rectangles.
Construct	Commands for constructing objects from existing objects—copy, fillet, chamfer, array.
Modify	Tools for editing objects—move, erase, stretch.
Data	Commands that access the properties of objects—colors, layers, linetypes, units, text styles.

Options   Drawing aids—grips, running object snaps, UCS icon.

Tools   Commands that run external applications and utilities.

Help   Access to on-line help.

Select the File pull-down menu (Figure 1.3). The first command, New, is one that you have already used. There is an ellipsis (. . .) after the word New. When you selected this option, a dialog box appeared in the middle of the screen, and you entered some information before beginning a new drawing. In the pull-down menus, an ellipsis following a command means that a dialog box will appear. In the File pull-down menu, a dialog box appears when you select the New, Open, or Save As commands.

Some selections have an arrow (>) after them. Select the word Import, and a menu *cascades* down from the word Import. Next, select the word PostScript. Another menu appears. The arrow means that a cascading menu is available with further options or command selections.

When you select a command from the pull-down menus, AutoCAD remembers your last selection. For example, if you last selected File Import PostScript Display, the next time you choose the File menu, all the cascading menus appear and the Import PostScript Display selection highlights. To repeat the previous selection, select the File menu heading a second time without traversing the cascading menus. To cancel a pull-down menu, select anywhere outside the menu or press the **Esc** key or the key combination **Ctrl-C.**

There is one special pull-down menu in addition to the ones listed above. It is the *cursor menu*. One of the mouse buttons normally activates the cursor menu. The cursor menu displays at the location of the cursor and normally lists special command modifiers for selecting points on objects. These command modifiers are discussed in Chapter 2.

The Dialog Boxes

Many commands or menu selections display dialog boxes which organize information graphically. Some are little more than menus, while others make it easy to scan through lists and change the settings of the items on the list. Still others, such as the 3D Objects dialog box, display graphic icons that depict the possible selections. Some dialog boxes even work dynamically to display the results of the selections immediately. The Dimension Control dialog box is an example of this type of dialog box (Figure 1.4).

Use dialog boxes to change settings, retrieve drawings, issue commands, or display other dialog boxes. Use your pointing device to navigate the dialog boxes. Or, if you prefer, you can use the Tab key to move between the various options or an Alt-key combination to move directly to the option you need. Each option title has an underlined letter. To select with the Alt-key combination, press and hold down the key marked **Alt** and type the

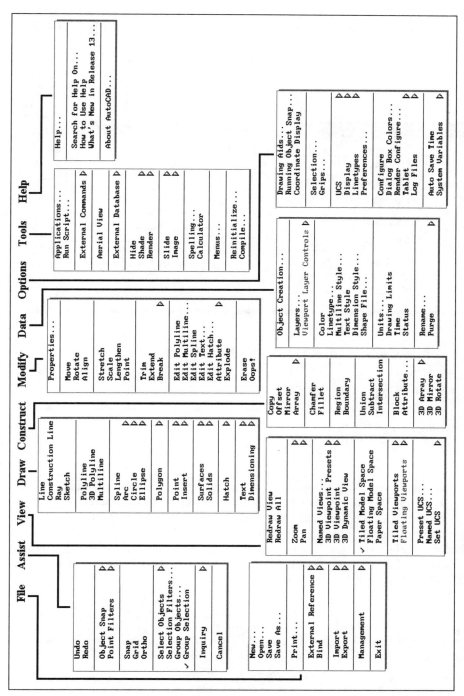

Figure 1.3 How the pull-down menus are organized.

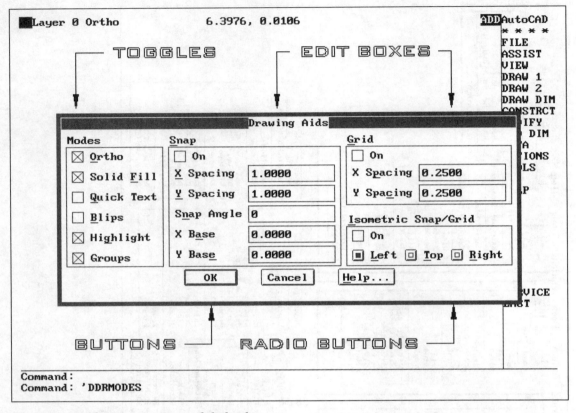

Figure 1.4   The Drawing Control dialog box.

underlined letter. You may cancel a dialog box by selecting **Cancel** or **OK**, by pressing the **Esc** key or by issuing the key combination **Ctrl-C.**

Chapter 7, "Customizing AutoCAD," introduces techniques for customizing menus and for creating command macros. Imagine a pull-down menu that has selections for hardware or symbols. You could choose a 1/4-20 socket-head cap screw from a menu and have that screw placed directly on your drawing at the location you specify.

> *Type the names of the dialog boxes directly from the command line. As you select from the screen and pull-down menus, keep an eye on the command line to see the actual command names. Try typing DDR-MODES at the command prompt.*

Dialog box tools have special names. A *button* performs a specific action. Most dialog boxes have buttons labeled OK, Cancel, or Help; still others may open other dialog boxes or issue commands.

A different kind of button, a *radio button,* selects one choice while deselecting another, similar to the buttons on car radios. In the Drawing Aids dialog box, radio buttons switch between the different isometric cursor modes.

Toggles, as noted earlier, turn features on or off. The No Prototype selection on the Create New Drawing dialog box is a good example of a toggle. An X in a toggle means it is ON.

Edit boxes accept specific input, such as number values, point locations, file names, and text strings. To change the information in an edit box, select anywhere in the edit box and use the arrow, Backspace, and Delete keys to change the value.

Dialog boxes can display an image, such as a hatch pattern or text font. An *image button* displays an image. Select anywhere within the image area of the image button to select the image. Dialog boxes sometimes request input from the graphic screen area. For example, to plot a specific area of a drawing, the area must be identified. One way to identify the area is by selecting a window that represents the area to plot. Choices that require point selections from the screen are identified by an arrow (<).

A *list box* displays a list of choices. When you select an item from the list, the item displays in an edit box. To accept the selected item, choose **OK.** Another way to select an item from a list is by selecting the item twice in rapid succession. This is known as *double-clicking.* Scroll bars, to the right of the list box, are used to move through the list. You can *drag* the *elevator* in the scroll bar by selecting and moving it while holding down your mouse button. Select the boxes at the top and bottom of the scroll bar to go through the list, one item at a time.

Another type of list box is a *pop-up list,* which looks like an edit box but has an arrow, pointing downward, to the right of the text. Selecting the arrow displays a list of choice options.

Using File Dialog Boxes

AutoCAD displays a dialog box whenever it needs a file name (Figure 1.5). Depending on the command, certain files display in the dialog box. For example, the OPEN command opens an existing drawing; therefore, the file list dialog box only contains the names of drawing files. Other commands list other types of files. Navigating through file listings, for this and other dialog boxes, can be a little tricky at first, especially if you are unfamiliar with **DOS** directory structures. At the top of all file list dialog boxes is the title of the dialog box. Below that is the word Pattern and an edit box. The pattern is equivalent to the DOS command that would display that particular file type. In DOS, the asterisk (*) or star represents a wild card, which

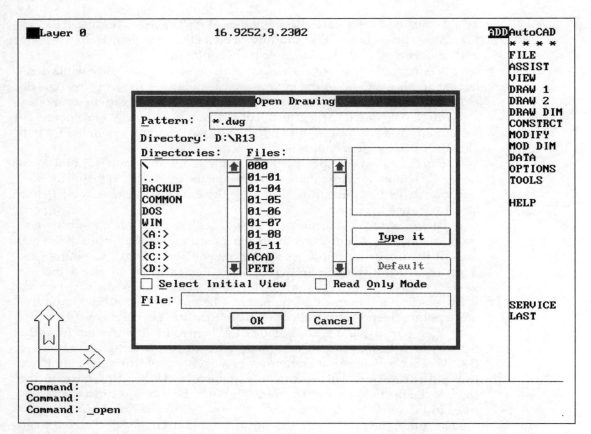

Figure 1.5 File Selection dialog box.

means that any number of characters can replace the star and any number of available character positions after the star. For the OPEN command, the pattern is *.DWG which lists all the files with a .DWG extension. The Pattern portion of the file listing dialog box may contain several patterns. To see only the AutoLISP programs, edit the pattern to specify *.LSP.

Below Pattern: is the word Directory, followed by the name of the current directory. Below that is the word Directories and a list box. At the top of the list box is a backslash (\) character. Selecting the backslash displays the root directory of the currently logged drive. Below the backslash character is a double dot (..) which, if selected, displays the parent directory (the directory that contains the current directory).

Below the list of files, if any, are the other drives that are available on your system. Your system may list drives <A:>, <B:>, <C:>, and so on. Selecting one of the drives changes directories to the currently logged directory on that drive. If your list of directories extends beyond what is displayed in the list box, use the scroll bar at the right of the list box to move through the list.

To the right of the Directories list box is the Files list box. This box displays any files that fit the pattern in the current directory. To choose a file, select it with your cursor so that it displays in the File edit box at the bottom of the dialog box. To finish the selection and close the File listing dialog box, select OK; or you can save a step by double-clicking on the file name.

The Command Line and Text Screen

The command line is at the bottom of your screen. This area normally displays up to three lines of text. On dual-monitor systems, the command line displays on a separate monitor. As you type in commands, they display on the command line so you can check your typing before issuing the command. The command line prompts you for information that you must supply or displays the options for the commands you issue.

The command line area is really only the last few lines of a much bigger screen called the text screen. The text screen automatically displays during certain commands. Commands that generate lists of information switch the display from the graphics screen to the text screen. Press the **F1** key to switch between the graphics screen and the text screen. Some versions of AutoCAD include a scroll bar on the text screen.

Before you can issue a command at the command line, you need to know its name. You can issue valid AutoCAD commands, system variable names, command aliases, or commands that have been loaded with an application. The command line displays the prompt Command: when it is ready to accept a command.

You cannot issue a command at the command line while a dialog box is open. You may cancel a command by selecting Cancel from the pulldown menus or by issuing the **Ctrl-C** key combination. If you mistype a command, you can use the Backspace and Delete keys to correct the error before pressing **Enter.**

To issue the LINE command at the Command prompt:

1. Press the **Ctrl-C** key combination to clear any previous commands.
2. Type **LINE** and press **Enter.** Commands and options are issued only when the Enter key is pressed.
3. Select the start point of the line.
4. Select the end point of the line.
5. Press the **Enter** key or the **Ctrl-C** key combination to terminate the line and the LINE command.

Certain keys, when pressed at a blank Command prompt, repeat the last command. The Enter key on the keyboard and on the keypad, the

Tab key and the Spacebar each repeat the last command. Additionally, one of the pointing device buttons normally reissues the last command.

▶ *When you know the name of the command you want to issue, type it at the Command prompt instead of selecting it from the menus. Typing commands is usually faster, especially if you know the options for the command in advance. Most advanced AutoCAD users avoid the menus and either type in the commands, use command aliases or macros, or select commands from the tablet. For instance, type SNAP at the Command prompt when you only need to change the snap increment. This is usually faster than opening the Drawing Aids dialog box. Remember, F9 or Ctrl-B toggles Snap on or off.*

To issue the SNAP command and see how the command line works:

1. Type **SNAP.** The following prompt is typical of the way AutoCAD displays command options:

    ```
    Snap spacing or ON/OFF/Aspect/Rotation/Style/<current setting>:
    ```

    The default value for any command, in this case SNAP, appears between the carets <>. To accept the default value for the Snap spacing, press **Enter.** To set a different value, enter the value.

2. To issue one of the other options, type in only the letter(s) that are capitalized. For example, to change the snap rotation, type **R.**

    The words ON and OFF are capitalized. Since they both begin with the letter O, typing O is ambiguous. Type enough characters to distinguish one response from the other. In this case, OF is enough to select off, but the whole word is capitalized for the sake of appearance.

    The Aspect option lets you set independent settings for X and Y spacing.

    The SNAP command, when issued from the command line does not have the X and Y origin options. Control this setting with the system variable SNAPBASE.

    The SNAP command has a Style option for Standard or Isometric. This is the equivalent of the Isometric Snap/Grid buttons on the Drawing Aids dialog box. Isometric snap is essential in isometric drawing.

3. Enter 0.125 to set the snap spacing.

NOTE   Certain commands may be issued *transparently*, while another command is active. In a previous example, you drew a line between two points. You selected the first point on the screen. But what would you do if the end point of the line were somewhere outside the screen area? By issuing a transparent ZOOM or PAN command you can change the display without interrupting the LINE command.

Transparent commands are preceded by an apostrophe ('). Use an apostrophe only if the command must be used transparently. For example, issue the command PAN without the apostrophe to adjust the display. Issue the 'PAN command with the apostrophe to adjust the display *while another command is active*.

You can display many dialog boxes transparently. To change the snap increment during the LINE command, issue the command 'DDRMODES to transparently display the dialog box for the snap increment.

The Screen Menu

The screen menu is AutoCAD's oldest user interface (Figure 1.6), but it is certainly not outdated. There are several special selections on the screen menu. At the top is the word AutoCAD, which you may choose at any time to go from a submenu to the main or *root* menu. Below the word AutoCAD are four stars (* * * *). Selecting the stars displays the Object Snap options menu. The word AutoCAD and the four stars remain available regardless of which menu displays in the screen menu area.

Another special selection on the screen menu is SERVICE. This selection displays the options for selecting objects and provides access to several dialog boxes. Below this selection is the word LAST. When selected, LAST displays the screen menu that appeared before the current screen menu. On high-resolution displays, the bottom of the screen menu displays the object snap modifiers for easy access.

The HELP menu item displays the on-line help dialog box that provides context-sensitive help for most commands and topics. Select this whenever you need clarification of a particular command or command option.

The screen menu does many things faithfully and efficiently. When you issue a command, it identifies the command and displays a menu with the options for that command. When you issued the LINE command earlier, the screen menu identified it and switched to the LINE options menu automatically.

The screen menu also intercepts the keystrokes as you are typing and tries to anticipate which command, on the current menu, you are preparing to issue. A *macro* is a keystroke or combination of keystrokes that represent

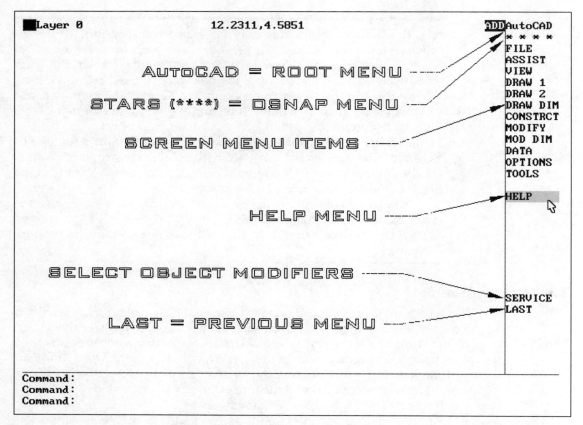

Figure 1.6 The screen menu area.

a command (or multiple commands) with fewer keystrokes than the command itself.

To demonstrate the screen menu macro feature:

1. From the top of the screen menu, choose AutoCAD to display the root menu.
2. Type the letter **D.** The word DRAW highlights.
3. Press the **Insert** key to display the DRAW menu.

Unfortunately, since several menu items may begin with the same letters, it is often easier to use the pointing device to select commands. For example, to distinguish the DRAW menu from the DRAW2 menu, you must type in the entire menu item name DRAW2. To display the DATA menu, you only have to type **DA** and press **Insert**.

> *To cut down on keystrokes, rename menu items so each has a unique first character. In Chapter 7, you learn how to modify the menus. A single keystroke and a press of the Insert key can open a menu or launch a command.*

You may access the screen menu area directly, without using the mouse, by pressing the **Insert** key. When you press the **Insert** key, the cursor disappears and a highlight bar appears on the screen menu. To make a selection in this way, use the cursor (arrow) keys to move the highlight bar to the item you want to select and press either **Insert** or **Enter.**

The Graphics Area

Your drawing displays in the graphics area. At the lower left corner of the graphics area is the User Coordinate System (UCS) icon (two wide arrows forming a right angle). The UCS icon shows the X and Y directions for the current coordinate system. The W indicates that the current coordinate system is the World Coordinate System (WCS). This means that a point represents 0,0 (expressed as X and Y coordinates respectively), and all points on the graphics screen are measured from that point. Later, you will learn how to set up and use your own coordinate system(s) using the UCS command.

The Concept of Scale

In AutoCAD scaling occurs at the plotter. Physical objects or parts are drawn at full scale. This makes it easy to combine parts from different drawings without having to scale the individual parts. Of course, not everything represented on a drawing is a physical object. Drawing elements like text, dimensions, and symbols are scaled according to the size of drawing.

How Scale Affects the Drawing

The rules for determining the scale of objects are:

- If it is physical, like a battleship, bolt, or building site, draw it at full scale (1:1).
- If it is not physical, text, dimensions, symbols, tables, title blocks, or other annotations, scale it according to the drawing scale.

With a few exceptions, these two rules cover all CAD drawings. As you develop drawings of parts, draw at full scale. It doesn't matter if you are drawing a paper clip or a battleship; draw anything that has a dimension at full scale. You may be wondering how you are going to plot a full-sized drawing of a bat-

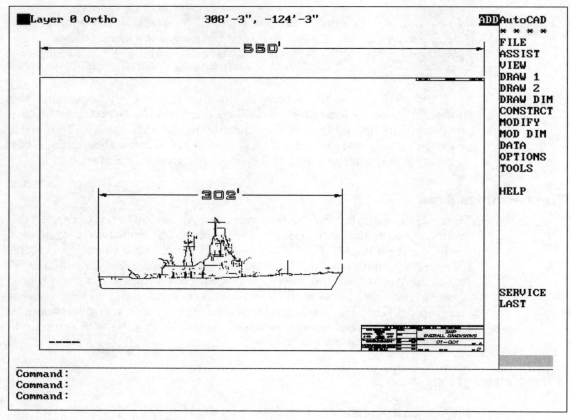

Figure 1.7 Plotting to scale.

tleship. Scaling occurs at the plotter. If the battleship is plotted on a D-size sheet of paper, the D-size sheet is scaled up to fit around the battleship (exactly the opposite of pencil drafting). At the plotter, you indicate the appropriate scale so the battleship and the D-size sheet will fit properly on the paper (Figure 1.7).

AutoCAD also has a feature called *Paper Space* which works more like pencil drafting. In paper space, the paper is represented at full scale. Although physical parts are also drawn at full scale, they are scaled as they are placed on the "paper" and the drawing is plotted at full scale.

Detailing at Different Scales

Details often have a different scale than the main drawing. To create a detail that is 4 × scale, relative to the main drawing, copy the detail area from the main drawing and use the scale command to increase its size by four times.

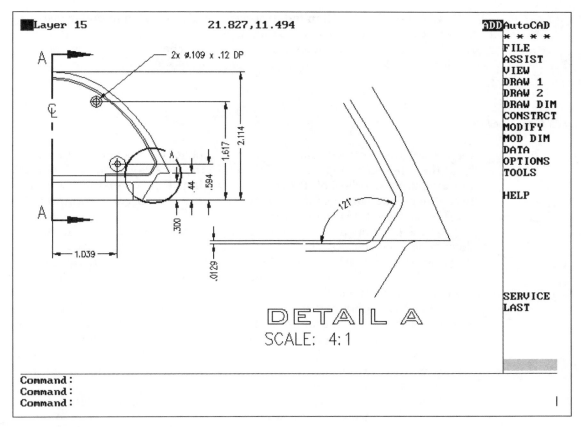

Figure 1.8   Scaling details.

All AutoCAD entities respond to the SCALE command. There is even a system variable for dimensioning scaled objects, so manual conversion of dimensions is unnecessary (Figure 1.8).

Scaling Drawings for Metric Units

Earlier in this chapter, you learned that the calculation of distances uses units that may or may not necessarily represent inches. When you develop metric drawings, you may decide that one unit represents one millimeter or one centimeter or one kilometer. To use metric units, adjust system variables to accommodate the metric unit you choose, then draw at full scale. If, however, you are going to combine parts created in millimeters with parts created in inches, you will have to scale the parts as you combine them.

Use the SCALE command to convert objects created in one measuring system to another measuring system. For example, to convert an object drawn in inches to millimeters, scale it by 25.4. Then, the object can be used on drawings that use millimeters as their unit of measurement.

Using Layers

Layers are a way of separating similar elements or objects on a drawing from the other elements on the drawing. In the past, layers were compared to transparent overlays of drawing information. This comparison was very two-dimensional, and as three-dimensional drawings became common, the overlay analogy didn't really work.

Think of layers as a way of grouping objects in space. Any criteria can determine how the objects are grouped. Sometimes, layers separate one drawing revision from another. Some CAD drafters put an entire project in a single drawing file (not recommended) and reveal the individual drawings by manipulating the layers.

The most common use for layers is to separate and group the drawing elements for editing and plotting. Establish layers for annotation, dimensions, title blocks, object lines, construction lines, and so on. Individual layers can be visible or invisible, selectable or not selectable. Layers can be plotted or only used for construction lines. A drawing may contain only one layer, or it may contain hundreds.

The first time you work on someone else's drawing, you will wish they organized their drawings the way you organize yours. Plotting someone else's drawing, for example, requires that you understand which layers represent object lines, dimensions, and construction lines. Only by understanding their layering system, can you assign the appropriate pen sizes to the elements of their drawing. Standardization is the key to a productive office. By developing and following layering standards, you and your colleagues will avoid potential headaches.

Why Use Layers?

The value of using layers to control a drawing becomes clear as complexity increases. A typical mechanical assembly may have several layers for each part in the assembly. Additionally, it will have separate layers for callouts, bill-of-materials, notes, and other information. Some layers may never make it to the final plotted drawing. Construction line layers, tool paths, vendor data, and other information are easily excluded from the plotted drawing while retained in the drawing file (Figure 1.9).

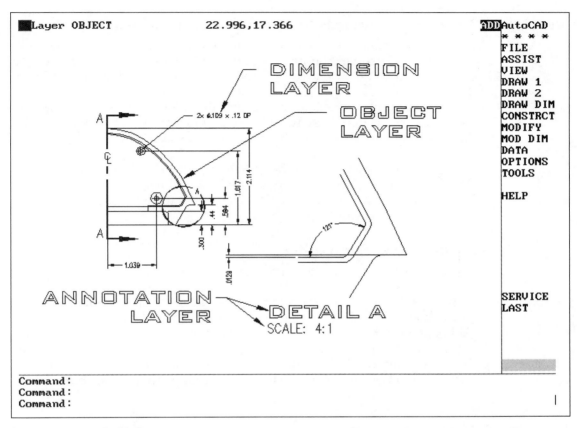

Figure 1.9 Utilizing layers.

Special Layers

AutoCAD creates several special layers. Layer 0, for example, is a special layer because it cannot be removed from the drawing. That is because Auto-CAD always requires a layer to work on. With each new release of Auto-CAD, special layers are introduced for AutoCAD's internal use. One such layer is DEFPOINTS. This layer captures the special point entities required for associative dimensioning. Layer DEFPOINTS does not plot.

Other layers that are internal to AutoCAD are added as AutoCAD needs them. For example, AutoCAD Designer creates, uses, and maintains information on a special layer that you should avoid thawing or using.

Developing Layering Standards for Mechanical Drawings

Layers may contain multiple colors and linetypes. They are versatile tools, but they can become a burden if not carefully managed. For this reason it is important to develop a conscientious method of establishing and controlling layers.

A mechanical drawing may require that plotted object lines use bold pen. Dimension lines may require a medium pen. Hatching may need a light pen. Layers can satisfy this criteria by associating a color (pen) with the objects on a particular layer.

A linetype is either specified by the object or controlled by the layer. Many CAD drafters create layers for the various linetypes. It is common to see drawings that have a HIDDEN layer, CENTER layer, and so on. Linetypes are discussed in Chapter 2.

Layer Names That Mean Something

Layers may have any name, but on most drawings, it is desirable to have the layer names describe the objects on the layer. For example, on a layer named DIM, you might expect to find dimensions. It is common to find layers on mechanical drawings that have names such as OBJ, TEXT, and DIM. Although layer names may be any length, there are reasonable limitations on how many characters are displayed in the status line and in the dialog boxes. The current limit for display is 16 characters. Keep in mind that you may have to type in the layer names from time to time. Short but descriptive names seem to work well.

Layering Schemes by Color

Many CAD drafters find it handy to associate a layer name with a particular color because the color of an entity determines which pen is used when the drawing plots. If you feel that you can easily identify the colors on the screen, you may want to explore this type of layering scheme. Although using this layering system doesn't give the layers descriptive names, it does give them meaningful names, at least during the drawing and drafting process. Learning the color numbers (at least the first eight), would make this type of layering scheme fairly easy to use. Table 1.1 shows one possible layering scheme based on color. Use it as a starting point for developing your own layering scheme based on color.

In the layering scheme in Table 1.1, it is possible to place object lines on layers that will plot using a bold, medium, or light pen. Obviously, all objects cannot be plotted with a bold pen (screw threads, for example). The unrestricted layers allow some flexibility on the part of the drafter.

Some drafters like to use certain colors for certain objects. Some colors are easier to see on the screen, so when you develop your layering

Table 1.1   Layering Scheme Based on Color

NAME	*COLOR*	*PEN*	*USAGE / RECOMMENDATIONS*
0	7 (White)	2-Medium	Construction (Not for final drawing)
1	1 (Red)	2-Medium	Unrestricted
2	2 (Yellow)	1-Light	Object Lines
3	3 (Green)	1-Light	Unrestricted
4	4 (Cyan)	3-Bold	Object Lines
5	5 (Blue)	3-Bold	Large text
6	6 (Magenta)	2-Medium	Notes, Text, Callouts, Annotation
7	7 (White)	2-Medium	Title block
8	8	1-Light	Unrestricted
9	9	1-Light	Unrestricted
10	10	3-Bold	Unrestricted
11	11	3-Bold	Section Lines, Breaks, Detail Bubbles
12	12	2-Medium	Object Lines
13	13	2-Medium	Unrestricted
14	14	1-Light	Hatching
15	15	1-Light	Dimensions and Dimension Text

scheme by color, take into consideration how the colors display on the screen. And, if your company shares drawings with others outside your company, consider their layering schemes.

The process of renaming the layers with more descriptive names, or names that adhere to the standards of the client is quite simple. If you develop a consistent layering system, the process of renaming layers can be automated.

Industry Standards

Although many people have tried to develop standards for mechanical disciplines, the engineering community has not embraced a definitive layering standard for mechanical drawings. This doesn't mean that layering standards are not important—imagine plotting drawings and getting different results each time.

Since there are no real industry standards in place, it is even more important to develop layering standards for your company. Should the industry ever adopt a standard that your company must adhere to, converting your existing drawings will be much easier if your drawings comply with some standard, even if it is only your own.

Because there are so many layering techniques, the best advice is just to decide on some reasonable layering scheme and stick to it. By knowing what layers to expect on your drawing, and what entities to expect on which layer, the process of layering and plotting is simplified. Remember, layers are tools that should simplify and clarify what you are doing.

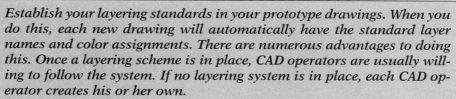

Establish your layering standards in your prototype drawings. When you do this, each new drawing will automatically have the standard layer names and color assignments. There are numerous advantages to doing this. Once a layering scheme is in place, CAD operators are usually willing to follow the system. If no layering system is in place, each CAD operator creates his or her own.

Custom menus and macros can become intuitive through the use of consistent layering. For example, selecting the dimensioning menu could automatically set the dimension layer before you begin dimensioning. This kind of automation not only enhances productivity, it improves overall drawing consistency. With a little customizing, you can simply draw and let the layers take care of themselves.

The importance of standardization becomes even more evident when you merge two drawings. If one of the drawings contains the layers OBJ, DIM, and TXT, and the other contains the layers OBJECT, DIMS, and TEXT, the new drawing will contain all six layers. Suddenly, anyone adding a dimension to the drawing must decide if the dimension belongs on layer DIM or on layer DIMS.

The LAYER Command

Access layers through the Layer Control dialog box by choosing Data Layers from the pull-down menus. Typing 'DDLMODES at the command line will also display the Layer Control dialog box. Additionally, you may issue the LAYER command (without the dialog box) at the command line.

The LAYER command has the following options:

SET	Sets the current layer.
NEW	Creates a new layer.
MAKE	Creates a new layer and makes it the current layer.
ON	Makes the layer visible.

OFF	Makes the layer invisible but includes it in the active object database.
FREEZE	Makes the layer invisible and excludes it from the active object database.
THAW	Unfreezes frozen layers.
LOCK	Prevents objects on the layer from being selected. Object snaps still work.
UNLOCK	Unlocks a locked layer.
COLOR	Establishes the color of the layer.
LTYPE	Establishes the linetype associated with the layer.
?	Lists all the layers on the drawing and their condition.

The Layer Control dialog box generally uses the same terminology as the LAYER command (Figure 1.10), although there are a few options that will be covered in later chapters.

To create a new layer:

1. From the Data pull-down menu, choose **Layers.**
2. Enter the new layer name in the edit box at the bottom of the dialog box. Layer names cannot contain spaces or periods. You can create multiple layers by separating the layer names with a comma.
3. Select **New** to make the layer name(s) appear in the layer list.
4. Select **OK** to close the layer control dialog box.

To define a layer's color:

1. From the Data pull-down menu, choose **Layers.**
2. Select the layer(s) from the layer list. AutoCAD will operate on any layers that are highlighted so multiple layers may be controlled at once.
3. Select **Set Color.**
4. Choose a color from the palette.
5. Select **OK** to close the Layer Control dialog box.

To define a layer's linetype:

1. From the Data pull-down menu, choose **Layers.**
2. Select the layer(s) from the layer list. AutoCAD will operate on any layers that are highlighted so multiple layers may be controlled at once.
3. Select **Set Ltype.**
4. Choose a color from the list.
5. Select **OK** to close the Layer Control dialog box.

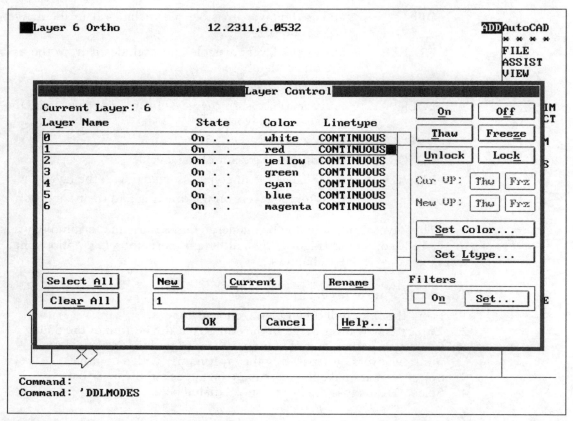

Figure 1.10 The Layer Control dialog box.

To make a layer current:

1. From the Data pull-down menu, choose **Layers.**
2. Select the layer from the layer list. Be sure it is the only layer highlighted. Only one layer may be current at a time.
3. Select **Current.**
4. Select **OK** to close the Layer Control dialog box.

To rename a layer:

1. From the Data pull-down menu, choose **Layers.**
2. Select the layer from the layer list. Be sure it is the only layer highlighted. Only one layer may be renamed at a time.
3. Type the new name in the edit box.
4. Select **Rename.**
5. Select **OK** to close the Layer Control dialog box.

> *You can choose **Select All** when selecting layers for some processes. This makes it easy to turn on all the layers at once or freeze all the layers except the current layer, which may not be frozen while it is current.*

Linetypes

In mechanical design and drafting, the proper use of linetypes is of significant importance. AutoCAD comes with many predefined standard linetypes and permits you to create custom linetypes.

Standard AutoCAD Linetypes

There are many standard linetypes, and the Continuous linetype is always available. Before you use a linetype, you must load it.

To load a standard linetype:

1. From the Data pull-down menu, choose **Linetype.**
2. Select **Load** from the Select Linetype dialog box.
3. Select the linetype to load, or choose Select All from the Load or Reload Linetypes dialog box.
4. Select **OK** to close the Load or Reload Linetypes dialog box.
5. Select **OK** to close the Select Linetype dialog box.

A linetype must be loaded before entities may use it. Before you can draw with a linetype, you must make the linetype current.

To make a linetype current:

1. From the Data pull-down menu, choose **Linetype.**
2. Select the linetype you want from the Select Linetype dialog box.
3. Select **OK** to close the Select Linetype dialog box.

Now, all new entities will use this linetype until you change it.

Linetypes can be BYLAYER. This means the linetype specification is in the layer definition. The LAYER command and the Layer Control dialog box allow you to specify a linetype for a particular layer. This is similar to setting the color for a layer. If you specify linetypes when you create your layers, then select BYLAYER for the current linetype.

Some linetypes are duplicated at different scales. The HIDDEN linetype, for example, also has HIDDEN2 (1/2 scale) and a HIDDENX2 (2 × scale) options. Linetype scaling can be global, based on the overall linetype scale factor. Linetypes can also receive their scaling information directly from the entity and independent of the overall linetype scale factor (Figure 1.11).

▶ *Develop a standard for layers, colors, and linetypes. It is easy to become confused when a drawing uses many different schemes. For example, you can define a color and a linetype for a layer. Additionally, an entity may have a color and a linetype independent of the layer settings. A drawing can have a red entity with a hidden line on a layer that is blue with a centerline linetype.*

If that isn't confusing enough, many plotters can define linetypes during plotting. Some color plotters also define colors independently of the drawing colors. So the Red/Hidden entity on the Blue/Centerline layer could plot as a green phantom line on the final plot. As with layers, a standard for creating, using, and plotting linetypes saves time and increases production.

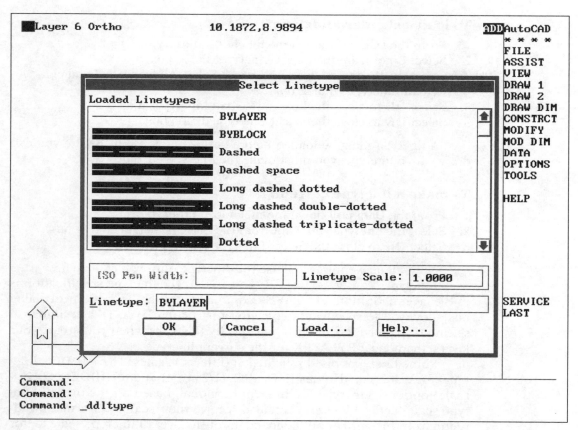

Figure 1.11   The Linetypes dialog box.

Scaling Linetypes

Linetype scaling is critical to mechanical drawings. Sometimes drawing specifications dictate the lengths of lines and dashes for a particular linetype. More often, linetype scaling has more to do with clarity and readability. A hidden line that shows a hidden surface may be too large, in scale, for the threads of a screw.

In AutoCAD release 13 linetypes scale globally or by the individual entity. Global linetype scaling is easy to set and adjust at plotting time.

To set the global scale factor for linetypes:

1. From the Data pull-down menu, choose **Linetype.**
2. Select the Linetype Scale edit box in the Select Linetype dialog box.
3. Enter the scale factor for all linetypes.
4. Select **OK** to close the Select Linetype dialog box.

To set the linetype scale for individual entities:

1. From the Modify pull-down menu, choose **Properties.**
2. Select the objects you want to change.
3. Select the Linetype Scale edit box in the Change Properties dialog box.
4. Enter the new linetype scale for those objects.
5. Select **OK** to close the Change Properties dialog box.

Creating Custom Linetypes

Many specialized types of drawings—patent drawings for example—require specific linetypes. Although there are many standard linetypes, you can create your own custom linetypes in AutoCAD. The basic rules for creating linetypes are:

- Specify lines with positive numbers indicating the length of the line.
- Specify spaces with negative numbers indicating the length of the space.
- Specify dots with a zero (0).

To create a custom linetype:

1. Issue the LINETYPE command at the Command prompt.
2. Type **C** for Create.
3. Enter the name of the linetype to create. Avoid using linetype names that are standard AutoCAD linetype names, although you can use variations of AutoCAD linetype names.

4. Enter a description of the linetype at the Descriptive text prompt. Linetype descriptions are normally combinations of dashes, dots, and spaces but you can use text descriptions such as threads or small dashes. The descriptive text is optional. If you don't want to supply descriptive text, press **Enter.**

5. Enter the linetype description for a single segment of the linetype. Use positive numbers for lines, negative numbers for spaces, and zeros for dots. Note that all AutoCAD linetype descriptions begin with the letter A followed by a comma. For example:

To define a centerline with a 2 unit line, a .5 unit space, a single dot and a .5 unit space, enter the following:

```
A,2,-.5,0,-.5
```

A linetype scale of 1.000 will generate the linetype using these values. A linetype scale of 0.5 will generate a 1 unit line, a .25 unit space, a single dot, and a .25 unit space centerline. Standard AutoCAD linetypes definitions are in the file ACAD.LIN, which is an ASCII (text) file that can edited with a text editor (in nondocument format) to include new linetypes.

Instead of changing the default linetype file, create your own linetypes and store them in their own .LIN file. Do this with a text editor or directly from within AutoCAD. The Load or Reload Linetypes dialog box includes a File selection option that allows you to recall and load your own linetypes easily.

Summary

AutoCAD is well suited for mechanical design and engineering. The design of the program and the user interface (environment) assists in and sometimes automates many aspects of the drawing process. AutoCAD's open architecture offers many options for command entry, settings, drawing, and editing styles, and even custom programming. Many tools for maintaining accuracy are available, including snap, ortho, and direct point entry.

AutoCAD's drawing editor places important information along the status bar at the top of the screen. Commands are issued from the pull-down menus, screen menus, or at the command line. Dialog boxes assist in grouping and displaying commands, command options, and system settings.

In AutoCAD, parts are drawn at full scale and are scaled to fit the paper at the time the drawing is plotted. Entities that are not parts are scaled based on the size of the drawing. AutoCAD works in units that make it relatively simple to generate drawings using different units of measurement.

Layers may be used to group and separate objects. AutoCAD can use and display an unlimited number of layers, which may be used to control visibility, selectability, or regeneration. Layers, colors, and linetypes can work together or independently. The use of layers and layering standards is critical in the productive use of AutoCAD.

Linetypes give you control over the appearance of your drawings. By independently scaling standard linetypes, or creating custom linetypes, you can display almost any type of line on your drawings.

Two-Dimensional Mechanical Drawings

With AutoCAD, you can generate *working* drawings, which in this sense, are two-dimensional representations of three-dimensional parts. In this chapter, you learn how to set up AutoCAD for two-dimensional drafting and how to use the commands for generating mechanical drawings in two dimensions.

> *As you set up your drawings, save your settings as a prototype drawing. For example, if you set up your system for a metric drawing, save the setup and recall it later as a prototype for any metric drawing.*

Setting Up AutoCAD for Mechanical Drawings

AutoCAD has no way of knowing in advance what type of drawing you are creating, and it's a good idea to take a few steps to set up the drawing before you begin to draw. As you learned in Chapter 1, AutoCAD has hundreds of settings that affect the way it works. Before you draw the first entity of the drawing, you should think about how to handle text height, dimensions, scaling, and units of measurement. Ask yourself: Will you represent distances in inches or millimeters or some other unit of measure? Will you plot the drawing at full scale or will you scale it at the plotter? What size should the text be on the final plot? What layers will you need?

Automating the Setup

Although you can manually define all the settings required for a particular drawing, the MVSETUP utility automates some of the process. MVSETUP.LSP is written in AutoLISP programming language which AutoCAD interprets internally. AutoLISP programs have the file extension .LSP and must be loaded before they are run.

To load MVSETUP:

1. From the Tools pull-down menu, choose **Applications.**
2. Select **MVSETUP** from the list box. If MVSETUP is not on the list, select **File.** Locate the file MVSETUP.LSP and select it. The MVSETUP.LSP file resides in the subdirectory COMMON\SUPPORT under your AutoCAD directory.
3. Select **Save List** if you want the MVSETUP.LSP application to appear in your Applications dialog box whenever it opens. Be sure an X appears in the Save List box.
4. Select **LOAD.**

When you specify the paper size, enter the true dimensions of the paper you are plotting on. If the paper actually measures 22 × 17, enter those numbers. MVSETUP multiplies the paper size times the scale factor. For example, if you are plotting your drawing at 1/2 scale, enter a value of 2 for the scale. MVSETUP sets up an area twice the size of the paper. When you plot the drawing at 1/2 scale, the drawing fits properly on the paper.

To begin the MVSETUP routine:

1. Issue the command MVSETUP.
2. Type **N** to use Model space. The text screen displays.
3. Type **D** to select Decimal at the prompt:

```
Units type (Scientific/Decimal/Engineering/Architectural/Metric):
```

4. Enter the scale you want to use. You don't have to pick from the scales offered but remember to use the inverse of the scale for the drawing. To use 10:1 scale, enter 0.1. To use 1/8:1 scale, enter 8.0.
5. Enter the width of the paper in inches.
6. Enter the height of the paper in inches.

AutoCAD switches back to the graphics screen and draws a rectangle representing the paper at the scale you have specified. If you specified 1/2 for the scale with a paper size of 22 x 17, the rectangle will measure 11 x 8.5.

Although MVSETUP sets the overall drawing size, you need to make a few more settings for a scaled drawing. If your drawing has dimensions, you need to set up the dimension scale.

Setting the Overall Dimension Scale

There are dozens of dimension variables or *dimvars* that affect dimensions. Chapter 3 describes the individual settings in detail and the use of dimension styles. Most dimension variables are adjusted to the scale of the drawing. Fortunately, you don't have to adjust each dimension variable. The dimensioning variable for controlling the scale factor for all dimension variables is DIMSCALE. For example, the dimensioning variable DIMEXO (EXtension line Offset) stores the size of the gap between the object and the extension line. At full scale (1:1), this value may be 1/16″. If the drawing scale is 4 ×, set of DIMSCALE factor is 4. On the drawing, the extension line offset measures 1/4″. When the drawing is plotted, the 1/4″ gap becomes 1/16″.

When the overall dimension scale is set, you should consider the size of the text for your drawing.

To set the DIMSCALE dimensioning variable:

1. Type **DIMSCALE** at the command prompt.
2. Set the Value. DIMSCALE values, like MVSETUP, are inverse of the drawing scale. For a 1/4 scale drawing, set DIMSCALE to 4.

Scaling Dimension Text

If the current text style uses a text height that is undefined, the dimensioning variable DIMTXT determines the height for dimension text created with that style. DIMSCALE affects the value of DIMTXT. The dimension text height will automatically be scaled to the drawing scale. If a text height is fixed, the value of the dimensioning variable, DIMTXT, does not affect the text height. Dimension text uses the value for the height that has been established in the text style.

In addition to dimension scaling, you have to determine scaling for other elements of the drawing. Text height is scaled according to the drawing scale.

Determining the Text Height

To maintain consistent text heights between drawings, scale text height based on the drawing scale.

To determine the height of the text for a scaled drawing:

1. Decide what height the text should be on the final plot.
2. Multiply the text height times the scale.

Example:
If the text on the final drawing should be 1/8″ high characters, and the drawing scale is 4:1, the text height is 1/8″ × 4 or 1/2″. Of course, a typical mechanical drawing usually requires several sizes of text and several different text styles. Each style establishes its own text height.

Setting the Snap

Snap lets you accurately pick points in the graphics area. Think of a snap point as a magnet that attracts your cursor. When Snap is on, the cursor moves on the snap points. You learned earlier that Snap toggles (turns on or off) with the F9 key or Ctrl-B. The SNAP command also turns Snap on or off. Additionally, the SNAP command can set the increment, aspect, and rotation of the snap points (Figure 2.1).

To see how Snap works:

1. From the Options menu, choose **Drawing Aids.**
2. Set the Snap increment to 0.125 in the X axis.
3. Set the Snap increment to 0.250 in the Y axis.
4. If the Snap ON toggle does not show an X, select in the box to turn Snap on.
5. Select **OK** to close the Drawing Aids dialog box. Move your cursor to see how it reacts to Snap. The coordinate display only shows values that are multiples of 0.125 in the X axis and 0.250 in the Y axis.

To rotate the Snap:

1. From the Options menu, choose **Drawing Aids.**
2. Enter a value in the Snap Angle edit box to change the Snap angle.
3. Enter values in the X Base and Y Base edit boxes to specify the point that will be the base point for the snap. The default setting for the snap base point is 0,0. By changing the base point, you control the start point for the snap increments.

Whenever you change a setting, you are really changing the value of a system variable. You can access most system variables directly from the command line. For example, to change the value of the system variable that controls the snap rotation, type **SNAPANG.**

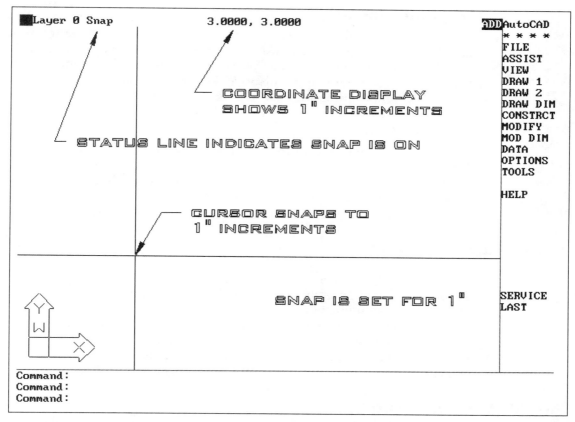

Figure 2.1 The effects of Snap.

Advanced AutoCAD users learn the names of the system variables that they use most often and set their values directly from the command line. If you need to set a system variable transparently, use the transparent command 'SETVAR to set the system variable value.

To change the snap rotation to 45 degrees, type SNAPANG at the command prompt. AutoCAD issues the following prompt which is similar to most system variable prompts:

```
New value for SNAPANG <0>:
```

Enter the value 45.

Displaying the Grid

Many engineers and designers don't leave home without a tablet of grid paper under their arm. In AutoCAD, the equivalent of grid paper is Grid. Just like some grid paper has bold lines and light lines, Grid and Snap work together to produce a similar affect. Make the grid some multiple of the snap. For example, if the snap is 0.125, set the grid to 0.5 or 1.0.

To set the Grid:

1. From the Options menu, choose **Drawing Aids.**
2. Set the grid increment to a multiple of the snap.
3. Select in the Grid toggle box. An X in the box means the grid is ON.
4. Select **OK** to close the Drawing Aids dialog box.

Controlling the System

If drawing and editing is a significant part of your work, you will appreciate AutoCAD's full set of drawing and editing tools. The process of drawing and editing is simplified by controlling the system properly.

With the snap set to 0.25 increments, it is easy to draw a rectangle that is 1.25 × 3.75. In mechanical drawings, geometry is not always that simple. Often, you must attach a line to the tangent of a circle, or draw two concentric circles. Frequently, lines must be parallel or perpendicular.

Snapping to Geometry

In most designs, objects don't usually conform to a particular snap increment. It is often necessary to find a specific point on the geometry—the end of a line or the center of a circle, for example. The tools for identifying these points are Object Snaps or Osnaps. An object snap takes precedence over other settings such as Snap or Ortho. Osnaps are modifiers that help you specify an exact point on existing geometry whenever a prompt requests a point (Figure 2.2). The Osnap modifiers are:

Endpoint	Finds the closest endpoint of an object.
Midpoint	Finds the midpoint of an object.
Intersection	Finds the intersection of two or more objects or elements.
Apparent Intersection	Finds the intersection of two or more objects even though they might not really intersect. If two objects intersect on the screen but are on different planes, the apparent intersection osnap finds the

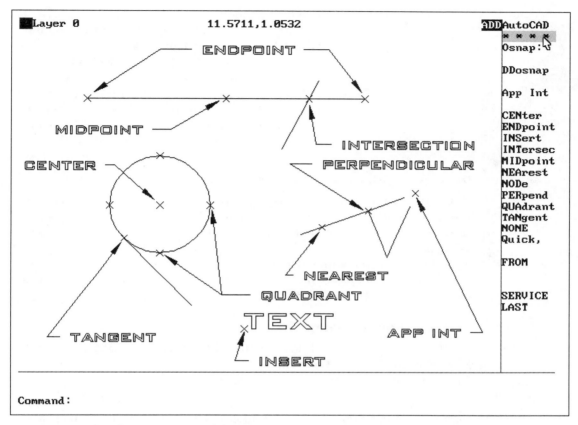

Figure 2.2 The Object Snaps.

	intersection as if the objects were on the same plane.
Center	Finds the center of a circle or arc.
Quadrant	Finds the closest quadrant of a circle or arc.
Perpendicular	Finds a point perpendicular to another point.
Tangent	Finds the tangent point of a circle or arc.
Node	Finds a point entity.
Insertion Point	Finds the insertion point for text or block entities. (Block entities are described later in this chapter.)
Nearest	Finds the point nearest to the cursor that is actually on the object.

Quick,   Used as a modifier for other object snaps. When multiple object snaps are set (See the "Running Object Snaps," section, next), Quick finds the first, but not necessarily the closest, object snap point.

From   Defines a temporary reference point for specifying subsequent points. Often, the From object snap modifier is used with other object snaps or as a basis for specifying a point using relative coordinates.

Running Object Snaps

Object snaps take two forms, running osnaps and interactive osnaps. Set running osnaps with the OSNAP command. Several running osnaps may be active at one time, and when they are, AutoCAD examines each point you select and determines if the object is within the aperture. If it is, AutoCAD determines which running osnap to apply.

Running osnaps are handy if you know in advance that you want to select multiple endpoints or center points.

To set a running osnap:

1. From the Options pull-down menu, choose **Running Object Snap.**
2. Select the Endpoint option.
3. Select **OK** to close the Running Object Snap dialog box.

Issue the LINE command and draw a line. Issue another LINE command and select a point near the middle of the line. The cursor snaps to the nearest endpoint.

Try setting multiple running osnaps. Good combinations are Endpoint, Intersection, and Center. Avoid using combinations that require AutoCAD to decide for you. A combination of Endpoint and Midpoint makes accurate selection difficult for short line segments.

You can change the size of the aperture from the Running Object Snap dialog box. In tight areas, a small aperture is desirable. A large aperture makes it easier to select objects when the area is not too dense.

Disable running osnaps with the Running Object Snap dialog box or by issuing the command OSNAP NONe.

NOTE Running osnaps can lead to problems. AutoCAD determines whether a cursor pick is close enough to an object to apply a running osnap. It does this by displaying an aperture at the cursor whenever running osnaps are active. AutoCAD applies the running osnap if an object falls within the aperture. If the object does not fall within the aperture, AutoCAD assumes that no object is available and places the point where you selected.

An error can occur when you think you selected a point on an object and AutoCAD "thinks" you didn't. AutoCAD assumes no object was there and places the point where you selected instead of on the object. Depending on your display resolution, the *missed* point could appear connected to the object and an error occurs.

Interactive Osnaps

A safer way to use object snaps is interactively. To snap to an endpoint, issue the Endpoint modifier before selecting a point on the object. When you use osnaps interactively, they are only active for a single selection. Instead of selecting an arbitrary point, AutoCAD displays an error message if no object is found. This method avoids the potential for errors described in the preceding note.

You can select osnaps from several menus. The cursor menu is the most convenient since it requires a minimum amount of motion to get to the object snap you need. A mouse button normally displays the cursor menu. If you are using a two-button mouse, hold down the **Shift** key and press the **Enter** button. If that doesn't work, try the Ctrl and Alt keys.

Osnaps also display at the bottom of the screen menu. To see these, however, you need a high-resolution (1024 × 768) display. The four stars (* * * *) at the top of the screen menu also display the osnaps. Another menu of osnaps is the Assist Object Snap pull-down menu. Of course, you can always type in the object snap you need. Use the following abbreviations (shown in capital letters) when typing osnaps at the command line:

ENDP	Endpoint (Although END will work, get in the habit of using ENDP because END is an AutoCAD command that ends the drawing.)
MID	Midpoint
INT	Intersection
APINT	Apparent intersection
CEN	Center
QUA	Quadrant
PER	Perpendicular
TAN	Tangent
NOD	Node
INS	Insertion point
NEA	Nearest
QUI,	Quick,

> *Program multiple interactive object snaps on your mouse buttons. This is done by modifying the AutoCAD menu file in a text editor. AutoCAD allows button assignments for Shift, Ctrl, and Alt keys in combination with the mouse buttons. For example, program the Shift-middle button to look for ENDP, INT, CEN, and the Shift-right button to look for MID, QUA, APINT.*

Selecting Objects

Whenever you must identify objects for editing, AutoCAD displays the *Select objects*: prompt. Since object selection is such a common activity, there are many ways to do it. The first is the most obvious: move the cursor to the object and select it. When the Select objects prompt is active, a pickbox, similar to the aperture used for object snaps, appears at the cursor. To select an object, move the pickbox over the object and select it.

Fortunately, you don't have to select objects one at a time. When you select objects, each object you select becomes part of a group of objects called a selection set. During the selection process, you may use any of the selection tools available to identify the selection set (Figure 2.3).

To explore the object selection tools, you need objects on your screen. Draw some lines and circles on the screen. Make some of the objects intersect.

Window   Creates a rectangle by selecting two corner points and selects any objects that are completely within the borders of the rectangle. When Implied Windowing is ON, in the Options Selection dialog box, Window selection mode is automatic when you pick the rectangle from left to right. When Implied Windowing is OFF, you must type the letter **W** to activate Window selection.

To select objects with a window:

1. Issue any editing command that prompts you to Select objects.
2. Select a window area around the objects by picking the two opposite corners.
3. Press **Enter** to complete the selection.
4. Continue the command.

Each of the following object selection modes works in the same way. You can combine modes during the selection process.

Crossing   Creates a rectangle by selecting two points. Crossing selects any objects that are completely within or intersect

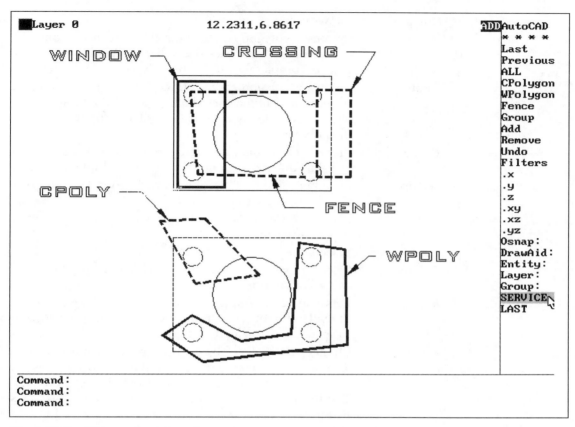

Figure 2.3 Object selection tools.

the borders of the rectangle. When Implied Windowing is ON, in the Options Selection dialog box, Crossing selection is automatic when you pick the rectangle from right to left. When Implied Windowing is OFF, you must type the letter **C** to activate Crossing selection.

AUTO — Determines if a selection was made on an object and selects the object. If the selection did not select an object, then the Implied Windowing mode activates and the selection point becomes the first point of the two point rectangle. Selecting a point to the right selects a Window, a point to the left selects a Crossing.

BOX — Same as AUTO above, except the first selection point is the first point of the rectangle.

SIngle	Allows only a single selection.
WPoly	Creates a polygon by selecting three or more points. A rubber band line closes the polygon. WPoly selects any objects completely within the polygon.
CPoly	Creates a polygon by selecting three or more points. A rubber band line closes the polygon. CPoly selects any objects completely within the polygon or intersecting the polygon.
Fence	Creates a line that intersects the objects you want to select. The line may be one segment or multiple segments.
Group	Prompts for the name of a named group (See the section "Creating Groups," next).
ALL	Selects all the objects on the drawing that are not on a locked or frozen layer.
Last	Selects the last object created.
Previous	Selects any objects that were selected during the previous selection operation.
Multiple	Lets you select multiple objects that are close to each other. Highlighting is disabled during multiple selection to speed up the selection process.
Remove	Changes the Select objects prompt to Remove objects. Remove allows you to use any of the methods in this list to select the objects to remove from the selection set. The Remove objects prompt continues until you press **Enter** to end the selection process or type **A** for Add (described next).
Add	Changes the Remove objects prompt to Select objects. Add lets you continue selecting objects to the selection set after a Remove option is entered.
Undo	Reverses the last selection operation.

Even with a formidable set of selection tools, objects that are very close together are difficult to select individually. There is another tool for selecting individual objects when multiple objects occupy the same area on the screen. Cycling lets you place your cursor in a crowded area of the drawing and cycle through the objects until the object you want highlights.

To try Cycling:
1. Issue an editing command that prompts you to Select objects.
2. Select a point in a crowded area while holding down the **Ctrl** key. (On some systems the **Alt** key will also work.)

3. Press the Pick button on the pointing device until the object you want highlights. Objects close to your selection are cycled.
4. Press **Enter** to select the object.

The way the object selection tools behave often depends on certain settings. To see the object selection options select the Options Selection pull-down menu (Figure 2.4).

Creating Groups

Even though it is fairly easy to select objects, it doesn't make sense to keep selecting the same groups of objects again and again. Fortunately, there is

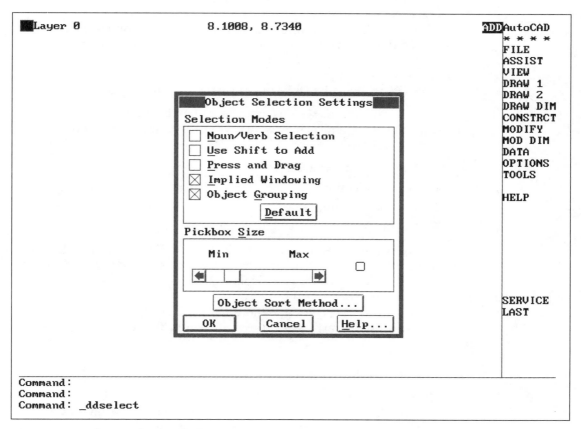

Figure 2.4 Object Selection dialog box.

a way of grouping objects for the purpose of selection. The rules for groups are:

- Groups are named or unnamed.
- Groups are selectable or not selectable. If the group is selectable, selecting a single member of the group selects the entire group.
- An object can belong to more than one group.

To create a group:

1. From the Assist pull-down menu, select **Group Objects.**
2. Enter the name of the group in the edit box labeled Group Identification. If you don't want to name the group, select Unnamed.
3. Specify whether the group is selectable. If the group is selectable, you may select the entire group by selecting any member of the group.
4. Choose **New** for Create Group.
5. Select the objects for grouping and press **Enter.** If you have already selected the objects, type **P** (for Previous) to recapture the previous selection set. Use any combination of selection tools to select the objects in the group.
6. Select **OK** to close the Object Grouping dialog box (Figure 2.5).

Group selection (as well as associative hatch selection) is affected by the PICKSTYLE system variable. PICKSTYLE accepts values of 0, 1, 2, or 3 and works as follows:

0 = No group or associative hatch selection

1 = Group selection

2 = Associative hatch selection

3 = Group and associative hatch selection

Before you select a group, set the PICKSTYLE system variable to 1 or 3. This permits the selecting of groups. Select a group by selecting an object in the group or by typing **G** (for Group) at the Select objects prompt, and typing in the name of the group.

Since objects may belong to more than one group, selecting a particular object won't necessarily select the right group. To identify the group you want, use Cycling.

To cycle through group selection:

1. Select the object.
2. Press and hold the **Ctrl** key while pressing the Pick button on your pointing device until the correct group highlights.
3. Press **Enter** to select the group (Figure 2.6).

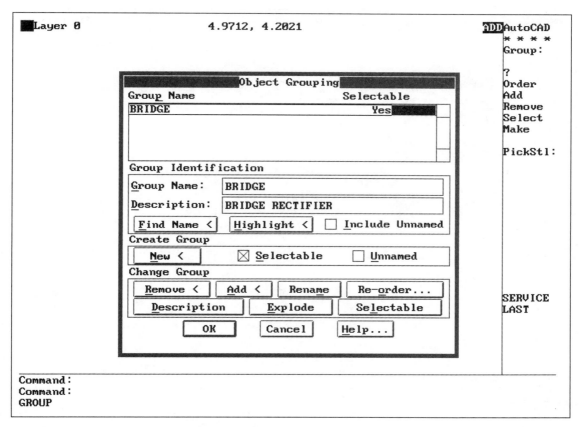

Figure 2.5 Object Grouping dialog box.

Filters

It is possible to select objects that meet a certain criteria. This type of object selection uses the 'FILTER modifier.

To select objects created with a particular color:

1. At the Select objects prompt, type '**FILTER.**
2. Select **Color.**
3. Choose the Select box (next to the Select Filter box).
4. From the color palette, select the color.
5. Select **Add to List** to use the Color filter.
6. Select **Apply** to apply the Color filter to the selections and to close the Object Selection Filters dialog box.

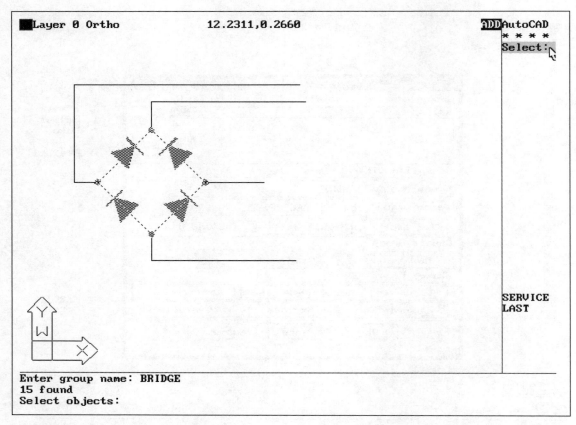

Figure 2.6 Group selection.

You can apply many types of filters to a selection. The following example selects all the red circles that have a radius larger than 1.25.

To use the 'FILTER modifier to set the above criteria:

1. At the Select objects prompt, type '**FILTER.**
2. Select anywhere in the Select filter edit box of the Object Selection Filters dialog box.
3. Select **Circle Radius** as the filter type.
4. Select the equal (**=**) symbol in the X= edit box.
5. Choose the greater than (**>**) symbol for the relational operator.
6. Change the value for X to 1.25.
7. Select **Add to List** to include the Circle Radius filter.
8. Select the Select filter box again.

9. Select **Color.**
10. Choose the Select box (next to the Select Filter box).
11. From the color palette, select color number **1** (Red).
12. Select **Add to List** to include the Color filter.
13. Select **Apply** to apply the Circle Radius and Color filters to the selections and to close the Object Selection Filters dialog box.

Now the object selection filters only allow the selection of objects that fit the criteria of red circles with a radius greater than 1.25. Objects not meeting this criteria are filtered out (Figure 2.7).

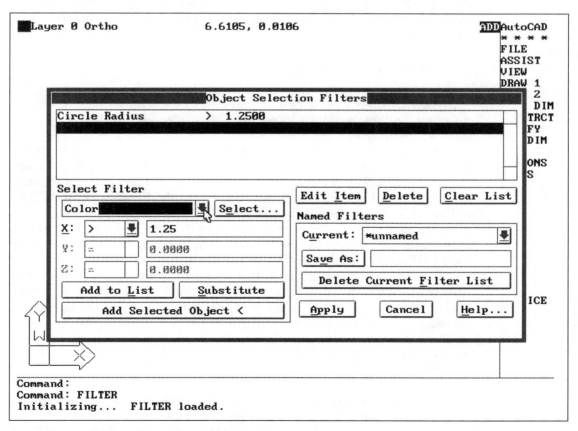

Figure 2.7 Object Selection Filters dialog box.

Controlling the Display

As you draw, the display sometimes requires adjustment to assist the drawing or viewing process. As you issue display commands, only the display of the drawing changes. The scale and relationship of the objects to any given point, or to each other, does not change.

You can use display commands to freshen the display (Redraw or Regen), change the display magnification (Zoom) or viewing direction (Viewpoint). You can save and restore a display (View) or display multiple screens at once (Viewports).

Redraw and Regen

Editing an object occasionally affects the appearance of the screen pixels which are the dots that make up the screen. When two objects share the same pixel(s), erasing or moving one of the objects may blank out the pixels for the second object. In such cases you can redraw the screen to restore the pixels.

To redraw the screen:

- From the View pull-down menu, choose Redraw View. You can also type **REDRAW** from the command line, or issue the REDRAW command transparently by prefixing it with an apostrophe ('REDRAW).

  You can also use Redraw to remove *blips* from the screen. Blips are small cross marks (+) used to mark the points you pick on the screen. The system variable BLIPMODE controls the display of blips. To avoid generating blips, set BLIPMODE to 0 (Off) or choose the Settings Drawing Aids pull-down menu and select the Blips toggle.

  The effects of changing magnifications, scaling linetypes, or manipulating layers are not visible until the drawing regenerates. When you issue the REGEN command, AutoCAD recalculates the entire drawing database and re-creates each entity. Depending on the drawing size, a regen can be time-consuming. For this reason, CAD operators have developed many tricks to avoid regens. Even AutoCAD's programmers are constantly looking for ways to minimize drawing regeneration.

To regenerate the drawing:

- Type **REGEN** at the Command prompt.

  Since unnecessary regens can affect productivity, it is desirable to control when regeneration occurs. There are two ways to force AutoCAD to ask for permission before regenerating a drawing. One is a command (REGENAUTO) and the other is a system variable (REGENMODE). Both work similarly.

To issue the REGENAUTO command:

1. Type **REGENAUTO** at the Command prompt.
2. Type **ON** for automatic regenerations or **OFF** for prompting before regeneration occurs.

To set the REGENMODE system variable:

1. Type **REGENMODE** at the Command prompt.
2. Type **1** for automatic regenerations or **0** for prompting before regeneration occurs.

NOTE   Redraw and Regen affect the current viewport. To Redraw or Regen all the viewports, use the REDRAWALL and REGENALL commands.

Using ZOOM to control display magnification

Use the ZOOM command to change the magnification of the display or the target of the display. To zoom transparently, prefix the command with an apostrophe ('ZOOM). When you select Zoom options from the View pull-down menu, the ZOOM command is automatically transparent.

The ZOOM command usually takes a modifier that indicates which part of the drawing to include in the new display. The ZOOM command modifiers are:

In	Zooms in using the center of the current display as the target. The zoom magnification factor is 2x. Double-click on the View pull-down menu for successive zooms. Zoom In is only available on the menus.
Out	Zooms Out using the center of the current display as the target. The zoom magnification factor is .5x. Double-click on the View pull-down menu for successive zooms. Zoom Out is only available on the menus.
Window	Prompts you to select a window area that specifies the display area. If you issue the ZOOM command without a modifier, the window option is the default. For consistent results, select a window that resembles the shape of your screen. Center your target in the window. AutoCAD uses the lower left pick point to identify the lower left corner of the new display and the height or width of the window to determine the display magnification.

All	Displays the entire contents of the drawing, plus the limits. Zoom All considers objects on layers that are OFF, even though they are not visible. Zoom All does not acknowledge objects on FROZEN layers. Zoom All always causes a regeneration of the drawing, regardless of the settings for REGENMODE and REGENAUTO.
Previous	Restores the previous display. AutoCAD saves up to ten previous displays.
Scale	Similar to Zoom In and Zoom Out except that you control the magnification. By default, the value calculates based on the limits of the drawing. To zoom into an area, enter a magnification greater than 1. To zoom out, enter a magnification of less than 1. Negative numbers are not valid but fractions are.
X, XP	Changes the magnification relative to the current view. The scale factor is followed by an X. AutoCAD has a feature called *Paper Space* that scales the model to the actual size of the paper. Enter XP after the scale factor to adjust the zoom magnification relative to paper space. (Paper space is described in a later chapter.)
Dynamic	Allows you to select the display area while viewing the entire drawing.

To change the magnification using Zoom Dynamic:

1. From the View pull-down menu, select **Zoom Dynamic** (Figure 2.8). The entire drawing displays. Crop marks indicate the extents of the drawing, the virtual screen area, and the current view. The virtual screen is that portion of the drawing that you can display without a regeneration. A window area marked with an X represents the display area, follows the cursor and controls the zoom magnification.
2. Press the Pick button of the pointing device and adjust the size of the window. The smaller the window, the greater the magnification. When you have adjusted the window size, press the Pick button again to lock in the window size.
3. Move the window over the area of the drawing you want to display. To display the area, press **Enter** or the Return button on the pointing device.

Center	Lets you specify the center of the new display. The Center option measures the current screen height. You can change the magnification by specifying a new screen height or by entering a new magnification.

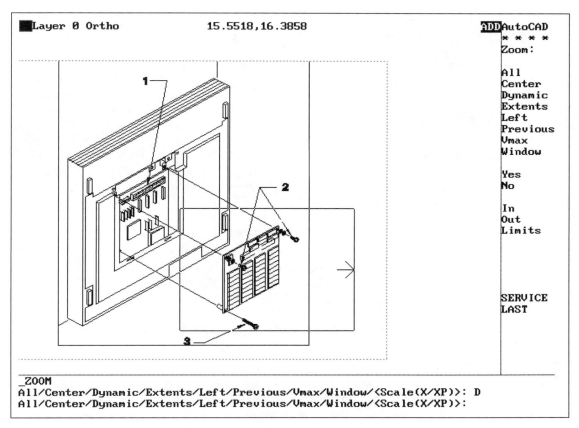

Figure 2.8   The Zoom Dynamic command.

Left	Same as the Center option except that you specify the lower left corner of new display.
Limits	Displays the drawing limits (as set with the LIMITS command).
Extents	Recalculates the outermost area of the drawing that contains entities, including layers that are off, and adjusts the display to show all the entities on the drawing. Zoom Extents will always cause a regeneration of the drawing, regardless of the settings for REGENMODE and REGEN-AUTO.
Vmax	Displays the virtual screen. The virtual screen is the largest area of the drawing that AutoCAD can display without regenerating the drawing.

> *Avoid unnecessary regenerations by carefully picking windows or by set-*
> *ting up views (See "Setting Up Views," later). When you pick windows,*
> *the display adjusts to the shape of your screen. The lower left corner is*
> *used as a start point. If the adjusted new display extends outside the vir-*
> *tual screen area then a regeneration will occur. Always pick windows*
> *that are the shape of your screen. Avoid picking tall, skinny windows or*
> *short, fat windows.*
>
> *By carefully selecting windows, you can avoid most regenerations.*
> *Another good tool for avoiding regens is the Zoom Dynamic option. Use*
> *the REGENMODE system variable or the REGENAUTO command to*
> *further control unnecessary regenerations.*

Controlling View Resolution and the Virtual Screen

The VIEWRES command controls the area of the screen that displays without causing a regeneration. This area is the Virtual Screen. VIEWRES also
controls how circles and arcs display on the screen. If arcs and circles appear segmented, you can adjust the number of line segments for the display.

To adjust the number of line segments for the display of circles and arcs:

1. Type **VIEWRES** at the Command prompt.
2. Answer Yes at the fast zoom prompt to activate the virtual screen or
   No to cause a regeneration whenever the display changes.
3. Enter a value for the circle zoom percent prompt. The value controls
   how many straight line segments are used to represent circles.

   Valid numbers are between 1 and 2,000. Increasing this number displays circles more accurately at the expense of performance. Decreasing
this number improves performance but causes circles to appear more segmented. This value does not affect how objects plot.

Setting Up Views

Views are snapshots of the display which simplify the process of moving
around your drawing. You can create and store named views, and you can
save any view as a named view. By using named views, you avoid unneces-
sarily regenerating the drawing. The command for saving and restoring
views is VIEW.

> *Use the VIEW command transparently to begin a command in one view*
> *and continue it in another.*

The VIEW command options are:

Delete   Deletes a named view.

Restore   Restores a named view.

Save   Saves the current display as a named view.

Window   Allows you to specify a named view by selecting a window.

To save a named view:

1. From the View pull-down menu, choose **Named Views.**
2. Select **New** from the View Control dialog box.
3. Enter the name of the view in the New Name edit window.
4. Select Current Display to save the current display as the new view or Define Window to select a window area for the new view. If you choose Define Window, the Window selection becomes active. The previously defined window coordinates are displayed in the boxes labeled First Corner and Other Corner. To define the window, select the Window selection box. You may also enter the window coordinates directly in the First Corner and Other Corner boxes. Select the window area for the new view from the screen.
5. Select **Save View.**
6. Select **OK** to close the View Control dialog box (Figure 2.9).

To restore a previously defined named view:

1. From the View pull-down menu, choose **Named Views.**
2. Select the named view you want to restore from the View Control dialog box.
3. Select **Restore.**
4. Select **OK** to close the View Control dialog box.

To delete a previously defined named view:

1. From the View pull-down menu, choose **Named Views.**
2. Select the view you want to delete from the View Control dialog box.
3. Select **Delete.**
4. Select **OK** to close the View Control dialog box.

By setting up and controlling named views, you can easily display different areas of your drawing one at a time. You can also divide the screen into multiple screens or *viewports*. Use viewports to display many areas of the drawing simultaneously. Viewports are discussed in Chapter 5.

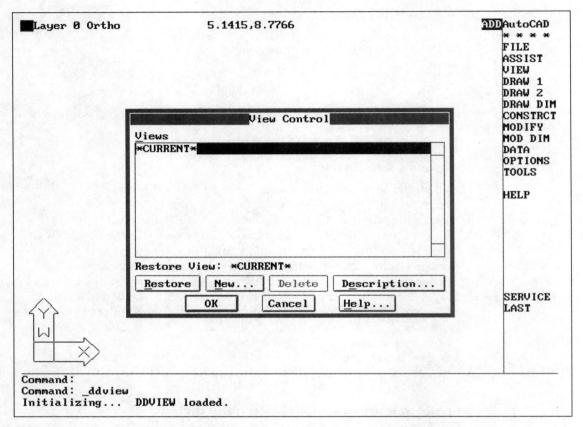

Figure 2.9 The View Control dialog box.

The Mechanical Drawing Command Arsenal

AutoCAD Release 13 supports a very robust mechanical drawing command arsenal. The programmers who developed AutoCAD Release 13 have worked hard to bring these specific mechanical capabilities to AutoCAD. Dimensioning is enhanced. Compliance with ANSI Y14.5 for geometric dimensioning and tolerancing has been a long-standing requirement. New commands provide construction lines, dimension leaders with multiple lines of text, solid modeling, and many features that directly benefit mechanical disciplines.

Drawing and Editing

It is difficult to make a clear distinction between drawing and editing. When you create a fillet or chamfer, you are actually modifying or editing the existing geometry to create a new feature. Although some commands are clearly for drawing and others are clearly for editing, many commands fall somewhere in between.

There are many ways to create geometry in AutoCAD. As you learn the commands, you will pick up techniques that simplify the drawing process. Many CAD operators learn one way to draw and never attempt to learn an easier way. Table 2.1 shows two ways to draw a rectangle.

In this example, the hard way is not the wrong way; it is correct since the geometry produced is accurate. The hard way just takes longer. There are many ways to issue and use the drawing commands presented in the following chapters. As you learn the commands, think of this example. In AutoCAD, if you think there should be an easier way to do something, there usually is.

Making a Point

The most primitive of the drawing primitives is the point. Use a point to identify locations or to place a handle on an object. Remember, the Node object snap finds point entities.

Since points are sometimes difficult to see on the screen, AutoCAD has two system variables that control the display of points. PDMODE, point display mode, lets you select any number of graphics to display a point. For example, if you set PDMODE to 3, points will display as an X. PDSIZE controls the size of the point display mode. A positive value for PDSIZE displays the points in units. A negative value displays points as a percent of the screen display. Note, however, that you have to regenerate your drawing before you can see the affects of PDMODE and PDSIZE changes. To select a point display type from a dialog box, type DDPTYPE at the Command prompt. Sometimes, AutoCAD uses points during certain commands. Two such commands are DIVIDE and MEASURE, discussed next.

Table 2.1   Two Ways to Draw a Rectangle

HARD WAY	*EASY WAY*
Command: LINE	Command: RECTANG
From point: 0,0	First corner: 0,0
To point: 0,4.5	Other corner: 6.5,4.5
To point: 6.5,4.5	
To point: 6.5,0	
To point: 0,0 (or C for Close)	

DIVIDE and MEASURE

For mechanical design, it is common to require accurate divisions along an object. The commands DIVIDE and MEASURE are two ways of dividing objects. They work exactly alike, with the following difference:

DIVIDE   Divides an object into equal divisions. You specify the number of divisions. Use DIVIDE to quickly draw sprockets, gears, or other objects where the number of increments is significant and the distance between them is secondary.

MEASURE   Divides an object into equal segments. You specify the length of the segments. Use MEASURE to accurately draw pictorial screw threads, chain links, or other objects where the distance between objects is significant and the number of objects is secondary.

Before you try DIVIDE and MEASURE, begin a new drawing or erase everything from your screen. You can issue the ERASE command with the All option to accomplish this easily.

To divide an object:

1. From the Options menu, choose **Display Point Style.**
2. Select a point style.
3. Select **OK** to close the Point Style dialog box.
4. Draw an object on your screen.
5. From the Draw pull-down menu, choose **Point Divide.**
6. Select the object.
7. Enter a value at the Number of segments prompt.

The block option places a symbol entity at each division. Blocks are covered in Chapter 4. You can use the block option of the DIVIDE command to create the illustration as shown in Figure 2.10.

Array

ARRAY creates multiple copies of objects in a circular or rectangular pattern at specified intervals. Array is much faster than Copy for creating large rectangular or circular patterns of objects.

Polar arrays copy objects in a circular pattern (Figure 2.11). You specify the center of the circle, the included angle, and whether to rotate the objects as they are copied. Use Polar Array to create sprockets, gears, spokes, or circular hole patterns. If you don't rotate the objects as they are copied,

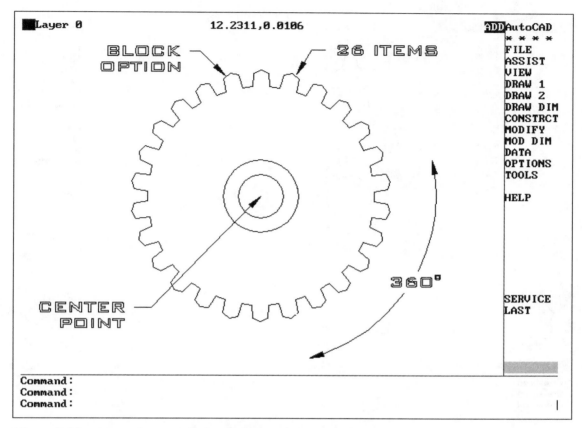

Figure 2.10 A gear drawn with the DIVIDE command.

the objects remain in the same orientation. This produces results like seats on a Ferris wheel.

To construct a polar array:

1. From the Construct pull-down menu, select **Array Polar.**
2. Select the object(s) you want to array.
3. Select the center point of the array.
4. Press **Enter** for a 360-degree array, or enter a smaller angle.
5. Press **Enter** to rotate the objects as they are copied.

Rectangular arrays copy objects in a rectangular pattern (Figure 2.12). You specify the number of rows and columns and the spacing between them. Use Rectangular Arrays to create rectangular holes or punch patterns, threads, springs, or banks of integrated circuits on printed circuit boards.

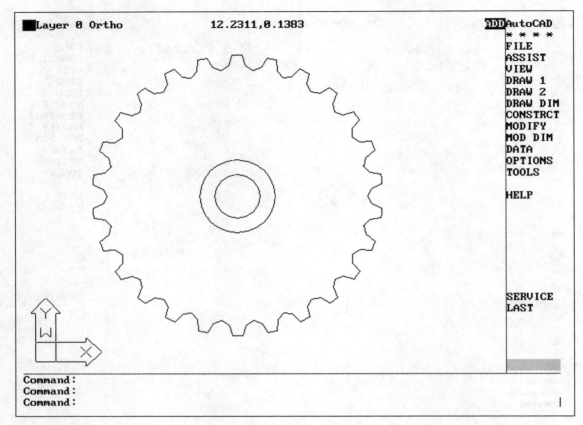

Figure 2.11 Polar Array options.

To draw a rectangular array:

1. From the Construct pull-down menu, select **Array Rectangular.**
2. Select the object(s) you want to array.
3. Select the base point, which represents the lower left corner of the array.
4. Enter the number of rows.
5. Enter the number of columns.
6. Enter the distance between rows. Positive numbers array in the positive Y direction; negative numbers array in the negative Y direction.
7. Enter the distance between columns. Positive numbers array in the positive X direction, negative numbers array in the negative X direction.

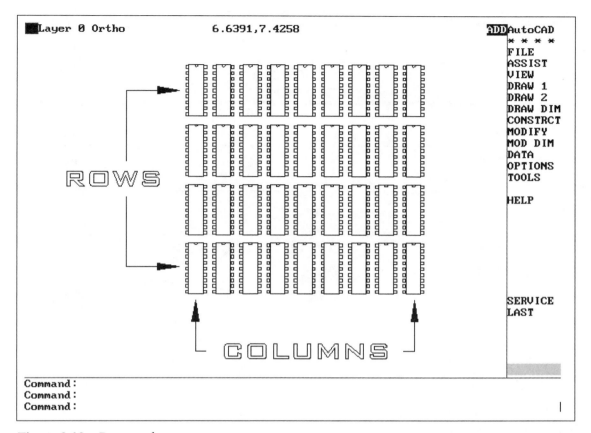

Figure 2.12 Rectangular array.

▶ *Use a rectangle to specify the distances between the rows and columns with two picks. At the distance between rows prompt, select the base point of your array. Create the rectangle to indicate the distances in the X and Y directions.*

▶ *Change the snap rotation to create a rotated rectangular array. AutoCAD creates rectangular arrays based on the snap angle. By changing the snap angle, you can rotate the rectangular array.*

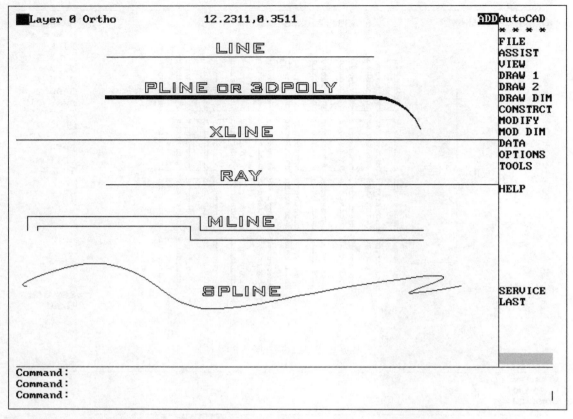

Figure 2.13 Lines available in AutoCAD.

Special Lines

There are many new types of lines available in AutoCAD Release 13 (Figure 2.13). Before you draw a line, you must decide which type of line to draw. Use the following brief descriptions to determine the different types of lines:

Line   Straight line segment between two points in three-dimensional space. Although the LINE command draws lines from point to point to point, each line segment is a separate entity. Use simple lines for individual straight line segments.

Pline   (Polyline) Straight or curved complex line that may have multiple vertices and varying width. Use plines for multiple straight line segments that can be treated as a single entity (a schematic resistor symbol for example), complex curves, or lines that require a width.

3-Dpoly   (3D Polyline) Similar to polyline (with some limitations) but permits vectors in three dimensions. Use 3-DPoly when you need a pline that moves in three dimensions; a tool path, for example.

Xline   Construction line that extends to infinity in each direction. Use xlines to quickly set up construction lines that you can trim later or for setting up diametric or trimetric drawings.

Ray   Construction line that begins at a point and extends to infinity in one direction only. Use rays for construction lines that originate at one origin, such as radial objects, or for setting up vanishing points for manually generated perspective drawings.

Mline   (Multiline) creates parallel lines. Use mline to create circuit board traces or wall thicknesses for plastic or sheet metal parts.

Spline   Creates true splined curves. Use splines to generate geometry for creating surfaces.

> *Set the system variable COORDS to a value of 2 to tell AutoCAD to display the length and angle of lines as you draw. Be sure each line you draw extends the entire distance you need to represent. Avoid creating a line segment out of smaller line segments. If it is a straight line between two points, only one entity should represent the line.*

Using Polylines

The PLINE command creates a complex line with characteristics not found in other types of lines. Unlike ordinary lines, which are made up of individual line segments, plines are a single entity comprised of multiple line segments. You will find this convenient when you use plines to create simple rectangles or complex tool paths. FILLET and CHAMFER commands can be applied to the entire pline at once or on the individual segments.

Plines can have a uniform or variable width. By selecting a starting and ending width, you can easily draw flow arrows, section arrows, or curved arrows. You can use plines with a uniform width for borders, section lines, or other wide areas that exceed the maximum pen width available for your plotter.

Plines can contain multiple vertices. Each vertex of a pline is a control point for various types of curves. By using the PEDIT command, you can create fit and splined curves. Cubic, quadratic, or bezier spline curves may be approximated by setting the SPLINETYPE system variable.

Grip editing can also edit plines. Grips appear at each vertex. For example, you can use the grip editing commands to stretch a vertex to a new location. Grips are described later.

> *Use polylines even when simple lines would work. When you encounter a situation where simple lines would have been a better choice—to offset a portion of the line, for example—use the EXPLODE command to convert the polylines to simple lines. You can always recreate the polyline. (See "Editing Polylines," next.)*
>
> *One uncommon use for polylines is quick tolerance studies. Set the width of the polyline to the allowable tolerance for the part. When you put mating parts together, you can easily see any interference between the parts. When you have completed your study, you can change the pline width to 0 (See "Editing Polylines," next).*

Editing Polylines

Polylines are line and arc segments with a vertex on the ends of each line and arc segment. Plines are complex entities and, as such, sometimes require extensive editing. The editing commands for polylines are available with the PEDIT command, and its editing options are:

Close/Open	Closes an open polyline or opens a closed polyline. If you select a closed polyline to edit, the Open option displays on the command line. If you select an open polyline, the Close option displays.
Join	Joins two or more polylines, lines, or arc segments arranged in a chain and connected to each other. A single point forms the connection for each segment.
Width	Sets the width for all the polyline segments, regardless of the width of the individual segments. To edit the width of individual segments, see the Width option of Edit Vertex in the following list.
Edit Vertex	See the description in the following list.
Fit	Fits a curve through all the vertices of the Pline.
Spline	Creates a curve that is controlled by, but doesn't necessarily pass through, the vertices of the pline.
Decurve	Displays the polyline using only straight line segments between the vertices.

LTgen	Controls whether a linetype applied to a polyline generates, based on the length of the polyline or on the length of each individual segment.
Exit	Exits the PLINE command.

The Edit Vertex options are:

Next	An X indicates the first vertex of the polyline. Type **N** to advance through the vertices of the polyline.
Previous	Selects the previous vertex in the polyline. Type **P** to move backward through the polyline vertices.
Break	Breaks a polyline segment between two specified vertices.
Insert	Inserts a new vertex in the polyline at the location you indicate.
Move	Moves the specified vertex to a new location.
Regen	Regenerates the polyline without leaving the edit vertex command option.
Straighten	Straightens polyline segments between two selected vertices.
Tangent	Sets a tangent direction for curve fitting.
Width	Sets the width for the pline segments between two vertices.

Often, it is easier to use simple entities for creating geometry. When you create geometry accurately, you can later join the objects to form a single polyline. Be sure the endpoints of adjoining segments share a common point.

You can create polylines from simple lines or arcs by using the PEDIT command.

To create a polyline from line or arc segments:

1. Draw two or more line or arc segments. Be sure their endpoints connect.
2. Type **PEDIT** and select one of the objects.
3. Type **Y** (or press **Enter**) at the prompt: Entity selected is not a polyline. Do you want to turn it into one? <Y>.
4. Type **J** to join the other segments.
5. Select the line objects you want to join to the new polyline.

Rectangles

Use the Rectangle command to draw rectangles whenever possible. It is fast and easy. Actually, rectangle is not really a command; it is an AutoLISP program that draws a rectangle using polylines. This means that the rectangle produced with this command will be a closed polyline in the shape of a rectangle and will have the width currently set by the PLINE command.

> *Although many AutoLISP programs must be loaded before they can be used, AutoCAD autoloads the rectangle program and several other AutoLISP programs.*

To draw a rectangle:

1. From the Draw pull-down menu, select **Rectangle,** or type **RECTANG** at the Command prompt.
2. Select one corner of the rectangle.
3. Select the opposite corner of the rectangle.

Construction Lines

Xlines and Rays are the two types of construction lines available in Auto-CAD. Xlines extend to infinity in both directions through a point. Rays extend to infinity in one direction through a point, similar to a vanishing point on a perspective drawing. Both have the following characteristics:

- Extend to infinity without affecting display commands. For example, the Zoom Extents command does not consider construction lines.

- Serve as boundaries for trimming objects or other construction lines, or offset at a distance or through another point. When trimmed, construction lines become ordinary lines.

- Object snaps work, with a few limitations. You can Osnap to intersections or perpendicular to construction lines. You can snap to the endpoint of a Ray (its origin) but not to the endpoint of an Xline. You can snap to the midpoint of an Xline (its origin) but not to the midpoint of a Ray.

Xlines and Rays have similar command options. The XLINE command has the following options:

Hor   Creates a horizontal Xline through a point.
Ver   Creates a vertical Xline through a point.

Ang	Creates an Xline at an angle through a point.
Bisect	Creates an Xline that bisects an angle.
Offset	Creates an Xline a specific distance from an existing object or Xline. The Offset option works like the **OFFSET** command.
Perp	Creates an Xline perpendicular to an existing object or Xline through a point.

Splines

Another type of line available is the spline. Use splines to construct or simulate surfaces, to indicate wires, or to draw irregular objects such as hands. You can create spline curves in two ways. The first way is by creating a polyline. You can use the PEDIT command to spline the polyline or the SPLINE command with the Objects option. The second way to create a spline is with the SPLINE command.

To create a splined curve:

1. From the Draw pull-down menu, select **Spline.**
2. Enter the points to define the spline. If you select the points on the screen, you can see the spline bend into shape as you move your cursor.

   The system variable, SPLFRAME, controls the display of the control polygon for the spline. You can edit splines with the SPLINEDIT command, whose options include:

Fit Data	Edits fit data such as fit points, fit tolerance, and tangents.
Close	Closes an open spline. If the spline is closed, this option changes to Open.
Move Vertex	Moves a control vertex.
Refine	Fine-tunes a spline definition.
Reverse	Reverses the direction of the spline.
Undo	Cancels the last editing operation.
Exit	Returns to the Command prompt.

To edit a splined curve's fit point:

1. From the Modify pull-down menu, select **Edit Spline.**
2. Select the spline curve to edit.

3. Select **F** for Fit Data.
4. Select **M** for Move Vertex.
5. Enter **N** until the vertex you want to move is highlighted.
6. Specify the new location for the vertex.
7. Enter **X** until you return to the Command prompt.

TRIM and EXTEND

In AutoCAD, it is common to create geometry by using existing geometry. Although much faster than creating new geometry, the resulting objects must sometimes be trimmed or extended. TRIM and EXTEND are two commands that work similarly. TRIM removes objects that extend beyond a boundary. EXTEND extends objects to a boundary.

To use Trim:

1. From the Modify pull-down menu, select **Trim.**
2. Select a cutting plane. The cutting plane is the line that the objects will be trimmed to.
3. Select the part of each line you want to remove.

Before you try Extend, draw a few lines. Now, draw a rectangle or a circle completely around the lines.

To use Extend:

1. From the Modify pull-down menu, select **Extend.**
2. Select the boundary edges. In this case, the boundary edge is the rectangle or circle.
3. Select near the end of each line you want to extend.

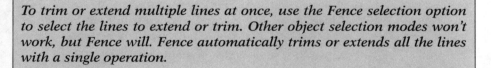

To trim or extend multiple lines at once, use the Fence selection option to select the lines to extend or trim. Other object selection modes won't work, but Fence will. Fence automatically trims or extends all the lines with a single operation.

Beginning with AutoCAD Release 13, Trim and Extend can use an *apparent intersection* for the boundary or cutting plane. This means that the boundary or cutting plane extends beyond the object and does not have to be at the same elevation as the objects you are trimming or extending.

FILLET and CHAMFER

Two more commands that work similarly are FILLET and CHAMFER. These commands are invaluable for mechanical drawings. Use FILLET to easily create corner bends for sheet metal parts, punched shapes, or corner radii for plastic parts. You can use FILLET and CHAMFER with wide polylines to create everything from printed circuit board traces to title block borders. You can even fillet to arcs and circles.

To use Fillet:

1. From the Modify pull-down menu, choose **Fillet.**
2. Type **R** to set the radius. Enter a value for the radius or select two points to specify the distance.
3. Press **Enter** to reenter the FILLET command.
4. Select two lines, arcs, a line and an arc, or an arc and a circle. The portion of the object you select is retained and the remainder is removed.

You can create quick corners with or without a radius by using the Crossing modifier to select two lines. This method automatically keeps the longest portion of the lines. Crossing only works with lines, not with arcs or circles.

Chamfers are commonly used to break sharp corners of sheet metal parts. As with FILLET, the uses for the CHAMFER command are endless.

To use Chamfer:

1. From the Modify pull-down menu, choose **Chamfer.**
2. Type **D** to set the distances. Enter a value for each distance or select two points. AutoCAD applies the first chamfer distance to the first line selected. If you want to specify an angle, type **M,** for method, and specify the angle.
3. Press **Enter** to reenter the CHAMFER command.
4. Select the two lines.

One of the options of the FILLET and CHAMFER commands is Trim. This controls the removal of any portion of the lines that extend beyond the fillet or chamfer. To avoid trimming the lines, type **T** and choose No Trim.

OFFSET

Offset is the workhorse of mechanical drafting. Offset accurately copies lines parallel to each other. Circles and arcs offset concentrically. Use the OFFSET command to generate tool paths, beveled edges, bezels, or concentric features. Offset curved plines to represent wires.

To use the OFFSET command:

1. From the Construct pull-down menu, select **Offset.**
2. Enter the offset distance.
3. Select the object to offset.
4. Select which side of the object to offset on.

You can continue offsetting objects at the same distance without leaving the command. Press **Enter** to end the command. Press **Enter** again to restart the command and supply a different offset distance.

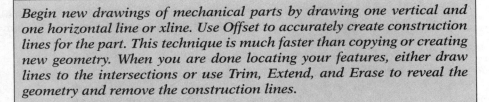

Begin new drawings of mechanical parts by drawing one vertical and one horizontal line or xline. Use Offset to accurately create construction lines for the part. This technique is much faster than copying or creating new geometry. When you are done locating your features, either draw lines to the intersections or use Trim, Extend, and Erase to reveal the geometry and remove the construction lines.

Editing with Grips

AutoCAD has an automatic editing feature called Grips, which can be very fast for certain commands. Whether you use Grips is usually a personal preference. Grips editing requires a few settings. Until now, you have been using the Verb/Noun editing mode. This means you issue a command first and select the objects second. Grips editing uses the Noun/Verb editing mode. When you use grips, you select the objects first and the editing command applies to the selected objects. You can perform multiple edits on the objects without reselecting them. To use Grips, set the system variables PICKFIRST On (1) and Grips On (1). These system variables are also accessible in the **DDSELECT** and **DDGRIPS** dialog boxes.

The Grips editing commands are:

STRETCH	Base point/Copy/Undo/Exit
MOVE	Base point/Copy/Undo/Exit
ROTATE	Base point/Copy/Undo/Reference/Exit
SCALE	Base point/Copy/Undo/Reference/Exit
MIRROR	Base point/Copy/Undo/Exit

Each command has options for establishing a new base point (other than the hot grip) or creating a copy (maintaining the original). The ROTATE and SCALE commands also have options for using reference information, just like the conventional ROTATE and SCALE commands.

To edit using Grips:

1. Select an object without issuing a command. The object will be highlighted and a small box or *grip* displays on significant points on the object. Grips appear on the points that correspond to the object snaps for the object. On lines, the endpoints and the midpoint have grips. On circles, the center and quadrants have grips. On polylines, each vertex has a grip.
2. Select one of the grips. It changes color and becomes a *hot* grip. The selection of a hot grip begins grip editing, and the hot grip defines the handle or default base point for the grip editing commands.
3. Press **Enter** to move through the grip editing commands until the one you want displays on the command line.
4. Move your cursor or enter a command option.
5. Select a point to complete the editing operation.

Experiment with Grip editing. When mastered, Grips can be a fast and easy way to edit for certain operations.

> *Grip editing commands do some things better than the equivalent conventional commands. Try the SCALE command with the copy option on a circle to create concentric circles very easily.*

Hatching

For mechanical drawings, crosshatching is an essential element of sectional views. You have tremendous control over AutoCAD Release 13's many new hatching features. You can choose from many predefined hatch patterns, or create your own pattern; and control the scale and angle of the pattern. The hatch pattern can be *associative* to the boundaries and islands of the part. If the boundary changes, the hatch pattern changes with it. You can even edit the hatch pattern or the type of hatch created.

The command for creating hatching is BHATCH (for Boundary Hatch). If you type HATCH, you will issue the old hatch command, which is still present for compatibility with third-party and custom programs. Create some closed objects on your screen. Two circles, one inside the other, will work just fine.

To see how boundary hatching works:

1. From the Draw pull-down menu, choose **Hatch** (Figure 2.14).
2. Select **Pattern** in the Pattern Properties box to see the predefined hatch patterns. Selecting a pattern name will display the pattern in the Pattern Type box. The pattern display doesn't show the scale or angle

```
Layer 0                    16.5422,2.8706                    ADDAutoCAD
                                                             * * * *
                                                             FILE
                                                             ASSIST
                                                             VIEW
              ┌──────────── Boundary Hatch ────────────┐    DRAW 1
              │ Pattern Type           Boundary         │    DRAW 2
              │                                         │    DRAW DIM
              │ ┌─────────────┐ ///    ┌─────────────┐  │    CONSTRCT
              │ │Predefined  ▼│ ////   │ Pick Points <│ │    MODIFY
              │ └─────────────┘ ////   └─────────────┘  │    MOD DIM
              │                        ┌─────────────┐  │    DATA
              │ Pattern Properties     │Select Objects<│ │   OPTIONS
              │                        └─────────────┘  │    TOOLS
              │ ISO Pen Width:         │Remove Islands<│ │
              │                        └─────────────┘  │    HELP
              │ Pattern:   ANSI31  ▼   │View Selections<│ │
              │                        └─────────────┘  │
              │ Custom Pattern:        ┌─────────────┐  │
              │ Scale:     1.0000      │ Advanced... │  │
              │ Angle:     0           └─────────────┘  │
              │ Spacing:   1.0000      ┌─────────────┐  │
              │ ☐ Double   ☐ Exploded  │Preview Hatch<│ │
              │                        └─────────────┘  │
              │                        │Inherit Properties<│ │  SERVICE
              │                        ☒ Associative   │    LAST
              │      Apply  Cancel  Help                │
              └─────────────────────────────────────────┘
Command:
Command: BHATCH
```

Figure 2.14 Boundary Hatching dialog box.

of the pattern, but it does give you an idea of its overall appearance. When you have selected a pattern, select in the Scale and Angle edit boxes to adjust them.

> *Avoid inserting* exploded *hatch patterns. An exploded hatch pattern is like an exploded block or an exploded pline. Inserting an exploded hatch pattern only inserts the entities that make up the hatch pattern. Instead of an* associative *hatch pattern, it creates individual entities (See "Associative Hatch Patterns," in the next section).*

3. Choose Pick Points in the Boundary box to select the internal point of a closed boundary. Choose Select objects to select objects on the screen that will define the boundary for the pattern.

4. Select inside the boundaries for the hatching. Press **Enter** when you are done. To see the hatch before actually making it part of the drawing, select Preview Hatch. Make changes to the pattern, scale, or angle and preview again.
5. When you are satisfied with the appearance of the hatch pattern, select **Apply.**

   You can copy the properties of an existing hatch pattern by choosing Inherit Properties. Select Advanced to set the features that control hatching style and island detection, and to define whether boundaries created for the purpose of hatching are retained as separate entities on the drawing.

> *Hatching originates from the point specified in the SNAPBASE system variable. By using a single point for the origin of all hatch patterns, AutoCAD ensures that hatching for mating or adjacent parts aligns properly. To adjust a hatch pattern, change the value of SNAPBASE and edit the hatch pattern.*

Associative Hatch Patterns

The Associative toggle of the Boundary Hatch dialog box determines if a hatch pattern will update when the boundary changes. Depending on the changes, the hatch pattern may require editing or updating. Only associative hatch patterns are available for editing. Before you edit your hatch pattern, use move or stretch to change the boundary or island locations on your drawing.

To edit an existing associative hatch pattern:

1. From the Modify pull-down menu, choose **Edit hatch.**
2. Select the hatch pattern to modify.
3. Make the modifications in the Boundary Hatch dialog box. If you just want to update the pattern to the revised boundary, don't make any changes.
4. Select **Apply.**

> *When you select an internal point for defining a boundary hatch, the point you select is important. AutoCAD remembers the point and, if boundary changes occur, the location of the internal point may affect the hatching, as the change may cause AutoCAD to hatch a different portion of the part. If this occurs, use Edit hatch to select a new internal point.*

You can define your own simple hatch patterns directly from within the Boundary Hatch dialog box.

To define your own hatch pattern:

1. From the Draw pull-down menu, choose **Hatch.**
2. Select on the arrow of the edit box in the Pattern Type box.
3. Select **User-Defined.**
4. Enter the Angle and Spacing in the Pattern Properties box.
5. Set the Double toggle. Double will create hatching at the angle you specified and at the angle opposite to the angle you specified.
6. Choose Pick Points in the Boundary box to select the internal point of a closed boundary.
7. Choose **Select objects** to select objects on the screen that will define the boundary for the pattern.
8. Select inside the boundaries for the hatching. Press **Enter** when you are done.
9. To see the hatching before actually making it part of the drawing, select **Preview Hatch.** Make changes to the pattern, scale, or angle and preview again.
10. When you are satisfied with the appearance of the hatch pattern, select **Apply.**

Text

Earlier in this chapter, you learned how to determine text height. There are many other factors that affect text besides its height. The factor that most affects the appearance of the text is the font. It makes a difference in the way your final drawings look, regenerate, and plot.

Fonts

AutoCAD has many standard fonts, many of which work well for mechanical drawings. When you select the fonts that you will use, consider the following criteria:

- Appearance: A clean and easy-to-read mechanical font is desirable, and will improve the appearance of plotted drawings. Eyestrain is a serious problem, especially with computers. If you find yourself straining to read the screen, try changing the font. SIMPLEX and ROMANS fonts are good choices for mechanical drawings based on appearance.
- Speed for Redraws/Regens: Some fonts regenerate very quickly; others regenerate very slowly. If speed is a consideration, try several fonts to see which works well. TXT font is very fast for regens because it

uses line segments instead of arcs and circles. It also plots very quickly, although it is not as pleasant to look at as SIMPLEX and ROMANS.

- Plotting: Some fonts plot faster than others. If you use a pen plotter, the TXT font is the fastest to plot. For raster plotters and printers, such as electrostatic plotters, ink jet plotters and all printers, the font has little affect on plotting speed.

To list the fonts:

1. From the Data pull-down menu, choose **Style.**
2. Enter a style name or press **Enter** to accept the default and display the Select a Font dialog box.

In the Select a Font dialog box, one of the selections is Bigfont file. Bigfonts are those that have more characters than normal. A standard font definition may have up to 255 defined characters, which is plenty for English fonts which have 26 uppercase characters, 26 lowercase characters, numerals, and punctuation. But AutoCAD is in use worldwide, so it must be capable of handling fonts that contain more than 255 characters, such as for Chinese. Bigfonts contain more than 255 characters.

In addition to the standard fonts, you may use postscript fonts and true-type fonts in AutoCAD.

Text Styles

Fonts work in conjunction with text styles. A text style is the combination of many factors that affect the appearance of the text. The font is only one of those factors. Other variables include the following:

- Height: Specifies the *fixed* height of the text. Enter a value of 0.00 for the text height if you want to use an undefined text height. AutoCAD will prompt you for the text height each time you create text in the drawing. See "Text Heights" on page 77.
- Width factor: Specifies a scale factor for the width. For example, a width factor of .8 makes the font appear narrower (80 percent of its defined width). A width factor of 1.2 makes the font appear wider (120 percent of its normal width).
- Obliquing angle: Specifies the angle for slanting the characters. A positive angle slants the top of the characters to the right; a negative angle slants the top of the characters to the left.
- Backwards: Characters are backwards. This is used to show text on the opposite side of an object; a printed circuit board, for example.
- Upside down: Characters are upside down.
- Vertical: Generates characters in a vertical line instead of a horizontal line.

By adjusting these variables, you can create many different appearances for any given font.

Creating a Text Style

Now that you know all the criteria for developing your own text styles, create a few text styles for your drawing.

To create a new text style:

1. From the Data pull-down menu, choose **Text Style.**
2. Enter the name of the style you want to create. When choosing a style name, use a name that describes the style. This will help you identify your text styles at a glance. You can rename text styles with the RENAME command.
3. Select the font you want to use from the list box.
4. Enter the Height, Width factor, Oblique angle, and so on. (See the previous section, "How Fonts are Affected by the Text Style.")

Whenever you create or redefine a text style, it automatically becomes the current text style.

Redefining a Text Style

It is sometimes necessary to redefine a text style, and you can do so at any time. Redefining a text style does not necessarily affect text already created with that style (See step 3).

To redefine a text style:

1. From the Data pull-down menu choose **Text Style.**
2. Type in the name of the style to redefine.
3. Select the font from the list box. When you choose a new font, all the text drawn with the style redefines automatically. If you do not change the font, existing text created with that style does not automatically change, but you can change it manually.
4. Enter the Height, Width factor, Oblique angle, and so on.
5. Type **REGEN** to regenerate the drawing. If the setting for the system variable REGENMODE is 1, the drawing regenerates automatically. You will not see the change until the drawing regenerates.
6. If you did not change the font, use the DDMODIFY or CHANGE commands to change the style of each text item individually.

Controlling the Text Height

Text heights are specified as part of the text style or defined at each text entry. There are advantages and disadvantages to each.

Text Heights

When you define a text style, you can establish a fixed text height as part of the text style. Optionally, you can leave the text height undefined. The advantage of using fixed text heights is that the text height is not specified for each text entry. This saves time and promotes consistency between text entities. The advantages of using undefined text heights are that text of varying heights uses a single text style, which saves space on the drawing; in addition, dimension text automatically scales.

Creating Text

There are several ways to create text in AutoCAD. The most common is the DTEXT or *dynamic* text command. DTEXT displays the text on the screen as you type it. You can create multiple lines of text and even backspace through them. When you use DTEXT, be sure to terminate the command by pressing **Enter** at a blank line. Otherwise, you will lose your text.

Another way to create text is with the TEXT command. TEXT displays the text on the command line as you type it. When you press **Enter,** the command terminates and the text is written to the screen. To continue creating text, press **Enter** again to reenter the TEXT command. If you want to continue beneath the text you just created, press **Enter** at the Start point prompt. With the TEXT command, you cannot backspace over multiple lines of text. Both DTEXT and TEXT have options for selecting a previously defined style and for selecting the justification of the text.

For multiple lines of text, you can also use the MTEXT command which uses the DOS text editor, or another editor that you can specify, to create the text. Once the text has been created, AutoCAD inserts the text on the screen.

To create text using MTEXT:

1. From the Draw pull-down menu, choose the **Text-Text** menu.
2. Select a window to define the length of the text lines.
3. Type the text in the DOS editor. Avoid using carriage returns. Type the text in a single line. The window you created determines the length of each line.
4. Save the file and exit the DOS editor.

MTEXT treats multiple lines of text as a single object. Selecting any part of MTEXT text selects all the text created with the MTEXT command. When you create text with MTEXT, AutoCAD ignores carriage returns. When you create your text, create it as a single line of text.

Editing Text

AutoCAD provides two ways to edit text. Both ways are accessed via the dialog boxes. The first method utilizes the DDEDIT dialog box.

To edit simple text using DDEDIT:

1. From the Modify pull-down menu, choose **Edit Text.**
2. Select the line of text to modify.
3. Use the dialog box to modify the text.
4. Select **OK** to keep the changes and select the next line of text.

To edit MTEXT text using DDEDIT:

1. From the Modify pull-down menu, choose **Edit Text.**
2. Select any line of text to modify. Ordinary text is edited in the DDEDIT dialog box. Selecting Mtext activates the DOS editor.
3. Modify the text in the DOS editor.
4. Save the file and exit the DOS editor.
5. Select **OK** to keep the changes and select the next line of text.

   The second way to edit text is with the DDCHPROP command.

To edit simple text using DDCHPROP:

1. From the modify pull-down menu, choose **Properties.**
2. Select the line of text to modify.
3. Modify the text in the text edit dialog box. With this command you can also change other properties of the text.
4. Select **OK** to save the edits and close the Change Properties dialog box.

Special Characters

It is sometimes necessary to create special characters that do not appear on the keyboard. Most fonts have provisions for this, which is why standard font definitions have up to 255 characters. Most standard fonts have the special characters that are used in mechanical drawings. These characters are shown in Table 2.2.

   AutoCAD also has the ability to create stacked text or stacked fractions. Stacked text uses the special character ^ to indicate where the selected text should be stacked. For example, to stack text to indicate a limits tolerance condition, separate the upper limit from the lower limit with a ^ character. For example, to create the text:

```
1.003
0.997
```

enter the text as:

```
    1.003^0.997.
```

Table 2.2   Characters Used in Mechanical Drawings

CHARACTER	TEXT OR DTEXT	MTEXT
Plus/minus symbol	%%P	\u+00B1
Diameter symbol	%%C	\u+2205
Degrees symbol	%%D	\u+00B0
Underscore	%%U	
Overscore	%%O	
Special Character	%%nnn, where nnn represents the code in the font definition file for the special character.	

AutoCAD can also stack fractions. To stack fractions, use the special character /. For example, to create the fraction ½, enter the text as 1/2.

General Readability

Fonts, style definitions, scaling, and text heights are a very important part of the drawing setup. If the text is too large or too small, or uses a style that is difficult to read, it detracts from the overall appearance of the drawing. For mechanical drawings, it is generally good practice to use clean and clear fonts that are easy to read and enhance the drawing's appearance.

Summary

AutoCAD has all the tools you need to accurately create two-dimensional working drawings of your designs. By using Snap, Osnap, Coords, and Grid, you can take advantage of AutoCAD's built-in accuracy tools.

When you draw objects in AutoCAD, you always draw at full scale. Drawings are scaled at the plotter. You can set up your CAD system with your particular requirements and save those settings in prototype drawings. The setup can easily control scaling of text and dimensions.

Whenever you edit objects, you must identify the objects for editing. AutoCAD's full set of selection tools permit you to select objects easily. Selected objects may be grouped or filtered out of a selection.

By controlling the display, you can adjust zoom magnification, set up prenamed views, control regeneration, and the virtual screen.

AutoCAD's mechanical command arsenal includes many tools that you can use to quickly create geometry. In addition to the commands themselves, there are many special entities that are useful for the development of designs. Xlines, rays, lines, polylines, splines, and other types of entities can be used for construction. Many commands modify existing entities. Other commands, such as BHATCH, embellish drawings so that they can be easily understood.

Every mechanical drawing requires annotation. AutoCAD has powerful text generation capabilities, and there are dozens of standard fonts with hundreds of third-party fonts available.

CHAPTER 3

Dimensioning

Since dimensions are such an important part of mechanical drawings, engineers, mechanical designers, and drafters take dimensioning very seriously. They should. Dimensions communicate the design so it can be manufactured.

Dimensioning usually must follow dimensioning standards. Companies have standards. Industries have standards. The government has standards. In most cases, you dimension your drawings according to some dimensioning standard. Since compliance with many standards is necessary, AutoCAD provides many tools and options for dimensioning.

Dimensioning with AutoCAD

For mechanical drawings dimensioning is critical. Dimensions have basically two requirements. First, they must be accurate. Second, they must be easy to interpret. AutoCAD easily handles the first requirement. Dimension accuracy, like drawing accuracy, is built into AutoCAD. It has features that control dimensional accuracy far beyond most engineering needs. Dimensional tolerancing and geometric tolerancing tools control features accurately. Alternate units of measure can accompany dimensions so that imperial and metric units can both appear on the same drawing.

The second requirement, interpretation, depends on you. How you dimension a mechanical drawing is almost as important as what you dimension. If the machine shop can't understand your drawing, what good is it? If you want to create drawings that others can understand, you must learn to control AutoCAD's dimensioning features.

NOTE   If you are running VGA resolution (640 × 480) you may not see the Draw, Dimensioning pull-down menu. Higher resolutions display the dimensioning commands on the pull-downs menus. Some of the examples in this chapter ask you to select dimensioning commands from the dimensioning pull-down menu. If your screen resolution does not display this menu, use the Screen menus to select dimensioning commands.

Concepts for Dimensioning

How you dimension your drawings may depend on many factors. There may be dimensioning standards for your office. You may have different dimensioning standards for different clients. Your personal preferences may serve as your dimensioning standards. Often, dimensioning must comply with military standards.

The dimensioning process is almost automatic if you create the geometry accurately. AutoCAD measures the distance between dimension points and uses this measurement for the default dimension value. Accurate geometry produces accurate dimensions.

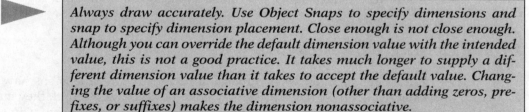

Always draw accurately. Use Object Snaps to specify dimensions and snap to specify dimension placement. Close enough is not close enough. Although you can override the default dimension value with the intended value, this is not a good practice. It takes much longer to supply a different dimension value than it takes to accept the default value. Changing the value of an associative dimension (other than adding zeros, prefixes, or suffixes) makes the dimension nonassociative.

Don't think of your drawing as simply instructions for making a part. People use CAD drawings in ways the originator did not anticipate. The minute you finish your drawing, someone else will ask you for a copy for a tolerance study or for use in another assembly.

Compliance with Military Standards

By controlling your dimensioning variables, you can create drawings that comply with most military standards. Your control over AutoCAD's dimensions and geometric tolerancing features allows your drawings to comply with ANSI Y14.5M (Engineering Drawings and Related Documentation Practices), DOD-STD-100 (Engineering Drawing Practices), and DOD-STD-1000 (Drawings, Engineering and Associated Lists).

AutoCAD Release 13 has added many dimensioning variables specifically designed for the purpose of compliance with military standards. For example, ANSI Y14.5M describes the handling of leading and trailing zeros in the following manner:

- **Millimeter Dimensioning:** "Where the dimension is less than one millimeter, a zero precedes the decimal point."

  "Where the dimension is a whole number, neither the decimal point nor a zero is shown."

  "Where the dimension exceeds a whole number by a decimal fraction of one millimeter, the last digit to the right of the decimal point is not followed by a zero."

- **Decimal Inch Dimensioning:** "A zero is not used before the decimal point for values less than one inch."

  "A dimension is expressed to the same number of decimal places as its tolerance. Zeros are added to the right of the decimal point where necessary."

AutoCAD handled the above specifications marginally in Release 12 with the dimensioning variable DIMZIN, which controlled leading and trailing zeros. As it is becoming common practice to include inches and millimeters on a single drawing, AutoCAD Release 13 has added several dimensioning variables to control decimal places and zero suppression:

- DIMTZIN controls leading and trailing zeros for tolerances.
- DIMALTZ controls leading and trailing zeros for alternate unit dimension values.
- DIMALTTD controls alternate unit tolerance decimal places.
- DIMALTTZ controls leading and trailing zeros for alternate unit tolerances.

ANSI Y14.5M also describes geometric tolerancing standards. AutoCAD Release 13 includes geometric tolerance frames as part of your dimensioning arsenal. Driven by dialog boxes, geometric tolerances are easy to create and comply with ANSI Y14.5M.

There are dozens of enhancements like the preceding examples for AutoCAD Release 13. Again, by controlling AutoCAD's dimensioning variables, you can comply with military, commercial, or other standards.

Conventional vs. Ordinate Dimensioning

AutoCAD provides two distinct types of dimensioning: conventional (arrowhead) dimensioning and Ordinate (datum) dimensioning. You must decide which type of dimensioning to use for each drawing. Conventional dimensioning works well for some types of parts. It allows you to tighten tolerances for some features and loosen tolerances for others, and you can include geometric tolerancing when necessary. Conventional dimensioning does require a little more setup because of the many features for each dimension. Does the dimension text belong above the dimension line or should it divide the dimension line? What size are the arrowheads? How far do the extension (witness) lines extend beyond the dimension lines?

Ordinate, or datum, dimensioning requires less setup and works well for some types of parts. Dimensions originate from a common base point (datum) and extend in both X and Y directions. You can control the placement of the dimensions and jog extension lines to improve readability. Conventional and ordinate dimensioning are described in "Dimensioning with AutoCAD," later in the chapter.

Setting Up for Dimensioning

Dimension setup often varies from drawing to drawing, and some parts may benefit from one dimensioning method while other parts may benefit from another. Drawing scale determines dimension scale. You will make many decisions before you place your first dimension.

Associative Dimensions

One decision you will make is whether to use *associative dimensions*, which are dimensions that dynamically change when the geometry of the part changes. Stretching or scaling a feature causes the dimension values to adjust. Associative dimensions cut down on editing. You can easily change the appearance of your dimensions when you use associative dimensions. The advantages of associative dimensions are numerous and far outweigh the disadvantages.

When you place an associative dimension, AutoCAD places points on the geometry where you specified the dimension. AutoCAD creates a special layer for these points which does not plot. The layer name is DEFPOINTS.

Associative dimensions are a special dimension entity. Unlike nonassociative dimensions, which are lines, arrowheads, and text, associative dimension work as a unit. Because of this, you can update their characteristics. For example, if you are half way through dimensioning a drawing and want to change the arrowhead size, you can update all the dimensions easily. With nonassociative dimensions, you would have to scale each arrowhead entity or re-create each dimension.

Dimension Styles

AutoCAD has dozens of dimensioning variables which control the appearance, tolerancing, text format, and every other aspect of dimensions. There are thousands of possible combinations for these variables, so when you decide on your favorite settings, you should save those settings as a *dimension style*.

A dimension style works much like a text style. A text style is a combination of many factors that control the appearance of the text, such as the font, height, width factor, oblique angle, and so on. A dimension style is the same concept except that many more factors control the appearance and function dimensions. You can set up dimension styles that work with most situations, and override specific dimension variables when necessary.

Dimension Style Families

Within each dimension style are families of dimension settings. A single dimension style may contain settings for linear dimensions, and different settings for radial dimensions. When you create a linear dimension, AutoCAD uses the settings for the linear family. When you create a radial dimension, AutoCAD uses the settings for the radial family. If the appropriate family is not available, AutoCAD uses the *parent* family definitions.

You can create dimension style families, based on the parent family definitions, for linear, radial, angular, diameter, ordinate, or leader dimensioning. For example, the dimensioning variable DIMUPT affects whether you will position the text on the dimension line manually. For linear dimensions, you may want AutoCAD to center the dimension on the dimension line automatically. For radial dimensions, you may want to position the text manually. You can use different settings within the same dimension style. When you draw linear dimensions, the Linear family activates and AutoCAD uses the appropriate setting. When you draw radial dimensions, the Radial family settings activate.

The Dimension Styles Dialog Box

The Dimension Styles dialog box provides easy access to the dimensions and their settings (Figure 3.1). The DDIM command opens the Dimension Styles dialog box. You can define most of your dimension settings from this dialog box, and each setting you change determines a value for one or more dimensioning variables. Before you begin dimensioning, open the Dimension Styles dialog box and take a look at the current settings.

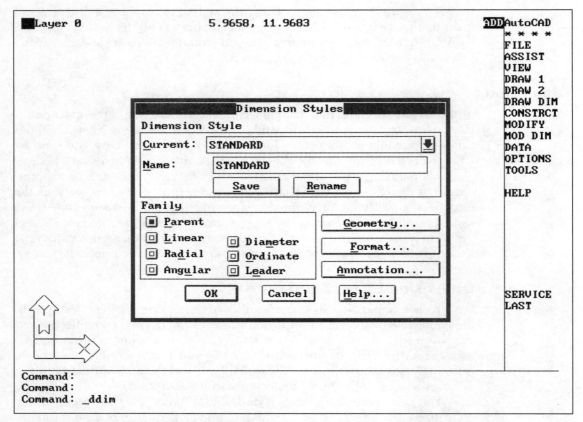

Figure 3.1   The Dimension Styles dialog box.

The Dimension Styles dialog box is an easy way to select or save a dimension style, then any dimensions can use a particular dimension style as a base. You can override the current settings for a dimension style; be aware however, that saving the dimension style with new definitions updates all dimensions created with that style. If you change your settings during a drawing, AutoCAD creates a new dimension style based on the current dimension style.

Under Dimension Style, in the first edit box, AutoCAD lists the current style. Below that, you can use the Name edit box to rename the current dimension style or save a new dimension style.

You cannot, however, rename the STANDARD dimension style. It is the AutoCAD default dimension style name. You can, however, change its definitions.

Below the Dimension Style edit boxes are the Family radio button boxes. Select these to make changes to a family for a dimension style.

To the right of the Family radio buttons are three selections, Geometry, Format, and Annotation. Each of these selections gives you access to the dimensioning variables that control the appearance of your dimensions. Many of the features include *image tiles* that allow you to preview the settings before accepting them.

> *Before setting up your dimension styles, select the Parent radio button. Make your changes to the Parent family first. When you are done, save your settings. Then select one of the other family radio buttons and make changes as necessary. Save your settings for each family that you modify.*

Geometry

The Geometry selection displays the Geometry dialog box (Figure 3.2). Within the geometry dialog box are features to control the dimension lines, extension lines, arrowheads, center marks, and overall scaling of dimensions. All values scale according to the overall scale factor. The following sections describe the geometry dialog box features:

Dimension Line

Suppress 1st and 2nd	Suppresses the first and second dimension lines when they are outside the extension lines. Sets dimensioning variable DIMSD1 and DIMSD2.
Extension	Specifies the distance to extend the dimension line past the extension lines. This feature is not desirable for arrowheads but is common for tick marks or other types of dimension terminations. Sets dimensioning variable DIMDLE.
Spacing	Specifies the spacing between dimension lines for baseline dimensions. Sets dimensioning variable DIMDLI.
Color	Specifies the color for dimension lines and arrows. Sets dimensioning variable DIMCLRD.

Extension Line

Suppress 1st and 2nd	Suppresses the first and/or second extension lines. Sets dimensioning variable DIMSE1 and DIMSE2.

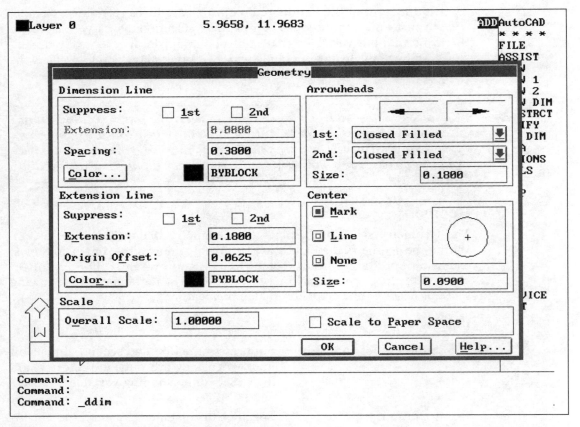

Figure 3.2 The Geometry dialog box.

Extension	Specifies the distance the extension lines will extend beyond the dimension line. Sets dimensioning variable DIMEXE.
Origin Offset	Specifies the distance from the origin point to the beginning of the extension line. Sets dimensioning variable DIMEXO.
Color	Specifies the color for extension lines. Sets dimensioning variable DIMCLRE.

Arrowheads

1st and 2nd	Displays the standard types for each arrowhead. Sets dimensioning variable DIMBLK, DIMBLK1, and DIMBLK2.

Size	Specifies the size of the arrowhead. Sets dimensioning variable DIMASZ.

Center

Mark	Selects a center mark for circles and arcs. Sets dimensioning variable DIMCEN.
Line	Selects a center mark and lines extending past the geometry of circles and arcs. Sets dimensioning variable DIMCEN.
None	Selects no mark. Sets dimensioning variable DIMCEN.
Size	Specifies the size of the center mark and the extension distance for the lines when you select the Line option. Sets dimensioning variable DIMCEN.

Format

The Format selection displays the Format dialog box (Figure 3.3), in which are features to control the formatting of the dimension. Formatting features control how the text, dimension, and extension lines work together.

User Defined	Overrides horizontal and vertical justification settings and places the text at the position of your cursor as you create the dimension. Sets dimensioning variable DIMUPT.
Force Line Inside	Draws the dimension line between the measured points even when arrowheads are outside the measured points. Sets dimensioning variable DIMTOFL.
Fit	Controls the placement of arrows and text, inside or outside the extension lines. Sets dimensioning variable DIMFIT.
Text	Specifies the orientation of text as follows:

Inside Horizontal: Specifies whether text inside extensions is horizontal. Sets dimensioning variable DIMTIH.

Outside Horizontal: Specifies whether text outside extensions is horizontal. Sets dimensioning variable DIMTOH.

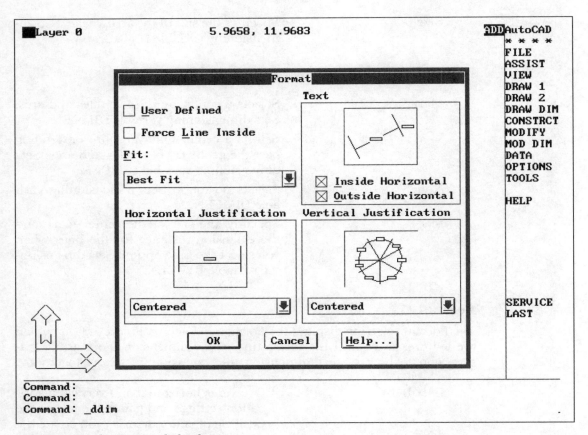

Figure 3.3   The Format dialog box.

Horizontal Justification	Specifies the horizontal justification for the dimension text. Sets dimensioning variable DIMJUST.
Vertical Justification	Specifies the vertical justification for the dimension text. Sets dimensioning variable DIMTAD.

Annotation

The Annotation selection displays the Annotation dialog box (Figure 3.4), which you use to control the actual dimension text. Within this box are features that control dimension units, alternate units, tolerance, and text.

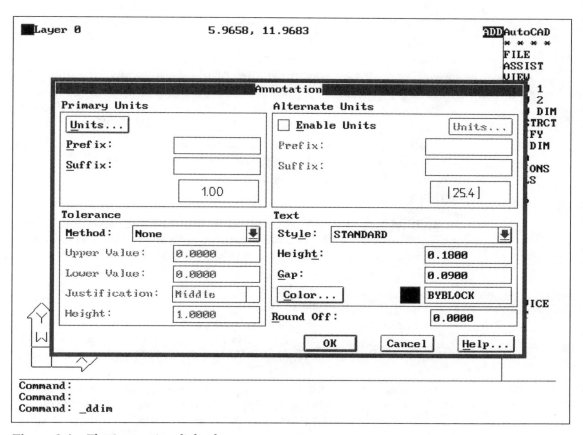

Figure 3.4 The Annotation dialog box.

Primary Units

Units   Displays the Primary Units dialog box. Use this to specify decimal, metric, or other unit types. Sets dimensioning variable DIMUNIT.

Prefix   Specifies the prefix for dimension text. Sets dimensioning variable DIMPOST.

Suffix   Specifies the suffix for dimension text. Sets dimensioning variable DIMPOST.

Alternate Units

Enable Units   Enables alternate units for dimensioning. AutoCAD displays alternate units in brackets [ ] after the pri-

	mary dimension. Sets dimensioning variable DI-MALT.
Units	Displays the Alternate Units dialog box. Use this to specify decimal, metric, or other alternate unit types. Sets dimensioning variable DIMALTU.
Prefix	Specifies the prefix for alternate unit dimension text. Sets dimensioning variable DIMAPOST.
Suffix	Specifies the suffix for alternate unit dimension text. Sets dimensioning variable DIMAPOST.

Tolerance

Method	Selects from None, Symmetrical, Deviation, Limits, and Basic dimension tolerance types. Depending on the method of tolerancing you select, other values in the tolerance box may become available.
None	No tolerance. Sets dimensioning variable DIMTOL = 0.
Symmetrical	Tolerance has plus and minus values that are the same. Sets dimensioning variables as follows: DIMTOL = 1, DIMLIM = 0, DIMTM and DIMTP = same value.
Deviation	Tolerance has plus and minus values that differ. Sets dimensioning variables as follows: DIMTOL = 1, DIMLIM = 0, DIMTM and DIMTP = different values.
Limits	Maximum dimension value is placed above the minimum dimension value. Sets dimensioning variables as follows: DIMTOL = 0, DIMLIM = 1, DIMTM and DIMTP have values.
Basic	Places a box around dimension values to indicate a basic dimension.
Upper Value	Specifies the upper tolerance value. Sets dimensioning variable DIMTP.
Lower Value	Specifies the lower tolerance value. Sets dimensioning variable DIMTM.
Justification	Controls justification for unilateral and bilateral tolerances. Sets dimensioning variable DIMTOLJ.
Height	Height factor applied to tolerance text. This value, multiplied by the text height, determines the height of tolerance text. Sets dimensioning variable DIMTFAC.

Text

Style	Specifies the text style. Sets dimensioning variable DIMTXSTY.
Height	Specifies the text height. Sets dimensioning variable DIMTXT.
Gap	Specifies the gap between the dimension line and the text. Sets dimensioning variable DIMGAP.

By using the Dimension Style dialog box, you can set up the appearance of your dimensions. Be sure to save your settings before selecting OK. Once you have set up your dimensions, you are ready to dimension.

Dimensioning with AutoCAD

There are two basic rules for dimensioning with AutoCAD:

- Draw accurately.
- Dimension to the geometry.

As you learned in Chapter 2, drawing accurately with AutoCAD is important for many reasons. If you draw accurately, the process of dimensioning becomes almost automatic. As you dimension an object, AutoCAD automatically measures the distance between dimension points for you. The measured distance becomes the *default* dimension. This means you can press **Enter** to accept the measured distance or supply your own value. Obviously, it is much faster to press **Enter** than to type in an adjusted dimension value for each dimension. Again, entering a different value undermines the integrity of associative dimensions.

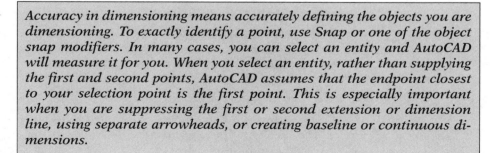

Accuracy in dimensioning means accurately defining the objects you are dimensioning. To exactly identify a point, use Snap or one of the object snap modifiers. In many cases, you can select an entity and AutoCAD will measure it for you. When you select an entity, rather than supplying the first and second points, AutoCAD assumes that the endpoint closest to your selection point is the first point. This is especially important when you are suppressing the first or second extension or dimension line, using separate arrowheads, or creating baseline or continuous dimensions.

Linear Dimensions

You create linear dimensions with the DIMLINEAR command. Linear dimensions use a new method for creating dimensions, called *dimensioning by inference.* When you specify a linear dimension, AutoCAD uses the dimension line placement point to determine whether you are creating a vertical or horizontal dimension. If the dimension line is placed to the left or right of the entity you are dimensioning, AutoCAD assumes you are creating a vertical dimension. If the dimension line is placed above or below the entity you are dimensioning, AutoCAD assumes you are creating a horizontal dimension. The DIMLINEAR command includes options that enable you to override the inference dimensioning mode and specify vertical or horizontal dimensions, dimensions at a specified angle, rotated text, or nondefault text values.

To create linear dimensions:

1. From the Draw pull-down menu, choose **Dimensioning–Linear.**
2. Select two points for the dimension. You may optionally press **Enter** to select an object to dimension. Remember to use Snap or object snap modifiers when selecting the points.
3. Select the location for the dimension.
4. Press **Enter** to accept the default value.

Baseline and Continuous Dimensions

You can use existing linear dimensions to create baseline and continuous dimensions. When you create a baseline dimension, AutoCAD uses the first dimension point of the previous linear dimension as the start point of the dimension. When you create a continuous dimension, AutoCAD uses the second dimension point of the previous linear dimension as the start point of the dimension. Optionally, you can select any dimension, rather than the previously created dimension, for baseline and continuous dimensions. AutoCAD remembers the order in which the points of the selected dimension were created. The dimensioning variable DIMDLI controls the spacing between dimension lines.

To create a baseline dimension:

1. From the Draw pull-down menu, choose **Dimensioning–Baseline.**
2. Select the second point to use the previous dimension, or press **Enter** to select a different dimension for the baseline. Select the second point.

To create a continued dimension:

1. From the Draw pull-down menu, choose **Dimensioning–Continue.**
2. Select the second point to use the previous dimension, or press **Enter** to select a different dimension to continue. Select the second point.

Radial Dimensions

Radial dimensions are easily created by selecting an arc or circle to dimension. AutoCAD automatically determines the radius for you. The value of the dimensioning variable DIMUPT controls whether you position the text or AutoCAD positions it for you. Set DIMUPT to a value of 1 to place the leader and text manually. Set DIMUPT to a value of 0 to have AutoCAD place the leader and text for you. This setting is also available in the Dimension Styles, Format, dialog box as the User Defined toggle.

For radial dimensions, AutoCAD automatically supplies the letter R for radius and the symbol Ø for diameter.

Leaders

AutoCAD's leader entity can be one of two types (Figure 3.5). A straight line segmented leader, typically used for mechanical drawings, can have multiple straight line segments. A curve leader, common on architectural drawings, is the second leader type. It uses AutoCAD's spline entity to draw the leader. Leaders are usually drawn with one of AutoCAD's standard arrowheads.

When you have specified the leader, press **Enter.** For straight line segment leaders, AutoCAD adds a short horizontal line segment at the end of the leader and prepares for the leader text. Leader annotation can be a single line of text or a multiple-line text object like the type created by the MTEXT command. You can append a copy of annotation that exists on your drawing to leaders. Additionally, you can use a tolerance control frame as part of the leader.

Ordinate Dimensions

Many mechanical drafters prefer to use *ordinate* dimensions, commonly known as datum dimensions, for dimensioning mechanical parts (Figure 3.6). The advantages of ordinate dimensions are:

- They are easy to create.
- They are easy to interpret.
- It is easier to set up for ordinate dimensions because they require fewer dimensioning variable settings.
- Drawings often look cleaner with ordinate dimensions.
- Machine shops prefer ordinate dimensions because they don't have to convert the dimensions for their equipment.

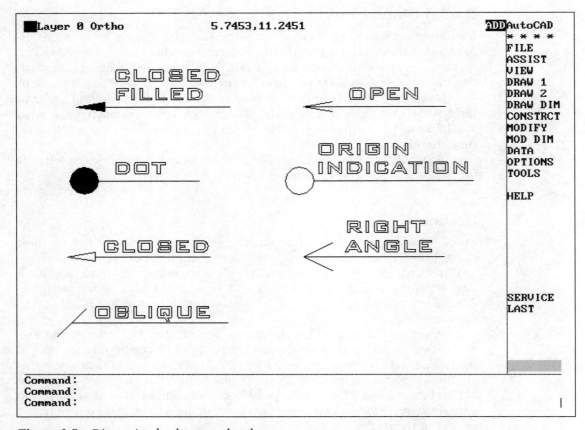

Figure 3.5 Dimension leader arrowhead types.

AutoCAD has a fairly simple way to generate ordinate dimensions. The process requires three basic steps.

1. Establish a UCS origin at the origin or datum point for the dimensions.

2. Identify the features to dimension.

3. Place the dimension text.

UCS, as noted in Chapter 2, stands for User Coordinate System. Among other things, you can use the UCS command to establish an origin other than 0,0 for point coordinates. By setting the UCS origin to the origin or datum point, you can measure all dimensions from that point. Chapter 5 describes the UCS command in detail.

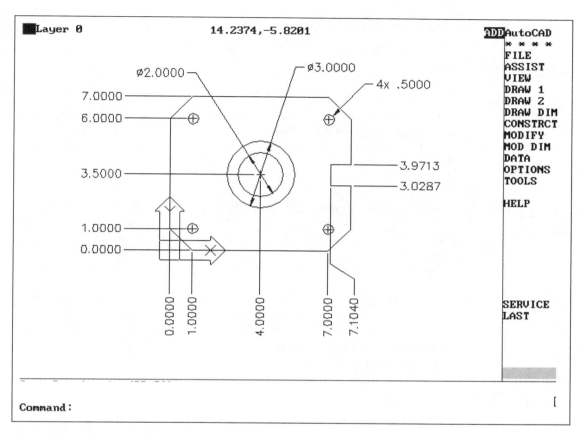

Figure 3.6 Ordinate dimensions.

To set the UCS origin:

1. From the View pull-down menu, choose **Set UCS–Origin.**
2. Select the origin or datum point for your ordinate dimensions.

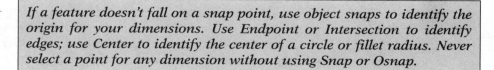

If a feature doesn't fall on a snap point, use object snaps to identify the origin for your dimensions. Use Endpoint or Intersection to identify edges; use Center to identify the center of a circle or fillet radius. Never select a point for any dimension without using Snap or Osnap.

To generate ordinate dimensions:

1. From the Draw pull-down menu, choose **Dimension–Ordinate.**
2. Select a point on the object to dimension.
3. Select the location of the text.
4. Press **Enter** to accept the dimension text.

For orthographic drawings, you must set the UCS origin for each view. The dimensioning variable DIMDEC controls the number of decimal places for the dimension text. Use this dimensioning variable to control toleranc-ing for ordinate dimensions.

Draw a temporary rectangle around the part you are dimensioning to help you align ordinate dimension text. When prompted for the dimension text location, use the Perpendicular object snap and select the rectangle.

AutoCAD places a jog in the extension line, when necessary, for ordi-nate dimensions when Ortho is off. To ensure that extension lines are cre-ated without a jog, turn Ortho on or use the Perpendicular object snap mode with the rectangle tip just given. To intentionally place a jog in an ex-tension line, turn Ortho off.

Geometric Tolerancing

In addition to dimension tolerances, AutoCAD can generate geometric tol-erance feature control frames that comply with ANSI-Y14.5M (Figure 3.7).

To generate geometric tolerance frames:

1. From the Draw pull-down menu, choose **Dimensioning–Tolerance.**
2. Select the tolerancing symbol for the geometric tolerance frame.
3. Specify the tolerance values, datums, and material conditions in the Geometric Tolerance dialog box.
4. Select **OK** to close the Geometric Tolerance dialog box.
5. Place the feature control frame on the drawing.

Editing Dimensions

If you use associative dimensions, the process of editing dimension values is automatic. As you stretch, extend, or trim geometry, the dimension values change with the geometry. If you choose not to use associative dimensions, you must edit the value of the dimension text manually, stretch the dimen-sion lines and, essentially, re-create the dimensions.

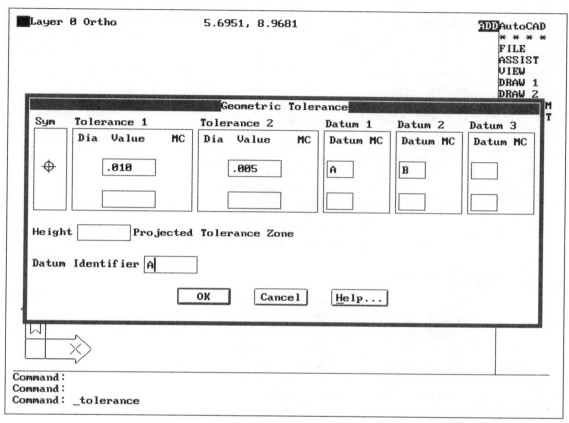

Figure 3.7 The Geometric Tolerance dialog box.

▶ *Always use associative dimensions. AutoCAD's associative dimensioning feature is a time-saver. By associating dimensions to the features they control, you can literally forget about editing dimension values when geometry changes. Nonassociative dimensions not only require extensive editing, they don't have any idea what they are dimensioning and don't even know that they represent a dimension. This means you cannot change the appearance of the dimensions without regenerating them. Also, avoid exploding dimensions. Exploding a dimension removes its association to the object being dimensioned.*

Changing Dimensions from One Dimension Style to Another

You can change the appearance of dimensions easily by changing the style used to create them. You can redefine the dimension style or change dimensions from one style to another. You can even create a new style, if necessary.

To change a dimension's appearance:

1. From the Data pull-down menu, choose **Dimension Style.**
2. Select the dimension style for the dimensions or override the settings to create a new dimension style.
3. Issue the DIMSTYLE command and select **Apply.**
4. Select the dimensions to change to the new dimension style.

You may optionally choose to change the dimensioning variable settings at the command line ("See Dimensioning Variables," next).

Dimensioning Variables

Some dimensioning variables are toggles. The values for toggles are 1 = ON and 0 = OFF. You can set dimensioning variables directly from the command line by typing the name of the dimensioning variable. To set a dimensioning variable transparently (during a command), use the transparent command 'SETVAR and enter the name of the dimensioning variable.

Although military standards usually represent guidelines or a preferred method for dimensioning, the following list notes the ANSI standard settings where they may apply.

DIMALT	Alternate units selected: Turn this on if you want to display two values for dimension text. AutoCAD multiplies the alternate units by the value of DIMALTF. Example: Use this feature to display inches and millimeters.
DIMALTD	Alternate unit decimal places: Specifies the number of decimal places for the alternate units.
DIMALTF	Alternate unit scale factor: AutoCAD multiplies the dimension value by this number to determine the alternate units. Example: To display millimeters as your alternate unit (assuming your drawing unit represents inches), enter a value of 25.4.
DIMALTTD	Alternate tolerance decimal places: Specifies the number of decimal places for tolerances of alternate units.
DIMALTTZ	Leading/trailing zeros: Specifies how AutoCAD handles leading and trailing zeros for alternate unit tol-

erances. See DIMZIN.ANSI = 3 for millimeters, 4 for decimal inches.

DIMALTU	Alternate units: Specifies the units for alternate dimensions.
DIMALTZ	Leading/trailing zeros: Specifies how AutoCAD handles leading and trailing zeros for alternate units. See DIMZIN. ANSI = 3 for millimeters, 4 for decimal inches.
DIMAPOST	Suffix for alternate text: Enter a value if you want to display a suffix for your alternate units. Example: Enter mm if you want alternate units to show mm (millimeters) as part of the dimension text.
DIMASO	Create associative dimensions: Turn this on to associate the dimension with the geometry.
DIMASZ	Arrow size: Specifies the size of the arrowhead. The size measures lengthwise along the arrow.
DIMAUNIT	Angular unit format: Specifies the format for angular dimensions. ANSI = 0
DIMBLK	Arrow block name: Specifies the name for a custom arrowhead block. See DIMBLK1 and DIMBLK2.
DIMBLK1	First arrow block name: Name of the custom arrowhead block for the first dimension line.
DIMBLK2	Second arrow block name: Name of the custom arrowhead block for the first dimension line.
DIMCEN	Center mark size: Size of the center mark for circles. The size measures from the center of the circle to the end of the mark. To produce a center mark that identifies the center of the circle and extends beyond the boundary of the circle, enter a negative value. The value controls the size of the center mark, the size of the gap, and the extension beyond the boundary of the circle. ANSI = Small center mark, exact size not specified.
DIMCLRD	Dimension line color: Specifies the color for dimension lines and arrows. Change this to control line widths when you plot.
DIMCLRE	Extension line and leader color: Specifies the color for extension lines and leaders. Change this to control line widths when you plot.
DIMCLRT	Dimension text color: Specifies the color for text. Change this to control text when you plot.

DIMDEC	Decimal places: Specifies the number of decimal places for dimension text.
DIMDLE	Dimension line extension: Specifies how far the dimension line extends beyond the extension line. Set this value to 0 to make dimension lines terminate at the arrowhead.
DIMDLI	Dimension line increment for continuation: Specifies the distance between dimension lines for baseline and continuous dimensioning. ANSI = not less than 6mm (.24 in.) between dimension lines. The first dimension line is not less than 10mm (.39 in.) from part.
DIMEXE	Extension above dimension line: Specifies the distance the extension line extends beyond the dimension line.
DIMEXO	Extension line origin offset: Specifies the distance between the geometry and the beginning of the extension line.
DIMFIT	Fit text: Fits the text in the available area. Not commonly used for mechanical drawings because it condenses or expands the text.
DIMGAP	Gap from dimension line to text: Specifies the distance between the dimension line and the text. ANSI = Visible gap, no specified value.
DIMJUST	Justification of text on dimension line: Specifies the text justification for dimension text.
DIMLFAC	Linear unit scale factor: Scale factor for linear measurements. Example: If you are dimensioning a detail on a drawing that is 2× scale, relative to the rest of the drawing, set this value for 0.5.
DIMLIM	Generate dimension limits: Creates limits tolerancing based on the values of DIMTM (minus tolerance) and DIMTP (plus tolerance).
DIMPOST	Default suffix for dimension text: Automatically attaches a suffix to dimension values. Example: mm adds the suffix for millimeters.
DIMRND	Rounding value: Used for rounding dimension values.
DIMSAH	Separate arrow blocks: Turn this on to use the arrowhead blocks specified in DIMBLK1 and DIMBLK2.
DIMSCALE	Overall scale factor: Scale factor for all dimensioning variable values. When you work on a scaled draw-

ing, adjust this value to the scale. Example: A drawing that is 2× scale reduces by half at the plotter. Set DIMSCALE to 2 so arrowheads, center marks, and other features scale properly when you plot the drawing.

DIMSD1   First dimension line suppression: Suppresses the first dimension line. The first dimension line is determined by the first point you select when specifying the dimension. If you press **Enter** to select the geometry to dimension, the first point is on the side closest to the point you selected.

DIMSD2   Second dimension line suppression: Suppresses the second dimension line. The second dimension line is determined by the second point you select when specifying the dimension. If you press **Enter** to select the geometry to dimension, the second point is on the side farthest from the point you selected.

DIMSE1   Suppress the first extension line: Suppresses the first extension line. The first extension line is determined by the first point you select when specifying the dimension. If you press **Enter** to select the geometry to dimension, the first point is on the side closest to the point you selected.

DIMSE2   Suppress the second extension line: Suppresses the second extension line. The second extension line is determined by the second point you select when specifying the dimension. If you press **Enter** to select the geometry to dimension, the second point is on the side farthest from the point you selected.

DIMSHO   Update dimensions while dragging: Turn this on to see associative dimension values change when you stretch a part. This works well with Snap but not too well without it.

DIMSOXD   Suppress outside extension dimension.

DIMSTYLE   Current dimension style (read-only): Displays the current dimension style. You cannot change this value directly.

DIMTAD   Place text above the dimension line: Values for DIMTVP affect this variable. ANSI = 0 preferred, 1 is OK.

DIMTDEC   Tolerance decimal places: Specifies the number of decimal places for dimension tolerances.

DIMTFAC	Tolerance text height scaling factor: Specifies the scale factor for tolerance text. Example: To make the tolerance text 3/4 size relative to the dimension text, enter a value of 0.75. ANSI = 1.
DIMTIH	Text inside extensions is horizontal: Specifies horizontal text for vertical, aligned, and rotated dimensions that are inside the extension lines. If you want your dimensions to align with the dimension line, turn this variable off. ANSI = 1.
DIMTIX	Place text inside extensions: When dimension lines, arrows, text, and gap spaces won't fit within the extension lines, this variable places dimension text inside the extension lines, and arrows and dimension lines outside the extensions.
DIMTM	Minus tolerance: Value for minus tolerance. DIMLIM and DIMTOL read this value.
DIMTOFL	Force line inside extension lines: Forces a line between the extension lines when the text and dimension lines are outside the extension lines.
DIMTOH	Text outside extensions is horizontal: Specifies horizontal text for vertical, aligned, and rotated dimensions that are outside the extension lines. If you want your dimensions to align with the dimension line, turn this variable off. ANSI = 1.
DIMTOL	Generate dimension tolerances: Generates nominal dimension with stacked plus and minus tolerances per the values of DIMTM and DIMTP. DIMTFAC controls tolerance text height. If the values of DIMTM and DIMTP are the same, AutoCAD displays a single tolerance value preceded by a plus/minus symbol.
DIMTOLJ	Tolerance vertical justification. Similar to DIMTVP.
DIMTP	Plus tolerance: Value for plus tolerance. DIMLIM and DIMTOL read this value.
DIMTSZ	Tick size: Size of the tick mark from the dimension line to the end of the tick mark. Tick marks are a type of arrowhead generally used by architectural disciplines.
DIMTVP	Text vertical position: Specifies vertical position of the dimension text. If you don't specify a value, AutoCAD centers the text on the dimension line.
DIMTXSTY	Text style: Dimension text style. The text style must be a valid, predefined text style.

DIMTXT	Text height: Dimension text height. If the current text style has a predefined text height, this value is not used.
DIMTZIN	Leading/trailing zeros: Controls how AutoCAD handles leading and trailing zeros for dimension text.
DIMUNIT	Unit format: Specifies the unit format for dimension values.
DIMUPT	User-positioned text: For radial dimensions, you may want to turn this on. Turning DIMUPT on allows you to adjust the leader length for the text. If DIMUPT is on for linear dimensions, the text goes where you select the dimension line location. Turn this off to center the text on the dimension line. ANSI = 0 is preferred, or 1 if text must be repositioned for readability.
DIMZIN	Zero suppression: A value of 1, 2, or 3 affects feet and inches dimensions (architectural units). A value of 4 suppresses leading zeros (to comply with military standards for decimal inch units). ANSI = 3 for millimeters, 4 for decimal inches.

CHAPTER 4

Blocks and External References

In AutoCAD, blocks and external references let you access geometry that is saved in your drawing file or in an external file. Blocks are multiple entities that are treated as a single object. For example, you can use lines and circles to draw a hex nut. Once drawn, the graphic elements can be captured as a block and saved as part of the drawing or as a separate drawing file. You can insert the block whenever you need to depict a hex nut. You can scale or rotate the block as you insert it.

You can create blocks as part of the current drawing, using the BLOCK command, or as separate drawing files with the WBLOCK command. The WBLOCK command writes a block definition to its own drawing file. Wblocking a block makes the block available for use in other drawings. You can group and organize blocks into block libraries, which may contain electronic, piping or weld symbols, hardware and fasteners, drawing formats or entire drawings.

An external reference (xref) is a drawing file that is linked to the current drawing. Unlike blocks, which become part of the drawing, xrefs display on the screen with your working drawing, but *do not become part of the drawing*. Each time you load your drawing, or reload the xref, the xref definition updates. Xrefs work like blocks in many ways. Although you insert blocks and attach xrefs to drawings, both require an insertion point, scale factor, and rotation angle. Both blocks and xrefs behave as a single entity, and you can use their elements for object snapping.

Xrefs make concurrent engineering possible so that while designers work on separate portions of an assembly, each designer's work is available to the other designers in reference form. As design changes occur, the results are available to the others on the design team.

Blocks

One of the most powerful tools in AutoCAD is the block. As just stated, a block may be a consolidation of many entities into a single object. Blocks are as simple as a single line or as complex as an entire drawing, and can use any number of layers.

In addition to graphic entities, blocks may contain visible or invisible text information called *attributes*. By using attributes, you can generate a report or a bill-of-materials. Often, attributes are used to help automate text entry.

You can insert blocks into a drawing at any scale or proportion and rotate them to any angle. You can also explode blocks. When you explode a block, it reverts to the elements that defined the block and loses any block and attribute information that it retained as a block.

Scaling Blocks

Before you create a block, consider its intended use. Different types of blocks can be scaled differently. There are three categories of blocks. The first is a *part*. A part is anything that has a dimension in the real world. This is similar to the discussion of scaling in Chapter 1. A part is a battleship, a screw head, or a pad on a printed circuit board. If you normally dimension it on a drawing, it is a part. When you create a part block, be sure to draw it at full scale.

The second type of block is a *symbol*. Symbols are things like arrows, bubble numbers, and schematic symbols. The scale of the drawing determines the scale of symbols. The factor that governs the symbol size is usually its readability on the final plot. Symbols scale based on the drawing scale.

The third type of block is a *parametric*. Parametric blocks are like parts except that typically measure one unit by one unit. Scaling occurs at insertion. For example, a parametric block that represents a hex head bolt is drawn at one unit across the corners. For this example, assume that the unit is one inch. A 1/4" bolt head, which measures 0.530" across the corners, can be created by inserting the block at a scale of 0.530. To represent a 7/8" bolt head, which measures 1.856 across the corners, scale the block at 1.856. The same block may be used for metric drawings and scaled in metric units.

Creating A Simple Block

Creating a block is not difficult. When you prepare your geometry for the block, consider how you will use the block based on the criteria just described. Then, draw accurately! Everyone in your firm may have to use the block.

NOTE When you create blocks, pay attention to the layer that the entities are on. Layer Ø is a special layer for blocks. If the entitites for your block are on layer Ø, they will inherit the characteristics of the layer on which the block is inserted. For example, if you insert the block on a red layer, the block will be red. If the entities for your block are on a layer other than Ø, they will retain the characteristics of the layer they were created on.

To create a block:

1. Draw the object you want to block.
2. From the Construct pull-down menu, select **Block.**
3. Enter the block name. Try to keep names within eight characters.
4. Select the insertion base point. This is the attachment handle for the block. If your block is a bolt, use the center of the bolt so you can align it with the center of the hole for the bolt.
5. Select the objects for the block. You can use any selection method to select the objects.

NOTE When you select the objects, the block disappears, but the definition for the block remains in the drawing. To redisplay the objects you used to create the block, type **OOPS**.

To place the block into your drawing:

1. From the Draw pull-down menu, select **Insert.**
2. Select **Block.**
3. Select the block name.
4. Select the point on the screen for the block.
5. Enter the X and Y scale factors.
6. Enter the rotation angle.

You can explode blocks to restore the entities that make up the block. When you explode a block, the entities return to the layer they were on when you created the block. Attribute values are lost but the attribute definitions are retained. Although you can explode blocks with uneven X, Y, and Z scale factors, the objects created may be unexpected. For example, if your block contains a circle and the scale factors cause the circle to look like an ellipse, the exploded block may include a series of arcs to represent the circle entity.

To explode a block:

1. From the Modify pull-down menu, choose **Explode.**
2. Select the block(s) to explode.

Why Use Blocks?

When you use blocks, you gain significant advantages over simply copying objects. When you create a block, AutoCAD stores the block definition in the drawing file or externally depending on the command used to create the block. There are several advantages to using blocks, including:

- Blocks save memory. When you begin a drawing, AutoCAD loads the drawing into memory (RAM). The larger the drawing size, the more memory it requires. This means less memory is available for AutoCAD commands and other functions. Blocks make your drawing smaller when multiple insertions of the block occur. The smaller the drawing, the less disk space you need to store the drawing.
- You can replace or redefine blocks. You can edit all the occurrences of a block with a single command. For example, all the slotted screw heads could be replaced with cross-recessed screw heads by redefining the block (see "Redefining Blocks," upcoming) or with the following command syntax:

```
INSERT OLDBLOCK=NEWBLOCK
```

- You can save blocks on your hard disk and create libraries of blocks to use in any drawing.
- You can add attributes to blocks to collect information from the user when the block is inserted in the drawing. Attributes can increase productivity by automating the gathering of information, displaying the information on the drawing, and extracting it for use in databases and spreadsheets.

Memory and Storage Savings

AutoCAD stores information for every entity on the drawing. For a simple line entity, AutoCAD stores the start point, end point, length, rotation angle, linetype, elevation, thickness, layer, color, and more. If you draw an object that uses ten lines and copy that object ten times on a drawing, AutoCAD stores the information for 100 entities.

If you create a block out of the ten entities and insert the block ten times in the drawing, AutoCAD stores the information for the first block definition, plus the information for each occurrence of the block, or 19 entities. Although it really isn't that simple, you can significantly reduce file size by using blocks. Smaller file sizes reduce loading times, storage space, and make more RAM available. More RAM means reduced virtual memory requirements (paging to disk) and enhanced overall performance.

Redefining Blocks

Changing the block definition automatically updates all the blocks that use that definition. A common trick is to define simple blocks during the early stages of the design process and replace them with complex blocks as the design nears completion. This speeds up overall performance during the design process.

To redefine a block:

1. From the Construct pull-down menu, select **Block.**
2. Enter the block name. If the block exists in the drawing, AutoCAD asks if you want to redefine the block. Answer Yes.
3. Create the new block just as you created the original block. All the blocks on the drawing redefine.

Writing Blocks to the Hard Disk

It wouldn't be of much advantage if block definitions were only good for a single drawing. Obviously, if blocks are reusable, there must be a way to save them independent of any particular drawing. The command for writing blocks to the hard disk is WBLOCK. When you Wblock a block, it becomes a separate drawing file. You can edit this drawing just like any other drawing, and you can insert any drawing file into another drawing.

When you insert a drawing file from the hard disk, you are inserting all the block definitions, layers, text styles, and other references that are in the drawing file but not on the current drawing. If any of the references already occur on the drawing, AutoCAD displays a message indicating that it ignores the duplicate definition.

To avoid generating block definitions with unnecessary information, the WBLOCK command automatically strips away any unreferenced information. This cleans up the block definition file and often makes it much smaller.

▶
> *Advanced AutoCAD users often use WBLOCK to save their finished drawings. In this way, they remove unreferenced information. This makes it easier to store and transport drawing files. See the WBLOCK * option later in the chapter.*

To write a block to the hard disk:

1. Issue the WBLOCK command at the command prompt.
2. Enter the name of the block at the file name prompt.
3. Enter the name of the block in the drawing that you are writing out to the hard disk. If the file name and the block name are the same, you can, instead, enter an equal symbol (=) instead of the block name.

The file name is the name of the drawing file on the hard disk. Make the name descriptive. If, for example, the bolt is a 10-32 pan head, try to work that into the name somehow. DOS only allows eight characters so try to work out a system in advance. If there is a file in the directory by the same name, AutoCAD will ask you for permission to overwrite it. Don't answer Yes unless you know what you are overwriting.

NOTE   Use caution when you WBLOCK a drawing, because you could overwrite a drawing file. A simple Yes could wipe out an entire drawing representing many of hours of work. WBLOCK does *not* create a backup! WBLOCK overwrites existing drawing files. It does not delete them so you can't use an undelete utility to restore them. Once it is gone, it is gone!

If you haven't created the block in the drawing, but want to write out a block definition, press **Enter** at the Block name prompt. AutoCAD then prompts for the insertion base point and the objects just like the BLOCK command.

Replacing Blocks

Suppose you have modified a part outside the drawing, and you would like to insert it into the drawing. When you issue the INSERT command, Auto-CAD first looks in the drawing for a block by the name you specify. If it doesn't find it, it looks in the current directory on the hard disk for the block. If it still doesn't find it, AutoCAD looks in each directory on the search path. The search path is determined by the SET ACAD = environment variable which is normally specified in the batch file that begins AutoCAD.

If you have already inserted a block by the same name in your drawing, AutoCAD assumes you just want to insert another block. To force AutoCAD to ignore the drawing's definition and look for the block on the hard disk, use the INSERT command, but when prompted for the block name, follow the block name with an equal (=) symbol. Example: BOLT= replaces the definition of the block in the drawing with the block from the hard disk.

You can also insert a block definition, sometimes called an exploded block, by prefixing the block name with an asterisk (*). Example *BOLT inserts the entities that were used to create the BOLT block. Block definitions are always inserted with equal scale factors.

Attributes

An attribute is text information that accompanies the insertion of a block. An attribute can contain information for a bill-of-materials or report or automate the insertion of a title block. Attributes can be constant or variable, visible or invisible. When you insert a block with attributes into a drawing, the attributes are displayed according to the block's scale, proportion, and rotation.

Why Use Attributes?

Perhaps you never create a bill-of-materials, or use a separate program for generating the bill-of-materials. Why use attributes? A good way to answer this question is with an example.

If you use a drawing title block *without* attributes, in the title block you must supply information specific to each drawing. Each time you insert the title block, you use one of the text commands to fill in the drawing number, drawing title, drawn by, date, revision, project number, next assembly, used on, and other information. This requires sizing and centering each piece of text for each title block at the particular drawing scale. If the drawing number should be bolder than the other text, you have to use a bolder text style or change the color for that text. When you are done, you have a graphic entity that represents a title block.

If, on the other hand, you use a title block *with* attributes, each time you insert the title block, a dialog box appears (or a prompt at the command line depending on your preference). You enter the information for each attribute. Each attribute has its own definition for text style, height, location and justification, and color. By simply supplying the information, you have generated a perfect title block that has capabilities beyond the graphic representation of the title block. The benefits of using attributes in this example then are:

- It's much faster to insert the drawing format.
- You get consistent text heights, styles, justification, colors, and so on.

- It's easy to use. You just type in an editable dialog box.
- You never forget to fill in the information because the dialog box lists everything required.
- You can extract the title block attributes to generate a report for each drawing in your company which lists each drawing name, drawing number, project number, revision, drafter, and date.

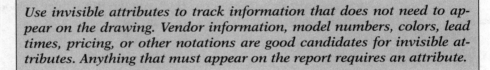

Use invisible attributes to track information that does not need to appear on the drawing. Vendor information, model numbers, colors, lead times, pricing, or other notations are good candidates for invisible attributes. Anything that must appear on the report requires an attribute.

Creating a Block with Attributes

Using attributes can result in significant savings in time. Visible attributes simplify the placement of text information by predefining the text size, style, justification, layering, and other characteristics of the text.

To define attributes from the command line:

1. Type **ATTDEF** at the command line. The options Invisible, Constant, Verify, and Preset toggle when you enter the letter **I, C, V,** or **P.** The default settings are No for all the options.
2. Press **Enter** to accept the defaults, or type **I, C, V,** or **P** to toggle the current settings.
3. Enter the attribute tag. The attribute tag is the field name for reports. If the attribute represents a size, then SIZE is a good tag name.
4. Enter the attribute prompt. At this point, you are the programmer. Since others may use your block, the prompt lets the user know what information to supply. If the user should supply the size, then "Size" or "Please enter the size" would be good prompts.
5. Enter the default attribute value. You can have a default value present each time you insert the block. If the value will change for each insertion, don't supply a default value. If a particular value is more common than other values, enter that value as a default.
6. Enter a modifier for the justification, if required. If the text should be middle justified, type **M.** If the text is left justified, skip this step; left justified is the default.
7. Select a start point for the attribute on your screen.
8. Enter the height of the text if you don't have a preset height defined in your text style. If you have a preset height, AutoCAD does not prompt for the height.
9. Enter the rotation angle for the attribute.

10. Repeat steps 1 through 9 for each attribute.
11. Create the block by selecting the objects and the attribute definitions.

To insert the block:

1. From the Draw pull-down menu, choose **Insert Block.**
2. Enter the block name.
3. Select an insert point on the drawing.
4. Supply the X and Y scale factor and Rotation Angle information at the prompts.
5. Supply the attribute information at the prompts.

As an exercise, use the procedure just defined to create a block called NOTE. Middle justify an attribute called NOTE in the center of a circle. When you create the block, select the attribute and the circle. See Figure 4.1.

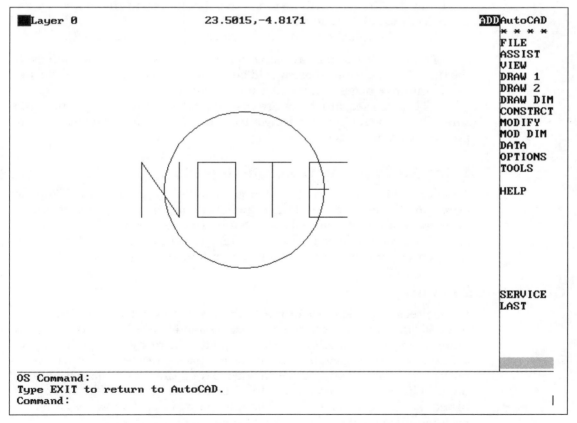

Figure 4.1 Note bubble with an attribute.

Try inserting several NOTE blocks with different values. Now try drawing a circle and place the text exactly in the correct position. Imagine how much time this simple block can save.

Explode one of your NOTE blocks. Erase the circle but leave the tag. Now put new circle around the tag—a triangle for example—and block it by a different name. The same tag works for multiple blocks.

Editing Attributes

Using attributes wouldn't make much sense if you couldn't edit them easily. AutoCAD provides a very easy way to edit attribute values.

To edit an attribute value:

1. From the Modify Attribute pull-down menu, select **Edit.**
2. Select the attribute to edit.
3. Change the value in the dialog box and select **OK** (Figure 4.2).

There are extra lines available for blocks with multiple attributes. In the title block example, there would be a value for each attribute in the title block. Multiple pages of attributes are available.

As you can see, attributes are easy to create and edit. They represent a substantial time savings. By using attributes, you can automate many of the time-consuming aspects of drawing.

Using Attributes to Generate Reports

Another significant element of attributes is the reporting feature. You can *extract* attribute values from the drawing and use them to generate a separate report or bill-of-materials. Attribute extraction requires an *extract template* file, which defines the attribute tags to extract and the size for each field. There are programs available that automate this process.

Generating a Report

In the preceding title block example, there are many attributes. You can extract the attributes to generate a report. Extracting attributes, for use in another program, requires an extract template. The extract template may not contain special characters, tabs, or extra spaces. Use only characters, numerals, and spaces, and do not include extra spaces after the last numeral on each line or at the end of the file. The extract template file, when completed, has the extension .TXT. The following example shows what the extract template for the title block might look like.

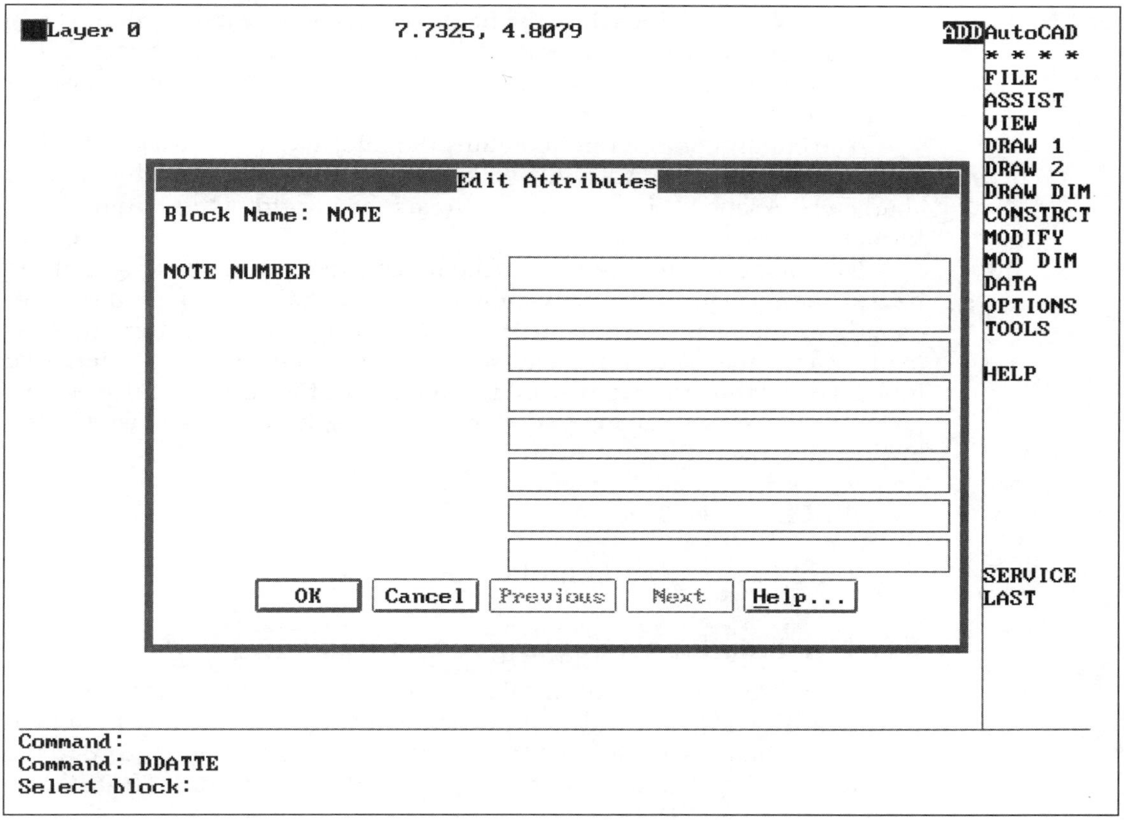

```
 Layer 0                    7.7325, 4.8079               ADD AutoCAD
                                                            * * * *
                                                            FILE
                                                            ASSIST
                                                            VIEW
                                                            DRAW 1
            ┌──────────────── Edit Attributes ─────────────┐  DRAW 2
            │                                              │  DRAW DIM
            │ Block Name: NOTE                             │  CONSTRCT
            │                                              │  MODIFY
            │ NOTE NUMBER        ┌───────────────────────┐ │  MOD DIM
            │                    └───────────────────────┘ │  DATA
            │                    ┌───────────────────────┐ │  OPTIONS
            │                    └───────────────────────┘ │  TOOLS
            │                    ┌───────────────────────┐ │
            │                    └───────────────────────┘ │  HELP
            │                    ┌───────────────────────┐ │
            │                    └───────────────────────┘ │
            │                    ┌───────────────────────┐ │
            │                    └───────────────────────┘ │
            │                    ┌───────────────────────┐ │
            │                    └───────────────────────┘ │
            │                    ┌───────────────────────┐ │
            │                    └───────────────────────┘ │
            │                    ┌───────────────────────┐ │
            │                    └───────────────────────┘ │
            │                                              │  SERVICE
            │  ┌──────┐ ┌────────┐ ┌──────────┐ ┌──────┐ ┌──────────┐ │  LAST
            │  │  OK  │ │ Cancel │ │ Previous │ │ Next │ │ Help...  │ │
            │  └──────┘ └────────┘ └──────────┘ └──────┘ └──────────┘ │
            └──────────────────────────────────────────────┘

Command:
Command: DDATTE
Select block:
```

Figure 4.2   The Edit Attributes dialog box.

DWG-NAME	C031000
DWG-NO	C010000
CAD-FILE	C012000
PRJ-NAME	C031000
DRAFTER	C003000
DWG-REV	C001000
DATE-REV	C008000
DATE-ISSUED	C008000
NEXT-ASSY	C008000
USED-ON	C008000

The column on the left is the name of the tag for each attribute. Only the attributes defined in the extract template appear in the report. If the drawing is a schematic that also has attributes, AutoCAD ignores those attributes for this report.

The column on the right contains the information for each field. The letter C indicates that AutoCAD will treat the information in this field as characters. A letter N in this location treats the information as numeric information; prices, for example.

The first three numbers after the letter C determine the length of the field. The first field is the drawing name and we have specified that it can contain as many as 31 characters. AutoCAD truncates characters that extend beyond the field limit. The second three numbers are for numeric input. They define the number of decimal places for numerals. If you have an entry that shows pricing in dollars and cents, it might look like the following example:

PRICE   N009002

The 2 specifies two decimal places.

File Formats for Extracting Attributes

There are three types of output file formats for extracting attributes: CDF, SDF, and DXF. CDF is the default format and stands for Comma Delimited File. This format uses a comma to separate the fields for each record in the output file. Many database programs and programs written in BASIC language understand CDF format.

SDF stands for Space Delimited File. SDF format separates the fields for each record with spaces. Many database programs, spreadsheets, and programs written in FORTRAN language can utilize output files in SDF format.

DXF stands for Drawing Interchange File and is a derivative of the AutoCAD DXF format for drawing files. It only contains block and attribute information. The advantage of DXF format is that it doesn't require a template file. The output file has the extension .DXX. DXF output files can be formatted using various programming languages.

NOTE Older versions of AutoCAD included a program written in BASIC language that generated a report from a DXF output file. The program, ATTEXT.BAS, is still available on some electronic bulletin boards and demonstrates how to use BASIC to format DXF output files.

Extracting Attributes

You can also extract attributes with the DDATTEXT command. DDATTEXT displays the Attribute Extraction dialog box. If you create a drawing that includes blocks with attributes and you have created the necessary extract template file, you can extract those attributes to generate a report or bill-of-materials.

> *To create a quick bill-of-materials directly on your drawing, extract your attributes with the SDF format. Use a text editor to edit the file, if necessary. Use the Import Text utility in AutoCAD to import the file directly into your drawing.*

Setting Up a Block Library

You will use some blocks in many drawings, and you can create a library for these types of blocks. For example, a library of fasteners might be a subdirectory on the hard disk, where each fastener is a separate drawing file containing a single block definition. Whenever you need to draw a 6-32 pan head screw, for instance, you insert it directly from the library on the hard disk.

Another method of creating block libraries does not use a separate directory or individual drawings for each block. The entire library is on a single drawing. As you create the blocks, they disappear, but their references remain in the drawing. The final block library drawing is blank but contains all of the block references. To insert a 6-32 pan head screw, you insert the entire library drawing first. Then, all the blocks are available for your drawing. The disadvantage of this method is that your drawing file may become quite large. Be sure to purge or Wblock your drawing when you are done. Don't purge or Wblock your block library file. All the block definitions on the block library file are unreferenced because the library drawing is blank. Purging or Wblocking the library drawing will remove the block definitions.

You can create dozens of block or symbol libraries. Some tips for creating a few types of libraries follow.

Fasteners and Hardware

In mechanical drawings, it is common to use different types and sizes of fasteners. One easy way to speed up the drawing and design process is to create a block library of fasteners. Fasteners are parts. When you create your fastener library, be sure to draw each fastener exactly to scale or use the parametric technique detailed previously.

▶ *Save a front and side view of each fastener head type. You may want to create blocks of the threads in the lengths and diameters you will be using. Place insertion points carefully. Use the centers of nuts, washers, and screw heads when drawn from the top. Include a point entity on each location to which you will be attaching (Figure 4.3). That way, you will be able to use Node object snaps to combine parts.*

If you want to generate a bill-of-materials from your drawing, you should add invisible attribute information to each block.

Welding Symbols

Welding symbols scale to the drawing. For these symbols, create a block for each element of the symbol or create a complete symbol for each type of

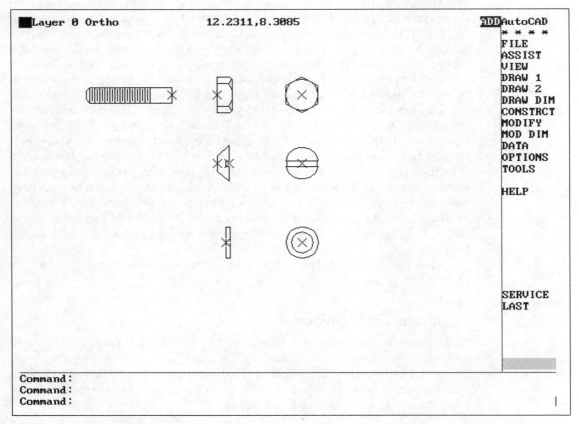

Figure 4.3   Fasteners and attachment points.

welding. Add visible attributes to your welding symbols. Attributes prompt you for the specific information required for each symbol and place the information in the correct location on the symbol automatically.

Scale welding symbol blocks for a full-size drawing. When you insert a welding symbol in a 4× scale drawing, insert it at 1/4 scale.

Electronic Schematic Symbols

Electronic schematic symbols also scale to the drawing. Create electronic schematic symbols for a full-scale drawing and insert them according to the drawing scale (Figure 4.4).

When you create schematic symbols, use visible attributes for the reference designators, values, wattage, and tolerances. Create two symbols based on their rotation in the schematic. For example, a resistor may be

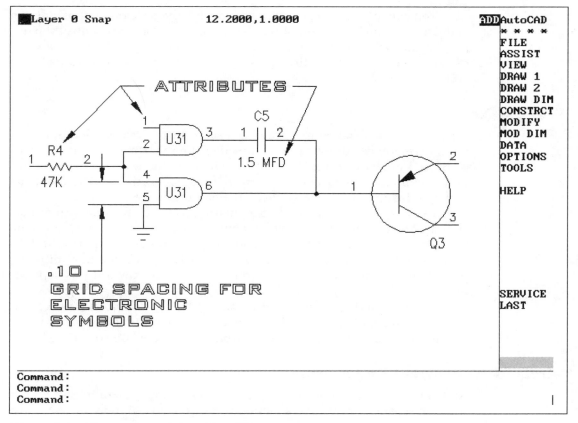

Figure 4.4   Electronic symbols with attributes.

vertically or horizontally oriented. Insert the appropriate symbol so the attribute text reads correctly.

You can generate a bill-of-materials directly from the schematic, which shows the reference designators, values, voltages, and tolerances for each component.

External References (Xrefs)

Xrefs are drawings that are linked to your drawing. They appear on your drawing but, unlike blocks, are not part of your drawing. Each time you load your drawing, the xrefs are loaded from the disk. Xrefs simplify the mechanical design and engineering process by allowing the concurrent engineering of parts and assemblies. They permit you to work on one aspect of a design while displaying drawings related to another. You could, for example, design a part while displaying the mating part(s) on the screen as you work.

You can attach Xrefs to a drawing during the development of a design and detach them at the end of the design process. You can control the display of the referenced drawing's layers with ordinary layer control commands. You can even identify and snap to specific points on externally referenced objects.

Why Use Xrefs?

When you attach an xref to a drawing, each time the drawing loads, the externally referenced drawings load directly from the hard disk, either locally or from a network drive. If a drawing changes, the updated drawing displays on all drawings where it is externally referenced. You can update an xref by reloading it; you don't have to reload the entire drawing.

By using xrefs, you can display mating parts for the part you are designing. You can snap to objects, manipulate layers, and plot xrefs. You cannot, however, alter the xref without opening the drawing file for the xref definition and altering the drawing. Unlike blocks, which can have different definitions within each drawing, xrefs are defined externally, as separate drawing files.

You can bind xrefs to your drawing, and doing so makes it part of the drawing instead of an external reference. This means that if the xref definition is later modified, those changes won't be reflected on your drawing.

Xrefs for Concurrent Engineering

Xrefs are a valuable tool for concurrent engineering. Several designers can work on separate drawings containing portions of an assembly without interfering with each other. The final assembly drawing can be a composite of xrefs. In a networked environment, you can update (reload) xrefs frequently to ensure that every member of the design team is working with the latest information.

As mentioned earlier, you cannot edit xrefs directly. To edit an xref, you edit the drawing file that is referenced. You can gain a level of security by limiting drawing file access to cognizant engineers.

Using Xrefs

Use xrefs for concurrent engineering of assemblies, designing for mating parts, or to visualize clearances in tight areas. If you are designing an alternator housing for an automobile engine, you can xref the entire engine compartment into your drawing so that you can verify the placement of other equipment, hoses, or wire harnesses. Xrefs may be *nested*. For example, you can develop a top assembly drawing by using xrefs of the sub-assemblies, each of which may contain additional external references.

The XREF command has the following options:

Attach	Attaches an external references to the drawing. Each time the drawing loads, or the xref definition reloads, the xref updates.
Overlay	Overlays an external reference. Overlay xrefs are useful for checking mating parts. Unlike an attached xref, you cannot nest an xref overlay. Referencing a drawing that contains an overlaid xref does not include the overlaid xref in the current drawing.
Reload	Reloads the xrefs. For concurrent engineering, this feature lets you update xrefs without reloading the current drawing.
Detach	Removes an attached xref definition from the drawing. Detach erases all occurrences of the xref from the drawing and marks the xref for deletion with the Purge command.
Clip	Controls clipping planes for viewing the xref.
Path	Establishes the path for xrefs. Although AutoCAD will attempt to find the required xrefs, you can use this feature to ensure that it finds the correct xref.
List	Lists the currently attached xrefs.
Bind	(Command line only) Binds an xref to the drawing. This is essentially the equivalent of inserting the xref drawing as a block. Bind does, however, affect layer names by including the source drawing name as part of the layer name.

Xref Bindings

The command sequence XREF Bind, binds an external reference to your drawing, making it part of your drawing. XBIND is a separate command that you can use to bind a *subset* of an external reference to your drawing. You can use XBIND to permanently bind blocks, dimension styles, layers, linetypes, and text styles to your drawing. If a block contains layers, linetypes, or text styles that are not in the current drawing, XBIND will also bind those elements to the drawing.

Xref Element Names

When you attach an external reference to a drawing, the xref brings its layer names with it. The xrefs name becomes a prefix to the layer name, separated by a bar (|) character. For example, if you attach the xref FLANGE, which contains a layer called HIDDEN, to your drawing, the layer name doesn't conflict with your own layer name. Your layer names may look like Table 4.1.

This makes it possible to control xref layers separately from the drawing layers. You can turn off the FLANGE|HIDDEN layer without affecting the HIDDEN layer. This naming convention extends beyond layers. Dimension styles, text styles, and linetypes also employ this type of naming for xrefs.

When you bind an xref or a subset of an xref to the drawing, the naming conventions change slightly. The characters 0 replace the bar (|) character. The zero character between the dollar signs may change from a zero to some other numeral. If you bind the previous xref to the drawing, the layer name FLANGE|HIDDEN will change to look like Table 4.2.

Again, the same naming conventions extend to dimension styles, text styles, and linetypes.

> *Use the RENAME command to rename the long names created by the xref BIND and XBIND commands.*

Table 4.1   Layer Names

LAYER NAME	*STATE*	*COLOR*	*LINETYPE*
0	On	white	CONTINUOUS
HIDDEN	On	red	HIDDEN
FLANGE|HIDDEN	On	blue	DASHED

Table 4.2   Changed Layer Names

LAYER NAME	*STATE*	*COLOR*	*LINETYPE*
0	On	white	CONTINUOUS
HIDDEN	On	red	HIDDEN
FLANGE0HIDDEN	On	blue	DASHED

The Xref Log

AutoCAD maintains an xref log file for drawings that contain external references. The xref log file uses the same name as the drawing, with the extension .XLG. The xref log resides in the current directory. Do not delete this file. Deleting the xref log file makes it impossible for AutoCAD to locate the external references for the drawing.

Summary

Blocks and xrefs are tools that help simplify the design process. Use blocks to develop parts and libraries of parts. You can create libraries of fasteners, electronic symbols, electronic parts, weld symbols, drawing formats, and other elements of your drawings that you will need.

When you create blocks, consider how you will use them. Draw parts at full scale. Symbols scale to the drawing. Draw parametric blocks as one unit and scale them as you insert them. Blocks cut down on file size when multiple insertions occur on a drawing. For editing, you can redefine all the block insertions at once.

Xrefs are entire drawings that appear as references on your drawing. Attach xrefs for concurrent engineering of parts and assemblies. Overlay xrefs to see how mating parts fit.

Xrefs are a good way to control drawing security and maintain drawing integrity. By using xrefs, you can restrict access to the source document while permitting access to the data.

CHAPTER 5

Working in Three Dimensions

You may be one of the many who wonder why anyone would ever want to construct three-dimensional (3-D) models of an object. After all, anything you create in three dimensions will still have to be put into two dimensions when it is plotted on paper. Designers, drafters, NC programmers, and machinists can all read two-dimensional (2-D) drawings, and few can actually generate a part from a 3-D model on a computer screen, so why create them?

There are many good reasons to create your models in three dimensions.

- Manually performing mass properties analysis on a part represented by 2-D views is far more difficult than having AutoCAD perform the same analysis on a 3-D part.

- Updating the top, front, and right views of an assembly after a change is something AutoCAD can do for you if your model is three dimensional. Accomplishing the same task on a model represented in a series of 2-D drawings requires time and a great deal of cross-checking.

- AutoCAD can create rendered images of 3-D models, which may be important if you have to sell your designs before you get to build them.

- Third-party applications can generate the NC code required to turn your 3-D models into prototypes.

These aren't processes you can automate if you create 2-D drawings.

Finally, the most important reason to consider constructing your models in 3-D is that it may actually be easier to generate and maintain a single 3-D model than it is to generate and maintain a series of 2-D drawings that represent a 3-D part.

In this chapter, and the two that follow, we introduce you to a selection of 3-D construction tools available from Autodesk. Some are easy to learn and are great for constructing simple models; some require a greater investment of your time but yield important benefits because they let you create families of 3-D models and associated drawings, or even produce machine-ready NC code.

Three Kinds of 3-D Models and Three Autodesk Applications

You can construct three kinds of 3-D models using tools available from Autodesk. In this chapter we introduce you to AutoCAD's standard 3-D commands. In the following two chapters we give you an introduction to Designer and AutoSurf. By reviewing these three chapters you learn which applications create which kinds of model, and you can determine which best meets your 3-D requirements.

Before you can decide which application you should use to develop your 3-D parts, you need to understand differences between kinds of 3-D models. You must select the type of model you want to create based upon what you intend to do with the model, and your choice of model profoundly influences which application you will use for design and modeling.

Wireframe models are composed of lines, arcs, and circles that represent the profile lines of a part. Wireframe models are called "wireframe" because you could construct the same kind of model in the real world by bending wire to represent the profile lines and by assembling the wire profiles to create a frame representing the complete part.

Wireframe models are the simplest kind of 3-D model, and they provide the least information. After all, the area between the profile lines of a wireframe model remain undefined. This means you don't know what these surfaces look like, and you don't have all the X,Y,Z coordinates required to cut a part. Wireframe models don't tell you which profile lines should be hidden when you examine a model from an angle thirty degrees above the drawing plane. They don't give you enough information to perform a mass properties analysis because the volume of the model remains undefined.

Nevertheless, wireframes are enough for some applications, despite their obvious shortcomings. Wireframe models you create in AutoCAD are useful for showing a part from a variety of angles. You can show the top, front, right, and isometric views of a wireframe model easily, and you can plot and even dimension these views.

Surface models of a part represent an object by describing its surfaces. They describe not only the profiles of a part, but also the area between those profiles. This kind of model can show you which lines are hidden when you view the model from a specific point of view, but it still can't be used to perform a mass properties analysis. Surface models describe the surface of a part, not the mass or volume of a part.

This kind of model is well suited for applications that generate NC code. Milling is nothing more than removing excess media from the surface of a part. With an accurate surface model you have enough information to know where the mill bit must ramp in, exactly how deep each cut should be, and where a tool change will be required.

You can use AutoCAD to create simple surface models, and AutoSurf to create much more sophisticated, mill-able, surface models.

Solid models of a part not only describe its profile lines and surfaces, but its volume as well. This kind of model contains enough information for you to calculate centroid, surface area, and mass. You can also generate accurate cross sections from a solid model. Solid models give you enough information to produce a surface model of a part, and therefore enough information to create the numerical control code required to cut the part.

Remember, you determine the kind of three-dimensional model to construct based upon the information you have available, and the use to which your model will be put. Sometimes a simple wireframe model is enough to tell your colleagues in marketing what a part will look like. On other occasions, you need a solid model so you can be sure a part won't be too heavy, or that it will spin about its anticipated center of gravity. Still other occasions warrant the investment required to generate a completely accurate surface model of a part, toleranced and refined until it leaves the drawing board to become code on the shop floor.

In the following sections you learn the commands available to you in AutoCAD for constructing 3-D wireframe, surface, and solid models.

AutoCAD Wireframe Commands

You can use almost all AutoCAD entities to construct wireframe models. Most commands let you specify X,Y,Z points to define objects. Some commands, like LINE and 3-DPOLY, let you enter points that vary on three axes simultaneously. You use these commands often when you create three-dimensional wireframe models.

To create a line by entering X,Y, and Z values:

1. From the Draw menu, choose **line.**
2. Enter the X,Y,Z coordinates for the start of the line.
3. Enter X,Y,Z coordinates for subsequent points on the line.
4. Hit **Enter** to exit the LINE command after the last coordinate (Figure 5.1).

Most other AutoCAD entities accept X,Y,Z values for at least one prompt. For example, you can place the center of a circle at any X,Y, or Z location, but AutoCAD constructs the remainder of the circle parallel to the current coordinate system. Later in this chapter you learn how to change your coordinate system or drawing plane to match any plane you can define in three dimensions.

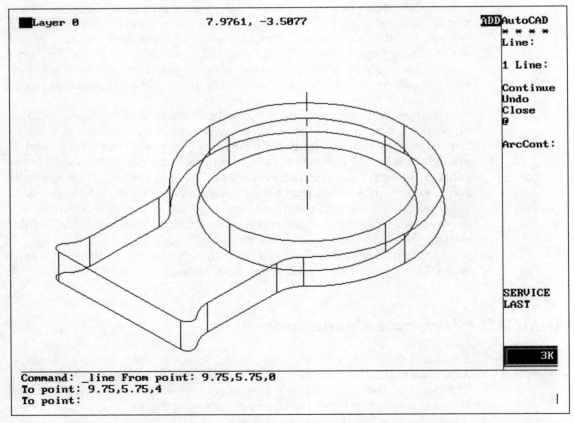

Figure 5.1 Enter X,Y,Z coordinates when prompted for the endpoints of a line.

To create a circle by entering X, Y, Z coordinates:

1. From the Draw Circle menu, choose **Center, Radius**.
2. Enter an X,Y,Z coordinate to establish the center point of the circle (Figure 5.2).
3. Enter a radius for the circle.

You can also use Object Snaps, like endpoint, center, and intersection to input X,Y,Z coordinates into commands. This allows you to create new three-dimensional objects based upon features of existing entities.

To create a circle on a new plane using Object Snaps:

1. From the Draw Circle menu, choose **Center, Radiu**s.
2. Hold down the Shift key and press **Enter** to bring up the Object Snap

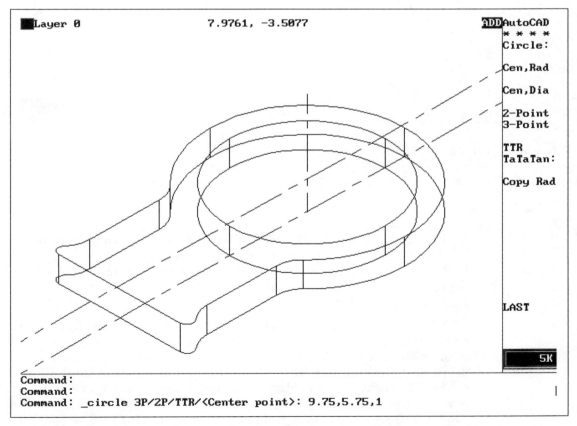

Figure 5.2 Many commands accept X,Y,Z coordinates as input for some prompts.

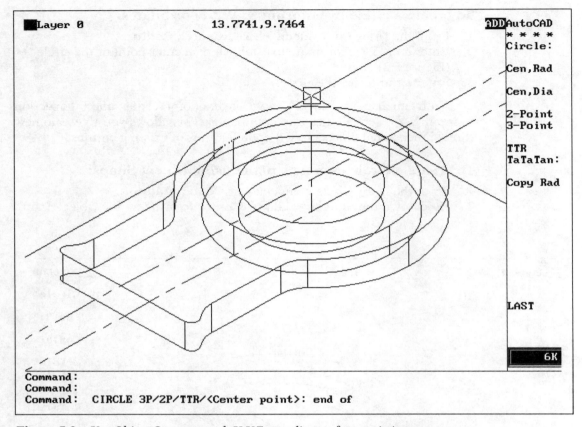

■Layer 0   13.7741,9.7464   ▌▌▌AutoCAD
                                                                * * * *
                                                                Circle:

                                                                Cen,Rad

                                                                Cen,Dia

                                                                2-Point
                                                                3-Point

                                                                TTR
                                                                TaTaTan:

                                                                Copy Rad

                                                                LAST

                                                                       6K

Command:
Command:
Command: CIRCLE 3P/2P/TTR/<Center point>: end of

Figure 5.3   Use Object Snaps to grab X,Y,Z coordinates from existing geometry.

        list. Select the desired Osnap. If you prefer, you may simply type the desired object snap at the command prompt.

3.   Select a point on an existing object to snap the circle's center point to this location (Figure 5.3).

4.   Enter a radius for the circle.

        Most editing commands, like MOVE, COPY, and ROTATE also work with entities created in three dimensions. Sometimes you may receive an error message that indicates that the object you are trying to edit isn't on the current drawing plane. If you see this error, it means that AutoCAD cannot edit the entity until you change the coordinate system to match the coordinate system the object was created on. The Entity option of the UCS command is specifically designed to let you return to the UCS on which an entity was created.

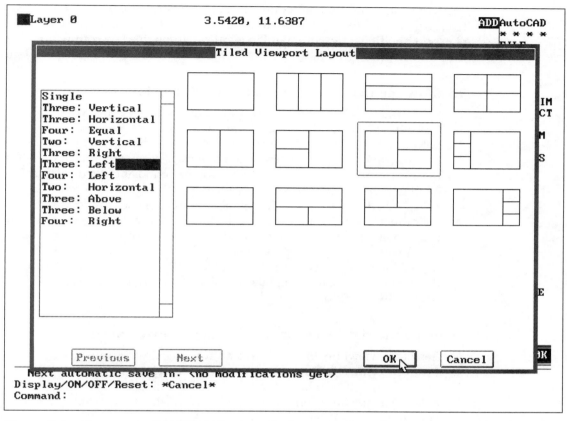

Figure 5.4   Choose one of the Tiled Viewport display options.

Displaying Multiple Views of Your Model

When you construct a three-dimensional model, you may not be able to see the effect of some commands because you are creating or modifying entities perpendicular to the drawing view. For best results, you should display a three-dimensional model in multiple viewports while you work. Many operators like to display the top and front views of an object as well as an isometric view. This lets them double-check the position of objects by examining the model from three points of view.

To show multiple views of your model:

1. From the Views Tiled Viewports menu, choose **Layout** (Figure 5.4).
2. Select the desired viewport configuration.
3. Select **OK** to exit this dialog box.

You can zoom, edit, and draw in each viewport. To make a viewport active, just select it with your mouse. You can start most commands in one viewport and finish the command in another, although a few commands, like ZOOM, will not allow you to change viewports in the middle of the operation.

To show the front view of your model in a viewport:

1. Select the viewport in which you want to display the new view.
2. From the View 3D Viewpoint Rotate menu, choose **Rotate.**
3. Select 270 on wide circle on the left side of the dialog box. Imagine that your model is at the center of the circle. When you pick a point on the circle that surrounds the object, you are choosing the direction from which you want to look at your model.
4. Select 0 as the angle on the X,Z plane from which you want to display your model. Imagine that your model lies at the center of your arc. If you pick a point at the top point of the arc you will be looking down on the top of your object. If you pick a point at the bottom of the arc, you will be looking up at the bottom of your object. By selecting 0 you indicate that you want to stare straight at the side of your object (Figure 5.5).
5. Select **OK** to exit this dialog box.

To show the right view of your model in a viewport:

1. Select the viewport in which you want to display the new view.
2. From the View 3D Viewpoint menu, choose **Rotate.**
3. Select 0 on wide circle on the left side of the dialog box.
4. Select 0 as the angle on the X,Z plane from which you want to display your model.
5. Select **OK** to exit this dialog box.

In addition to using the dialog box just illustrated, AutoCAD lists the most common views in the View Viewpoint Presets menu.

To show an isometric view of your model in a viewport:

1. Select the viewport in which you want to display the new view.
2. From the View Viewpoint Presets menu, choose SE Isometric. This indicates that you wish to view your model from the southeast at a 45 degree angle above the drawing plan (Figure 5.6).

Coordinate Systems

The X,Y drawing plane on which you normally create entities is called the World Coordinate System (WCS). All other coordinate systems are defined

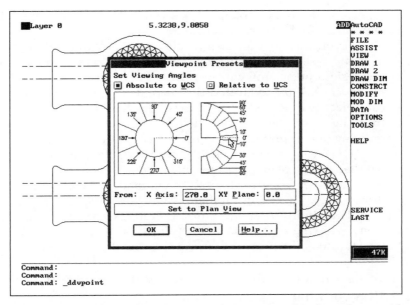

Figure 5.5 Select the direction you want to view the object from, and then the angle off the X,Y plane.

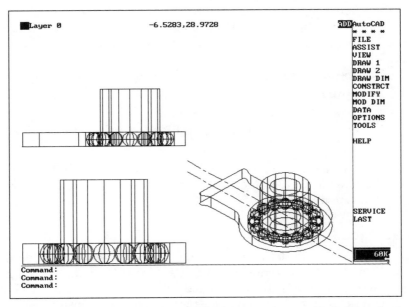

Figure 5.6 Use the View Viewpoint Presets options to display standard views.

relative to this default plane. When you create 2-D drawings, all the entities are drawn on the World Coordinate System.

If you wish to draw on any other plane, you must define a new user coordinate system. This can be as simple as selecting three points that lie on the desired plane. You can also define a new user coordinate system by rotating the X,Y plane around the current X, Y, or Z axis. If you prefer, you can select two points on the Z axis. The X and Y axis will then be derived from the Z axis you just identified. You can return to any previously defined drawing plane simply by selecting an entity drawn on the desired UCS.

Once you change to a UCS, or drawing plane, all the entities you create will be on that plane. For example, although you can't enter X,Y,Z coordinates at the prompts for the ARC command, you can define a new UCS and draw an arc. The points on that arc will lie on the new coordinate system.

The ability to create any 2-D AutoCAD entity on any three-dimensional drawing plane means that all AutoCAD drawing commands are, in effect, three-dimensional drawing commands.

To define a new drawing plane with the option 3Point of the UCS command:

1. From the View Set UCS menu choose **3Point.**
2. Select a point to define the origin of the new UCS. The point you select will be 0,0,0 for the new drawing plane (Figure 5.7).
3. Select a point to define the direction of the positive X axis. You can use Osnaps, if you like, to snap to existing geometry (Figure 5.8).
4. Select a point to define the direction of the positive Y axis (Figure 5.9).

To display the plan view of the new coordinate system in a viewport:

1. Select the viewport in which you want to display the plan view.
2. From the View 3-D Viewpoint Presets menu, choose **Plan** (Figure 5.10).

Note that the crosshairs in the isometric view reflect the orientation of the new drawing plane, and that any 2-D entity you draw will now be on that drawing plane.

AutoCAD Surface Commands

If you want to define the surface area between the profile line of a wireframe model, you must use AutoCAD's surface commands. All surfaces created in AutoCAD are constructed with an entity called a 3-D Face. 3-D Faces can be imagined as triangular pieces of opaque plastic. They are defined by three vertices, which is to say that each point of a 3-D Face has an X, a Y, and a Z coordinate. The 3DFACE command lets you construct a face be-

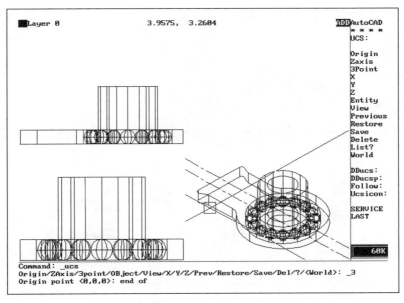

Figure 5.7   Use the Osnaps to grab the origin of the new coordinate system.

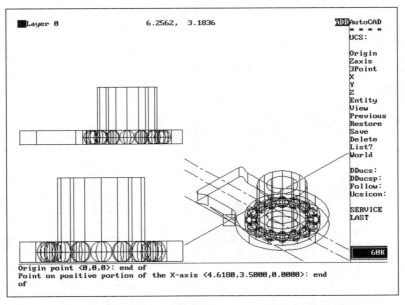

Figure 5.8   Use the Osnaps to grab a point on the X axis of the new coordinate system.

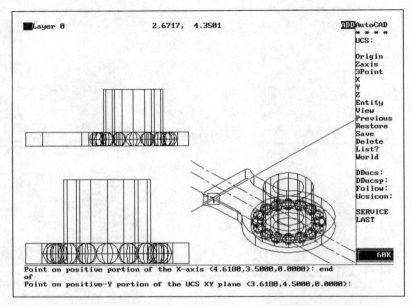

Figure 5.9 Use the Osnaps to grab the Y axis of the new coordinate system.

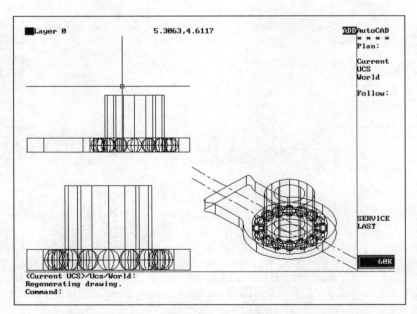

Figure 5.10 The PLAN command displays the top view of the current UCS.

tween any three points in three-dimensional space. AutoCAD's surface commands create meshes composed of 3-D Faces.

One simple way to construct a surface is to extrude a 2-D entity. When you extrude a 2-D entity, it is extended in the positive or negative Z direction from the current coordinate system. Though extruded entities are constructed of 3-D Faces, these faces cannot be manipulated or adjusted.

To extrude a 2-D entity into a 3-D object:

1. From the Modify menu, choose **Properties.**
2. Select the entity you want to change.
3. Enter a new value in the Thickness edit box. The value you enter here can be positive or negative. Negative values extrude the object in the negative Z direction. Positive values extrude the entity in the positive Z direction (Figure 5.11).
4. Select **OK** to exit this dialog box (Figure 5.12).

The Elevation edit box in the Properties dialog box lets you move entities up or down along the Z axis. If you want to move an object up off the current drawing plane, enter a positive value representing the desired Z coordinate in the elevation edit box. Negative values move the entity down.

You can extrude objects only if the current UCS matches the coordinate system active when the 2-D object was created.

In addition to surfaces created by extrusion, AutoCAD also incorporates a host of prebuilt surface primitives, which you can find by selecting Draw Surfaces, then choosing Primitives. In addition to these simple surface models, you can create more complex surface models by:

- Revolving a curve around an axis.
- Extruding a curve along a direction vector.
- Creating a surface defined by two curves.
- Creating a surface defined by four curves.

NOTE   Using these four tools to create surfaces sometimes requires you to join entities created with lines and arcs into multisegment polylines. To do this, you use the PEDIT command to identify one component of the curve, then specify the Join option and identify the lines or arcs you wish to join to the first entity. If all the entities you select are touching endpoint to endpoint, the PEDIT command will join them into a single polyline.

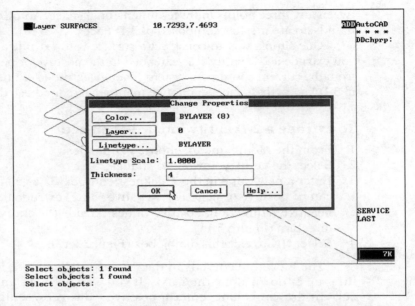

Figure 5.11 Change the thickness value to extrude an object, and the elevation value to raise an object off the ground.

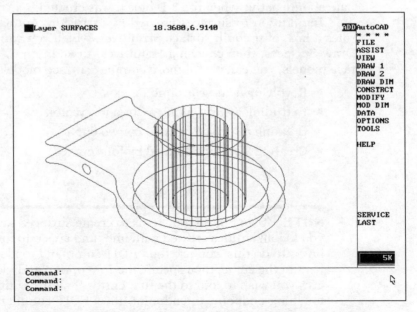

Figure 5.12 Changing the thickness of an object extrudes it perpendicular to the current X,Y coordinate system.

Revolving a Curve around an Axis

To create a surface of revolution, you must identify an open or closed curve and an axis of revolution. Unlike solids, surface models don't have to be closed entities.

To create a surface by revolving a curve around an axis:

1. From the Draw Surfaces menu, choose **Revolved Surface.**
2. Select the curve you want to revolve (Figure 5.13).
3. Select the axis you want to revolve around (Figure 5.14).
4. Enter the start angle.
5. Enter the angle you want include in your revolution (Figure 5.15).

Extruding a Curve along a Vector

To define a swept surface, you identify the curve and a line indicating the direction the curve should be extruded. Sweeping surfaces along a direction vector, in many instances, looks much like simple extrusion. The difference is that you can only extrude entities perpendicular to the current coordinate system, while you can sweep curves along any direction vector. This means that the swept surface can be at any angle to the current coordinate system.

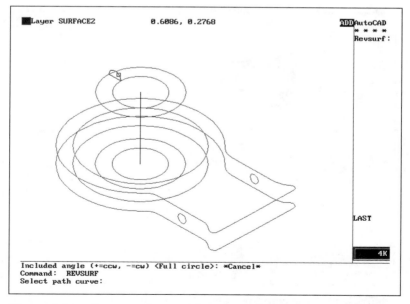

Figure 5.13   Create surfaces with open or closed curves.

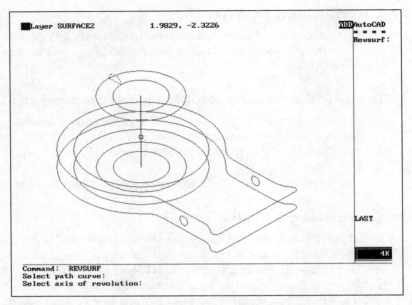

Figure 5.14   Use a line to define the axis of rotation.

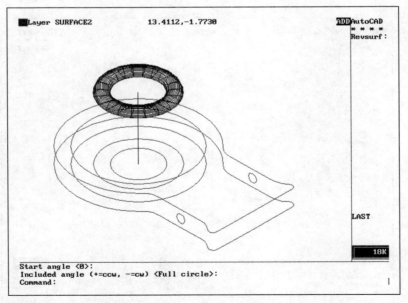

Figure 5.15   You can determine how far your curve revolves to create a surface.

To create a surface by sweeping a curve along a direction vector:

1. From the Draw Surfaces menu, choose **Extruded Surface.**
2. Select the curve you want to sweep (Figure 5.16).
3. Select the line representing the direction vector (Figure 5.17).

Creating a Surface Defined by Two Curves

You can create a surface between any two curves. Use the RULESURF command when you have the edges, or profile lines, of a part and you want to create a surface model. This command is called RULESURF because the surface created has only one set of surface lines, rather like the lines on ruled paper.

To create a surface defined by two curves:

1. From the Draw Surfaces menu, choose **Ruled surface.**
2. Select the first curve of the ruled surface (Figure 5.18).
3. Select the second curve of the ruled surface (Figure 5.19).

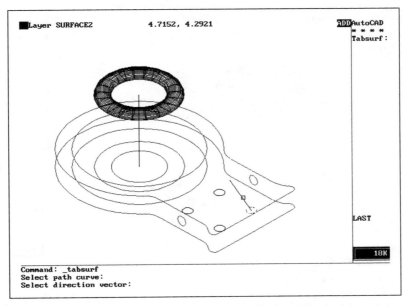

Figure 5.16 Use TABSURF to create surfaces that follow a direction vector.

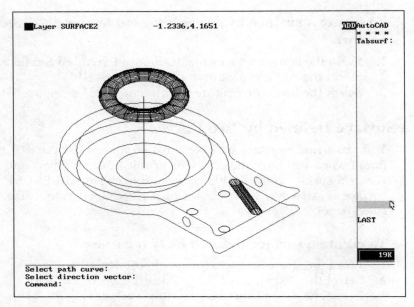

Figure 5.17 TABSURF can extrude curves at any angle to the current coordinate system.

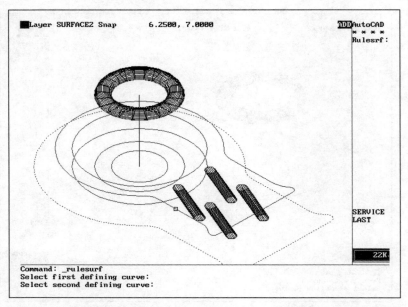

Figure 5.18 Use RULESURF to construct surfaces between two curves.

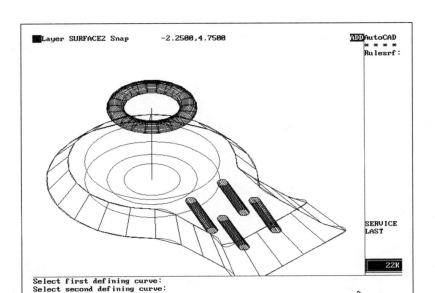

Figure 5.19   Define a plane with only two curves, or use four curves for a better fit.

Be sure to select both points on the curves near the same side. The points you select help to determine which ends of the lines are connected. If you pick points on opposite ends of the two lines, you'll end up with a spiderweb effect.

Creating a Surface Defined by Four Curves

The EDGESURF command creates a surface based upon four edges. These edges can be on any coordinate system, but they must meet at their endpoints. This command accepts only four curves as input, and prior to processing the curves it checks to be sure that the curves share endpoints. If one or more curves do not share an endpoint, an error message will indicate which edge fails the test.

To create a surface by extrapolating a surface based on four edges:

1. From the Draw Surfaces menu, choose **Edge Surface** (Figure 5.20).
2. Select the four lines (Figure 5.21).

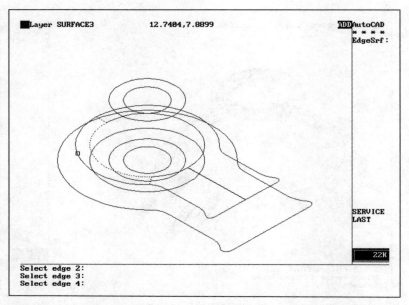

■Layer SURFACE3   12.7404,7.8899   ⒶⒹⒹAutoCAD
                                                 * * * *
                                                 EdgeSrf:

                                                 SERVICE
                                                 LAST

                                                 22K

Select edge 2:
Select edge 3:
Select edge 4:

Figure 5.20 Use EDGESURF to construct a surface from four curves that share endpoints.

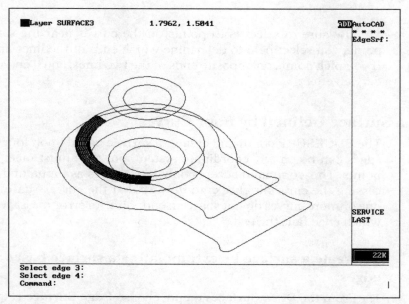

■Layer SURFACE3   1.7962, 1.5041   ⒶⒹⒹAutoCAD
                                                 * * * *
                                                 EdgeSrf:

                                                 SERVICE
                                                 LAST

                                                 22K

Select edge 3:
Select edge 4:
Command:

Figure 5.21 The edges of this mesh were defined with four polylines.

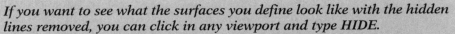

If you want to see what the surfaces you define look like with the hidden lines removed, you can click in any viewport and type HIDE.

Assign higher values to the system variables SURFTAB1 and SURFTAB2 to increase the number of 3-D Faces used to construct the surface.

Using 3-D Faces, extrusion, and these four types of surfaces you can create very complex surface models of objects. You can render these models, show hidden-line isometric and perspective views of the objects, and even export them into other applications like 3D Studio for use in creating computer animations (Figure 5.22).

AutoCAD Solid Modeling Commands

Previous versions of AutoCAD featured an add-on application, called the Advanced Modeling Extension (AME), which allowed users to construct solid models. The Advanced Modeling Extension incorporated many useful features, like the ability to cut one model out of another, or create a solid based upon the volume that two overlapping models had in common. Many mechanical users found AME an efficient tool for constructing 3-D models,

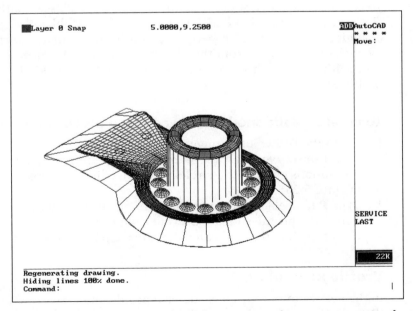

Figure 5.22 Use AutoCAD's surface commands to construct simple surface models.

and relied upon the add-on to help them design parts more quickly in 3-D than they did in 2-D.

AutoCAD Release 13 replaces AME with new solids modeling technology. AutoCAD now incorporates the nonrational bspline technology (NURBs) purchased for use in the parametric solids modeling application designer. The primary difference between the new ACIS based solid models and the solid models create by AME, is that the ACIS models are generally smaller for complex assemblies, and they are more accurate.

In addition to a fleet of solid primitives, like cones, wedges, and spheres, you can create solids by:

- Sweeping a profile along a path.
- Revolving a profile around an axis.

In the sections that follow, you learn the fundamentals of constructing solid models using these techniques, and how to combine simple solid models to create more complex objects. Whenever you create a solid model using the techniques outlined in the upcoming sections, make sure that the profile you use in the operation is closed. Only closed profiles can be used to create solid models.

Sweeping a Profile along a Path

To create an extruded solid, you must first create a closed continuous curve. Note that this extruded entity is a solid object. Unlike objects created by changing the thickness property of an entity, or tabulated surfaces created by choosing Tab Surf from the 3D Entities menu, this procedure creates a solid with mass. In this example, we show you how to identify a path for the profile to follow.

To create a solid model by sweeping a profile along a path:

1. From the Draw Solids menu, choose **Extrude.**
2. Select the curve you want to extrude. This entity must be a closed continuous curve like a circle, polygon, ellipse, or closed polyline (Figure 5.23).
3. Type **P** to specify that you want to use a curve to define the path along which the profile should be swept (Figure 5.24).
4. Select the line that indicates the extrusion path (Figure 5.25).

Revolving a Profile around an Axis

In the next example, we constructed a profile and then drew a line to define the axis of rotation. If you prefer, you may identify the current X, Y, or Z axis as the axis of rotation. This technique is more flexible than using an

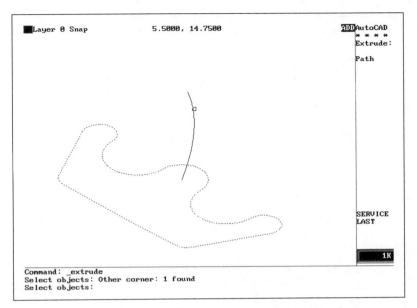

Figure 5.23 Select the profile you want to extrude, which must be a closed curve.

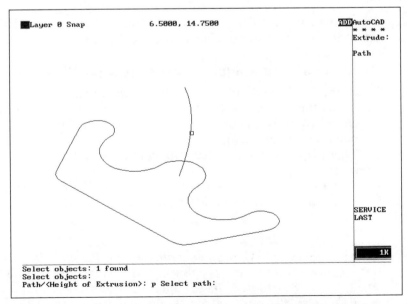

Figure 5.24 Use polylines and other curves to define the extrusion path.

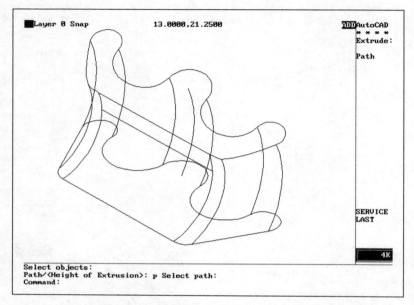

Layer 0 Snap   13.0000,21.2500   AutoCAD
* * * *
Extrude:

Path

SERVICE
LAST

4K

Select objects:
Path/<Height of Extrusion>: p Select path:
Command:

Figure 5.25 Extrude solid models from a closed profile and a path
curve.

axis of the current UCS as the axis of rotation because you don't have to re-
orient the axis in order to change the specification of the solid.

To create a solid model by revolving a profile around an axis:

1. From the Draw Solids menu, choose **Revolve.**
2. Select the edge of the entity you want to revolve. This entity must be a
    closed continuous curve like a circle, polygon, ellipse, or closed
    polyline (Figure 5.26).
3. Type **Object** to specify that you want to use a line to define the axis of
    rotation.
4. Select the line you wish to use as the axis of rotation (Figure 5.27).
5. Enter the revolution angle (Figure 5.28).

▶

> *You should retain the profiles, paths, and other entities you use to con-
> struct your solid models. If you want to change or refine these models in
> the future, you will need these components. You may find it most conve-
> nient to keep these objects on a construction layer so they can be dis-
> played or hidden upon demand.*

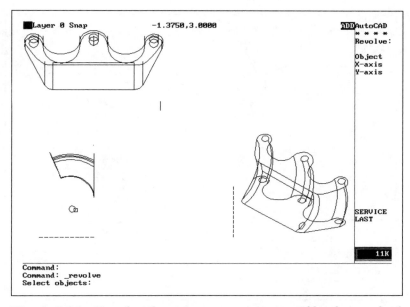

Figure 5.26 Use closed continuous curves as profiles for revolved solids.

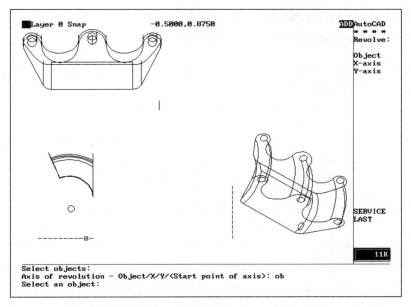

Figure 5.27 Use the Object option to select a line as the axis of rotation.

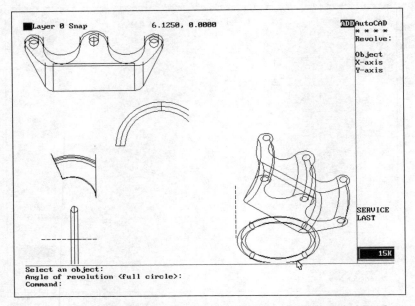

Figure 5.28 Revolved solids can reflect any included angle less than 360 degrees.

Combining Simple Solid Models to Create Complex Solid Models

There are three ways you can combine simple solid shapes to create more complex assemblies.

- You can add two objects together to create a solid model that has the mass of both objects.
- You can construct a solid model by subtracting one model from another. In order for this operation to be successful, the two models must overlap. The volume the two models have in common will be subtracted from the first object.
- You can construct a solid model by retaining only the volume that the two models have in common.

Together, these three methods of combining solid models are called the Boolean operations.

To construct a new model using Boolean subtraction:

1. From the Construct menu, choose **Subtract** (Figure 5.29).
2. Select the solid you want to keep (Figure 5.30).
3. Select the solid you want to subtract (Figure 5.31).

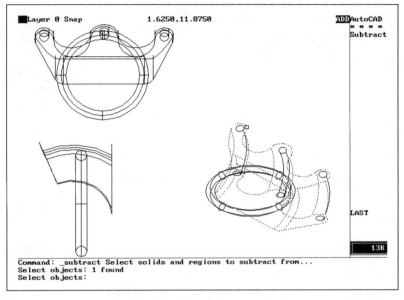

Figure 5.29 First select the object you want to keep, then the object you want to subtract.

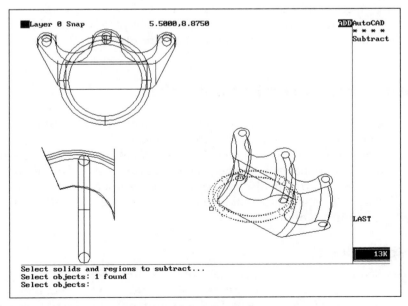

Figure 5.30 SUBTRACT subtracts the volume the two objects have in common from the first object.

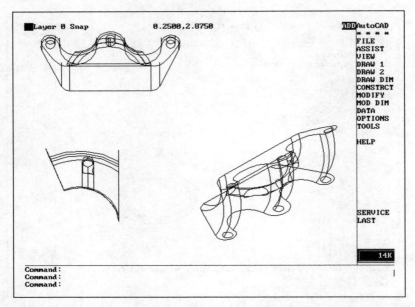

Figure 5.31 Make sure solids overlap before performing a subtraction operation.

Remember, it is only where the two objects overlap that the subtraction occurs. If you subtract an object completely inside another object, you will create a hollow area inside the first object.

Slicing and Sectioning Solid Models

AutoCAD lets you cut a model into two parts using the SLICE command. You should use this command when you need to show a cutaway view of a model, when you wish to cut a model cleanly in half so you can show two cross sections simultaneously, or when you wish to discard part of a model permanently.

AutoCAD can also generate an independent 2-D cross section of a solid model. This is useful when you wish to crosshatch or dimension a sectional view for use on a detail.

Slicing a Solid Model

Before you can slice a model, you must first create a cutting plane. The easiest way to define this plane is simply to create a rectangle on that plane using the UCS and RECTANG commands. Although you can use other methods to define the cutting plane, an X, Y, or Z axis for example, using the Rectangle means that you can use normal AutoCAD editing commands to rotate, move, and mirror the plane into its final position.

To slice a solid model:

1. From the Draw Solids menu, choose **Slice.**
2. Select the solid you want to slice.
3. Type **O** to specify that you want to use an object to define the cutting plane.
4. Select the rectangle (Figure 5.32).
5. Select the side of the model you want to keep. If you prefer, you may retain both parts of the sliced model by typing **B** (Figure 5.33).

Sectioning a Solid Model

As just outlined, the easiest way to define the plane through which the cross section should be generated is simply to construct a rectangle on that plane. You may even want to create a cross section construction layer where you retain these rectangles for future use. That way, if you change the model, you don't have to redefine the cutting planes.

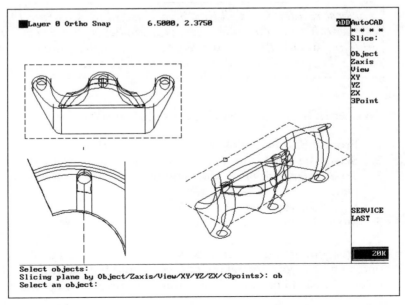

Figure 5.32 Use a rectangle as a cutting plane for slicing operations.

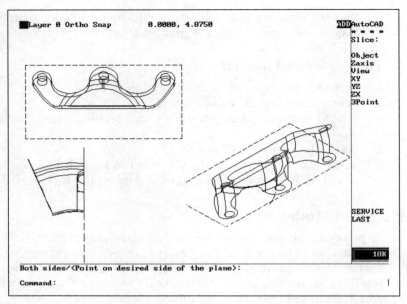

Figure 5.33 Discard either side of a sliced model, or keep both.

For best results, you will find it very useful to construct the sections on a layer other than the one where your model is stored. This allows you to hide the model after the procedure is complete, which makes it easy to move the new 2-D cross section to its final position.

To create a cross section of a solid model:

1. From the Draw Solids menu, choose **Section.**
2. Select the solid from which you want to construct a cross section.
3. Type **O** to specify that you want to use an object to define the cutting plane.
4. Select the rectangle (Figure 5.34).
5. Move the model aside to reveal the cross section.

Assuming you constructed this cross section on a layer other than the one on which your model resides, you could hide your model by turning its layer off instead of moving your model to reveal the cross section.

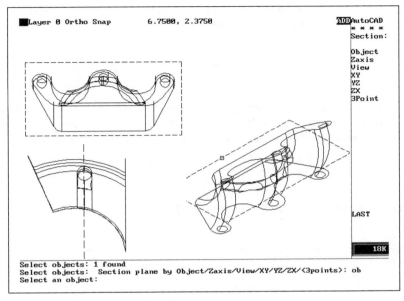

Figure 5.34 Use a rectangle to define the cross section plane.

Calculating Mass Properties of Solid Models

Since solid models define not only the profile lines and surfaces of a model, but the mass of the object as well, AutoCAD can calculate the mass properties for the object. Mass properties for an object include moments of inertia, mass, surface area, and centroid. This information can help you ensure that your model meets your design requirements.

To calculate mass properties:

1. From the Assist Inquiry menu, choose **Mass Properties.**
2. Select the object for which you want to calculate mass properties.
3. Type **F** to write the Mass Properties to a data file.

You can use AutoCAD's text import commands to import the mass properties data file into the drawing if desired.

The mass properties of the part shown in the figures is provided in Table 5.1. Note that mass properties data files have the extension .MPR.

Summary

In this chapter you reviewed many of AutoCAD's 3-D commands. More important, you learned that AutoCAD can construct three types of models, and you learned that some models are better than others for specific purposes. In

Table 5.1   Output from Mass Properties Operation

SOLIDS

Mass:	23.2435
Volume:	23.2435
Bounding box:	X: 3.8968 — 11.6032
	Y: 8.1250 — 12.2977
	Z: 0.0000 — 4.4281
Centroid:	X: 7.7513
	Y: 10.2487
	Z: 1.2992
Moments of inertia:	X: 2506.6565
	Y: 1543.4378
	Z: 3938.8339
Products of inertia:	XY: 1846.5166
	YZ: 314.6253
	ZX: 234.0921
Radii of gyration:	X: 10.3848
	Y: 8.1488
	Z: 13.0177
Principal moments and X-Y-Z directions about centroid:	I: 26.0443 along [1.0000 0.0007 0.0002]
	J: 110.4560 along [-0.0005 0.8802 -0.4746]
	K: 98.1801 along [-0.0005 0.4746 0.8802]

the following two chapters you will learn about other Autodesk applications designed to meet the needs of mechanical users. AutoSurf lets you construct very accurate surface models, and together with its companion product AutoMill, helps you develop numerical control code. Designer lets you construct sophisticated parametric solid models, smart enough to change when you modify a dimension value, and clever enough to use ASCII text files holding dimension values to produce a family of parts drawings.

CHAPTER 6

▲

Designer

Parametric Solids Modeling

Autodesk's new solids modeling product, Designer, lets you build intelligent 3-D models. Designer models, unlike the surface and solid models created using standard AutoCAD commands, are parameter driven. Each component of a Designer model is defined by a number of dimensions, and changing the value associated with a dimension changes the model.

Dimension values can be constants or variables defined by equations. Equations can be interdependent, which means that changing a single parameter can update an entire model. You can export dimension values and equations to ASCII data files, and modify them using a standard text editor. You can also use database and spreadsheet applications to generate data files, which is useful when you need to construct a family of parts or compare competing designs.

Designer also incorporates automated drafting commands that let you create working drawings from a solid model. Unlike AutoCAD's powerful, but somewhat difficult to follow Tiled Model Space, Paper Space, MVIEW, and viewport specific layering commands, Designer has a selection of simpler and more sophisticated layout utilities. You specify scaled orthographic, cross-sectional, and isometric views from within a dialog box. You place scaled views of your model on a drawing sheet with your mouse.

If you change a Designer model, the automatically generated views of the drawing also update. The automated drafting features also manage the dimensions displayed in any view and control the display of the layers containing solid features.

Designer is a very useful tool for engineers looking for a way to speed up the design process. Intelligent models help enforce design objectives and eliminate the double checking usually required to be sure a plotted drawing accurately reflects the current version of the model. Automated drafting commands reduce layout time and increase productivity. (Note: Designer for AutoCAD Release 13 was not available prior to the publication of this book. The features and methods illustrated in this chapter are illustrated using Designer for AutoCAD Release 12.)

Learning Designer Terms

To use Designer, you must first become familiar with some new terms. In many cases these words are familiar to mechanical designers, but their meanings have been tailored to fit Designer's specific requirements. In the sections that follow we review the terms below in some detail, but this list will serve as a quick reference and an introduction to Designer's drawing environment.

Sketch	An inexact 2-D drawing of a component created with standard 2-D drawing commands like LINE, ARC, CIRCLE, and POLYLINE.
Profile	A sketch to which Designer has applied constraints. Profiles must have enough dimensions and constraints to completely define all the geometry in the profile. Only profiles can be turned into features.
Feature	A feature is a parameter-driven solid model. By changing the dimensions associated with a feature, you change the model. Features can be joined to the existing part, subtracted from the existing part, or used to create a new solid based upon the volume that two or more features have in common.
Part	A part is a complete component defined by one or more features.
Dimension	Designer creates two kinds of dimensions: *Parametric dimensions*, created using special dimensioning commands, control profiles, and features. *Non para-*

metric dimensions, created using normal AutoCAD dimensioning commands, do not control features or profiles.

Constraint
: A constraint is a rule imposed upon a profile. You can create quite a variety of constraints, including those that force circles to remain concentric and lines to remain parallel.

Parameter
: Parameters are variables you assign to a dimension. Sometimes parameters are set to a constant, sometimes they are values based upon an equation.

Work Plane
: A work plane is a parametric plane defined relative to at least one other plane in a part. You construct profiles on work planes. You can define work planes to be offset from an existing plane, be tangent to a curve, or even pass through a feature at an angle. *Note that a UCS is not a work plane.* You must construct work planes using Designer commands, not standard AutoCAD commands.

Sketch Plane
: At any given time, one work plane in a drawing is defined as the sketch plane. Only sketches created on this sketch plane can be turned into profile, constrained, dimensioned, and finally be turned into a feature. Designer forces you to define each work plane used as the sketch plane relative to a previous feature. This ensures that no matter how the values controlling your part change, Designer knows the position of each feature because it knows the position of each work plane.

If these terms are somewhat confusing, the following sections should serve to clarify them.

Designing with Designer

Using Designer to create complex solid models, called parts, almost always requires you to follow the same sequence of steps.

1. You create a sketch of the solid on the sketch plane.

2. You convert the sketch into a profile, which lets Designer apply some constraints to the model. You can change or add to these constraints to enforce additional rules you want the part to obey.

3. You add dimensions to the profile. These dimensions can have constant values, be dependent upon other dimensions, or they can be

dependent upon parameters. Parameters are variables defined by an equation.

4. When the profile is completely defined by constraints and dimensions, you convert the profile into a solid, called a feature. You can create features by extruding profiles, revolving profiles around a centerline, or sweeping profiles along a path. As part of this process, you determine if the new feature is added, subtracted, or intersected, with the existing features that make up the part.

Each feature of a part is constructed following these steps, except for the few features that Designer can construct without sketches profiles and constraints—Holes, Fillets, and Chamfers are such well-defined terms that Designer can create them without much help from you. For example, to place a fillet on the edge of a part, Designer needs to know only the edge you want to fillet and the radius you want to apply.

When you are ready to create working drawings of the model for the first time, you use the automated drafting utility to define the base view of the model. This is usually the top view of the model, and it is the view from which all other views are constructed. After creating the base view, you can create orthographic or isometric views of the model simply by selecting the base view and determining the direction from which the new view is calculated.

In the sections that follow, you learn how to create sketches, apply constraints, add dimensions, and construct features.

Creating Sketches

You can create a sketch using lines, polylines, arcs, and circles. You can combine these entities using any of the standard AutoCAD editing commands including TRIM, FILLET, CHAMFER, COPY, or MIRROR. The final version of the sketch should be a single, closed, continuous curve.

Don't worry about making your sketch completely accurate. Designer automatically cleans up some problems, like lines that don't quite meet in a corner, when you convert the sketch into a profile. You can add constraints and create dimensions to clean up other problems later on.

To create a sketch:

1. From the Designer Sketch menu, choose **Sketch Plane** and define the sketch plane as a plane on an existing feature or a previously created work plane. (You can skip this step when you create the first feature of a part. The sketch plane in this case is automatically defined as the World Coordinate System.)
2. Create the closed shape of the sketch using Lines, Arcs, Polylines, and Circles (Figure 6.1).

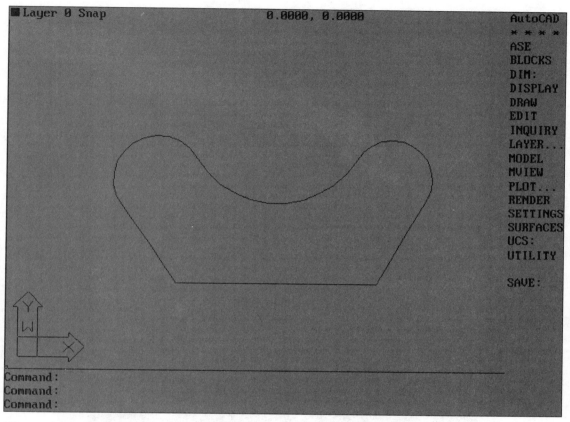

Figure 6.1 Create sketches with standard AutoCAD drawing commands.

Unlike AME, which lets you create a feature based upon a two closed curves one inside the other, Designer requires that you loft only one closed curve at a time.

Creating a Profile

After you make a sketch of the feature you want to create, you must convert the sketch into a profile. When you do so, Designer automatically enforces the following rules by applying some standard constraints:

- Lines sketched nearly vertical are vertical.
- Arcs, circles, and lines sketched nearly tangent are tangent.
- Two arcs or circles whose centers are sketched nearly coincident are concentric.

- Two lines sketched nearly overlaying one another are collinear.
- Lines sketched nearly parallel are parallel.
- Lines sketched nearly perpendicular are perpendicular. In order for one line to be constrained to remain perpendicular to another, they must touch one another.
- Any arcs and circles sketched with nearly the same radius will have the same radius.
- If two lines almost meet in a corner, they will be joined at their endpoints.
- If one line almost touches another, Designer will move the endpoint of one object so it touches the near point of the other.

Although Designer automatically applies these constraints to your sketch, you can remove them later if desired. You can even create new constraints, if you want, to enforce additional rules that you want your feature to obey. An overview of the constraints you can apply or remove from a profile is provided later in this chapter.

To convert a sketch into a profile:

1. From the Designer Sketch menu, choose **Profile.**
2. Select the entities that make up your sketch (Figure 6.2).

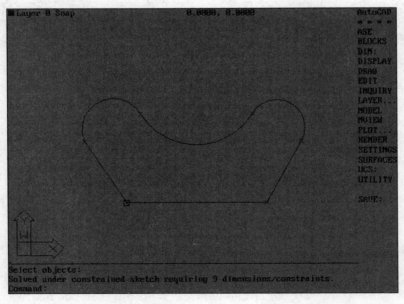

Figure 6.2 Designer applies constraints to your sketch as it turns it into a profile.

Applying Dimensions to a Profile

You control a profile by applying dimensions to the entities that make up the profile. Later, when the profile becomes a feature, the dimensions control the feature.

To create a parametric dimension:

1. From the Designer Sketch menu, choose **Add Dimension.**
2. Select the entity you want to dimension. You may select two entities if you want to show the distance or angle between them (Figure 6.3).
3. Place the dimension by selecting a point near the dimensioned entity. Note that Designer will try to guess the kind of dimension you want to create based upon where you click. For example, if you click on a point immediately to the left or right of the entity you are trying to dimension, Designer will create a vertical dimension. You can change the type of dimension that Designer creates after the dimension is placed.
4. Enter the dimension value (Figure 6.4).

When you have added enough dimensions and constraints to control the part, AutoCAD tells you the profile is *fully constrained* (Figure 6.5). You can edit dimension values after you enter them by choosing Change Dimension from the Designer menu. This only lets you change the dimension

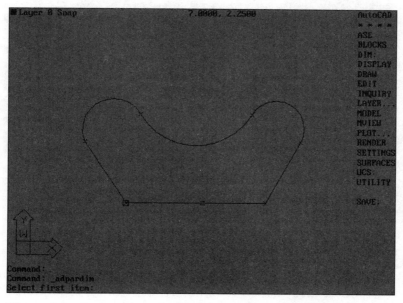

Figure 6.3 Designer's parametric dimensions control profiles.

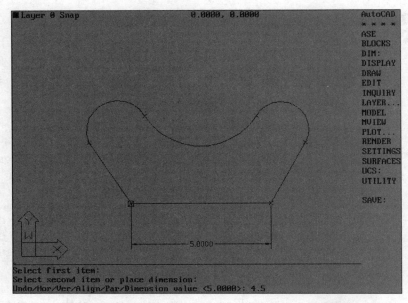

Figure 6.4 Changing the dimension value changes the profile.

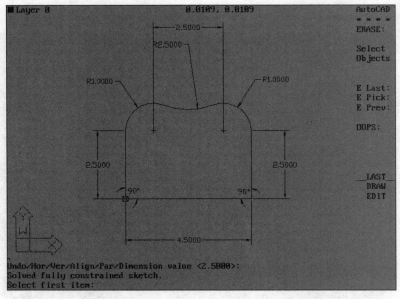

Figure 6.5 You should only use fully constrained profiles to create features.

values for a profile. To change the dimension values that control a feature, choose Edit Feature from the Designer menu.

Dimension values can be constants or parameters. Sometimes a parameter does nothing more than make one dimension value equal another dimension value. But you can also establish more complex equations that incorporate trigonometric functions, exponents, and previously defined parameters.

By default, all dimensions are assigned a name beginning with a lowercase d (Figure 6.6). For example, the first dimension applied to the first profile is called d1. If you want the second dimension applied to a profile to always have the same value as the first dimension, enter **= d1** when prompted for the value of the second dimension.

Before a profile can be extruded, swept, or revolved into a feature, it must be completely constrained. This means that your profile must have enough dimensions or constraints to define all the relationships between all the entities in the profile. If you create a feature from a less than fully defined profile, later changes to the dimension values may have unpredictable results.

It is possible to over-define a profile such that there is no solution that satisfies all the constraints and dimensions applied to the profile. If this happens, Designer will warn you that the profile is over-defined. If you ac-

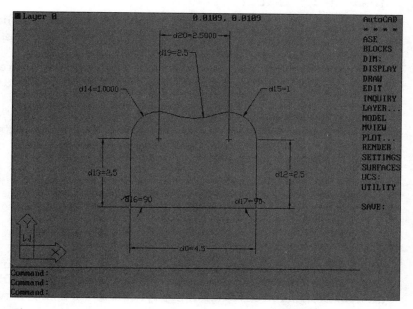

Figure 6.6 Designer assigns all dimensions a parameter name beginning with a lowercase d.

cidentally over-define a profile by adding too many dimensions, you can remove the excess dimensions using AutoCAD's ERASE command.

It is also possible to define a profile such that there is only one solution to the dimensions and design constraints. Designer does not warn you about this problem, but when you try to manipulate the resulting feature later, you discover that any change you make results in an error message saying that the profile is over-defined. If this happens, you must re-create the feature starting with the re-creation of the profile. You cannot change dimensions and constraints you originally applied to the profile. To avoid this problem, save your Designer drawing to a new name prior to turning each profile into a feature. If you run into an over-defined feature, at some future date, you will not have to recreate the 2-D geometry.

Creating an Extruded Feature

There are three ways to turn profiles into features. You can extrude the profile, revolve it around a centerline, or sweep it along a path. When you define a feature, you determine if the feature is joined to the existing part, cut from the existing part, or if a new solid is created that is based upon the volumes the two features have in common. This latter option is defined as a *solid based upon intersection*.

To create an extruded feature:

1. From the Designer Features menu, choose **Extrude.** You don't have to select the profile you want to extrude because *only* the profile on the active sketch plane will be extruded (Figure 6.7).
2. Specify whether the extruded feature will be a Base feature, Joined to the existing part, Cut from the existing part, or Intersected with the existing part.
3. Specify whether the extruded feature extends to the specific Depth indicated in the Distance edit box, extrudes to the Mid Plane, extrudes to a Selected plane, or passes Through the part no matter how thick the part gets.
4. Specify the Draft Angle, if any, that should be applied to the extruded feature.
5. Select **OK** to exit the dialog box (Figure 6.8).

Creating a Revolved Feature

To create a revolved feature, you must create a profile as outlined earlier in this chapter. You must also create a centerline for the profile to revolve around. Designer needs to know not only the relationships between entities in the profile, but the relationship the profile has to the centerline. This means that if the centerline is not a part of the profile boundary, you must

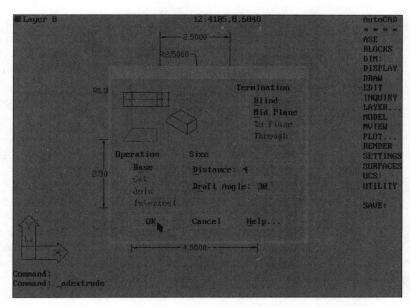

Figure 6.7 You can define draft angles and Boolean operations for extruded features.

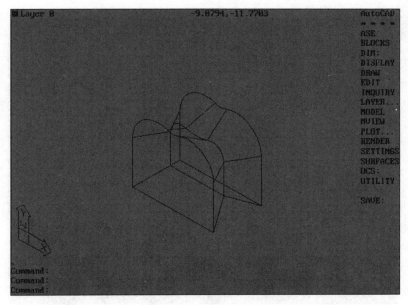

Figure 6.8 From the Designer Part Viewing menu, choose Iso to display an isometric view of a part.

create a dimension that specifies the distance between the profile boundary and the centerline.

Note that if the centerline is not part of the profile boundary, it must be in a linetype other than the sketch linetype that is defined with the ADSKSTYLE system variable (Figure 6.9).

To create a revolved feature:

1. From the Designer Features menu, choose **Revolve.** You don't have to select the profile you want to revolve because only the profile on the active sketch plane will be revolved (Figure 6.10).
2. Specify whether the revolved feature will be a Base feature, Joined to the existing part, Cut from the existing part, or Intersected with the existing part.
3. Specify the termination of the revolved feature. If you select By Angle, Designer will rotate the profile the amount specified in the Angle edit box. If you select Mid Plane, Designer will revolve the feature in both directions around the centerline, terminating at the specified angle in the Angle edit box. If you select To Plane, Designer lets you select a plane that will determine the rotation angle. Full specifies that the profile should be rotated a full 360 degrees around the centerline.

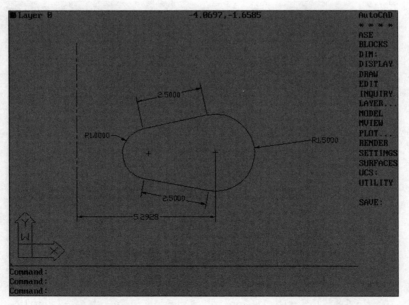

Figure 6.9 Define centerlines in a linetype other than the linetype used to draw the profiles.

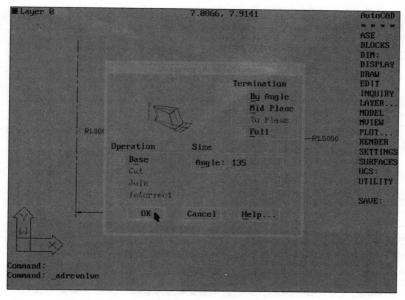

Figure 6.10 You can define revolved solids that incorporate less than 360 degrees.

4. Specify the angle, if necessary, that should be used to determine the termination of the revolution.
5. Select **OK** to exit the dialog box (Figure 6.11).

Creating a Swept Feature

In addition to creating extruded and revolved features, Designer creates swept surfaces. To create a swept surface, you define not only a profile, but also a parameter-driven path for the profile to follow.

To create a sweep path:

1. From the Designer Sketch menu, choose **Sketch Plane** to define a sketch plane if the swept feature is not the base feature of a part.
2. Use Lines, Arcs, Circles, and Polylines to sketch the sweep path (Figure 6.12).
3. From the Designer Sketch menu, choose **Path.**
4. Select the start point of the path.
5. From the Designer Sketch Constraints menu, choose **Add** from the pull-down menus and add any required constraints to the sketch.
6. From the Designer Sketch menu, choose **Add Dimension** and add dimensions until the sketch is fully defined (Figure 6.13).

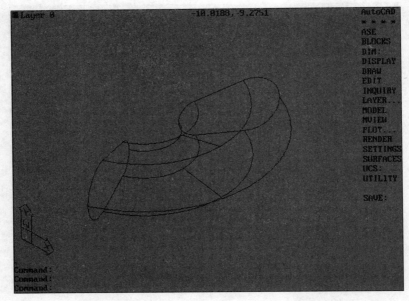

Figure 6.11   A revolved feature need not sweep a full 360 degrees.

After you define the path, you define the profile that will follow that path. To do this you create a sweep profile work plane on the path at any point. This is the work plane that you define as the sketch plane, and this is where you sketch the profile that will follow the path.

To create a profile for the swept feature:

1. From the Designer Features menu, choose **Work Plane** (Figure 6.14).
2. Select Sweep Profile to specify that the new work plane should be normal to the path at the point you select.
3. Select **OK** to exit this dialog box.
4. Select one item in the sweep path.
5. From the Designer Part Viewing menu, choose Iso to display an isometric view of your sweep path and work plane (Figure 6.15).
6. From the Designer Sketch menu, choose **Sketch Plane** and select the edge of the new work plane. This is easiest to do in an isometric view.
7. Type **R** to rotate the plane if necessary.
8. Use Lines, Arcs, Circles, or Polylines to define the new profile.
9. From the Designer Sketch menu, choose **Profile** from the command column.

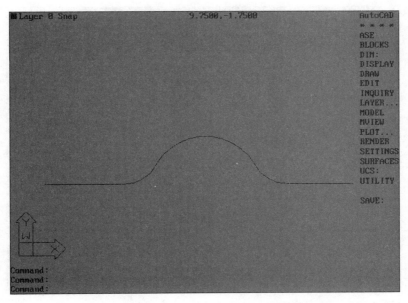

Figure 6.12 Use Lines, Arcs, Circles, and Polylines to create the sweep path.

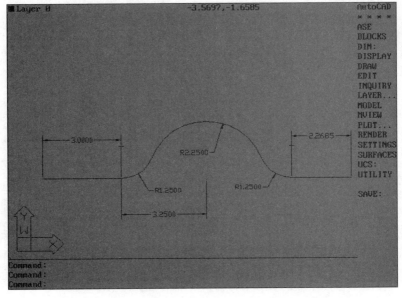

Figure 6.13 Dimension sweep paths like profiles.

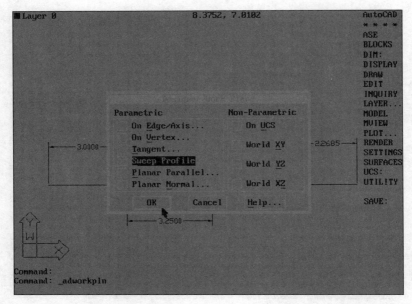

Figure 6.14 Define a sweep profile work plane on the starting point of the path.

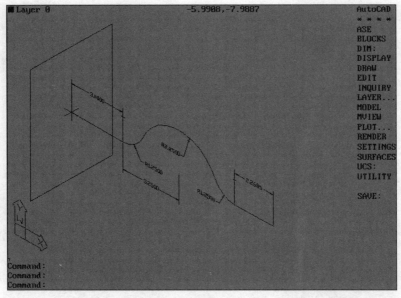

Figure 6.15 Display an isometric view to make it easier to select the new work plane.

10. From the Designer Sketch Constraints menu, choose **Add** and include any constraints required by the profile.
11. From the Designer Sketch menu, choose **Add Dimension** and add enough dimensions to fully constrain the profile (Figure 6.16).

Once the path and the profile are defined, you define how you want the profile to follow the path and whether the new feature should be added, subtracted, or intersected with the previous components of the part.

To create a swept feature:

1. From the Designer Features menu, choose **Sweep** from the command column.
2. Select the sweep path.
3. Select the sweep cross section profile.
4. Type **P** to keep the profile parallel to its starting orientation as it follows the path, or **Enter** to rotate the profile so it always stays Normal to the path.
5. Select **OK** to exit this dialog box (Figure 6.17).

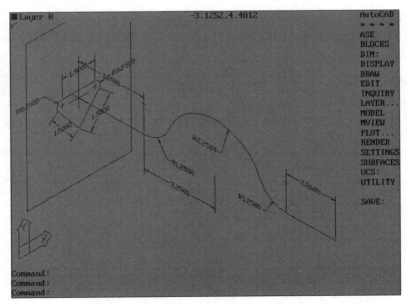

Figure 6.16 You must dimension and constrain sweep profiles prior to creating a feature.

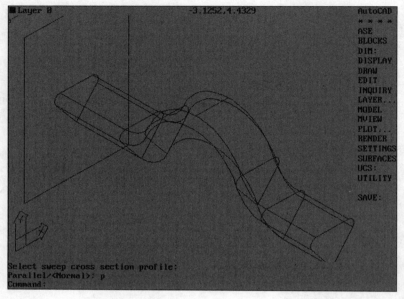

Figure 6.17 Sweep profiles can rotate to remain perpendicular to the path.

Viewing and Removing the Constraints Applied to a Profile

Constraints are rules you want the entities of a profile to obey. For example, you may want to ensure that two arcs always have the same radius, or that two lines always remain parallel. In order to implement these rules, Designer lets you apply constraints to a profile, and in fact automatically applies the most commonly used constraints to your sketch when you convert it into a profile.

Sometimes, however, Designer applies unwanted constraints to the profile. For example, it may force a line to be vertical when you want to control the angle of the line with an angular dimension. When this happens, you can remove the constraint and create a new constraint or even a dimension instead.

To see the constraints applied to your profile:

1. From the Designer Sketch Constraints menu, choose **Show**.
2. Type **A** to see all the constraints applied to your profile, or **S** to select an entity and see its constraints. Press **Enter** to see the next entity's constraints (Figure 6.18).

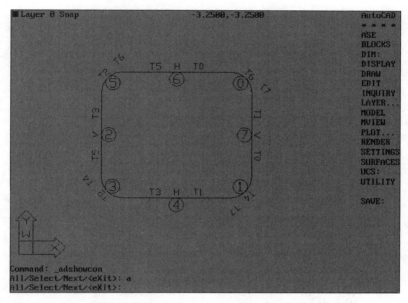

Figure 6.18 The circled number near each entity identifies the entity.

The constraint symbols are defined as follows:

H	Horizontal
V	Vertical
L	Perpendicular
P	Parallel
C	Collinear
N	Concentric
I	Projected
R	Same Radius
T	Tangent
X	Same X Coordinate
Y	Same Y Coordinate

These constraint codes are placed near the entity the constraint is applied to, and they may be shown with a number. The number indicates the other entity in the constrained relationship. For example, in Figure 6.18, T3 indicates that entity two is constrained to remain tangent to entity three.

To remove a constraint:

1. From the Designer Sketch Constraints menu, choose **Delete.**
2. Select the entity you want to free from a constraint, or type **A** to remove all constraints from the profile (Figure 6.19).
3. Select the constraint you want to remove.

Adding Constraints to a Profile

In addition to viewing constraints automatically applied to a profile, you can add constraints to a profile.

A horizontal constraint forces lines to remain parallel to the X axis.

A vertical constraint forces lines to remain parallel to the Y axis.

A perpendicular constraint forces two lines to remain at right angles to one another.

A parallel constraint forces two lines to always have the same slope and orientation.

A tangent constraint forces the slope of two entities to be identical at the point where they meet. This constraint can only be applied to two arcs, circles, or one line and one arc or circle.

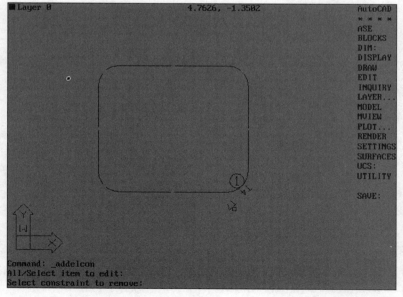

Figure 6.19 You may find it necessary to remove constraints that Designer automatically applies.

A collinear constraint forces two entities to fall on the same line.

A concentricity constraint forces two arcs and circles to have coincident center points.

A projected constraint forces the selected point of one entity to touch a second entity.

A joined constraint forces two endpoints to be coincident.

An X value constraint forces the center point of two circles to have the same X coordinate.

A Y value constraint forces the center point of two circles to have the same Y coordinate.

A radial constraint forces arcs and circles to have the same radius. You can apply this constraint only after you apply a dimension to one of the arcs or circles.

You should add constraints when you want to ensure that an entity or entities always obey a rule. If you always want two circles to have the same radius, create a radial constraint to enforce that rule. But be careful. When you turn a constrained profile into a feature, you can't go back and remove the constraint. Make sure that any constraint you apply represents a rule that you won't want to change later.

To add a constraint to a profile:

1. From the Designer Sketch Constraints menu, choose **Add.**
2. Specify the type of constraint you want to add.
3. Select the entity, or if the constraint requires two entities, the two entities to which you want to apply the constraint (Figure 6.20).

Even if you apply a constraint to an entity, you can still use dimensions to make adjustments to that entity. For example, if you constrain two arcs to share the same X value, you can create a dimension that controls the center point of one arc. The second arc's center point will also be controlled by this dimension.

Creating, Listing, and Deleting Parameters

Every dimension you create is assigned a parameter, a variable value based upon an equation. Usually, the equation for a dimension parameter is fairly simple; the dimension parameter is equal to a constant. Dimension parameter names always begin with a lowercase d followed by a number. The first dimension created in a part, for example, has the name d1. Usually, the equation for a parameter looks something like d1=5.

But you can also create more complex relationships between dimensions by assigning more complex equations to dimension parameters. For

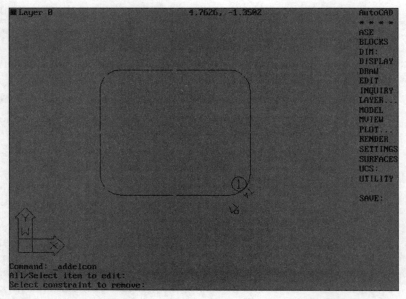

Figure 6.20   Add constraints to a profile to establish rules that you want Designer to enforce.

example, you may make the third dimension you create, d3, have twice the value of the first dimension you created. In this case, when prompted for the dimension value for d3 you might enter =**2*d1.**

You can also create parameters that are not immediately dependent on a specific dimension. These parameters, called global parameters, are usually defined to control the most important facets of a design. For example, you might ensure that a triangle remain a right triangle by creating a parameter defined as follows:

```
HYPOTENUSE = sqrt(SIDEA^2 + SIDEB^2)
```

where **SIDEA** and **SIDEB** are parameters that control the sides of the triangle. By assigning the **HYPOTENUSE** parameter to the hypotenuse of a triangle with sides controlled by SIDEA and SIDEB, you ensure that Designer always creates a right triangle. You can also type parameters to specify values in dialog boxes (Fig 6.21).

In this case changing the values assigned to the global parameters SIDEA and SIDEB will make the part grow thicker and thinner based upon the new distance value.

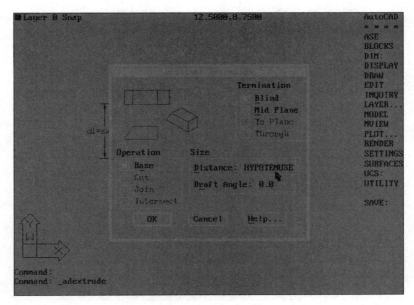

Figure 6.21 Parameters can be based upon equations involving other parameters.

To create a global parameter:

1. From the Designer Parameters menu, choose **Create.**
2. Enter the name of the parameter, followed by an equal sign (=), followed by the equation that defines the parameter (Figure 6.22).

Follow this procedure to redefine parameters as required.

Setting dimension values equal to global parameter names lets you define systems of equations that control your part.

Importing and Exporting Parameters

Designer lets you export global parameters to an ASCII text file with the extension .PRM. Use a text editor to open the text file and modify the parameters. You can then import the parameter file back into Designer and the model will change to reflect the new values. You can use the import and export utility to create a family of drawings, as follows:

1. Create a parametric model using Designer.

2. Export the parameters to a .PRM file.

3. Make one or more duplicates of the drawing containing the model.

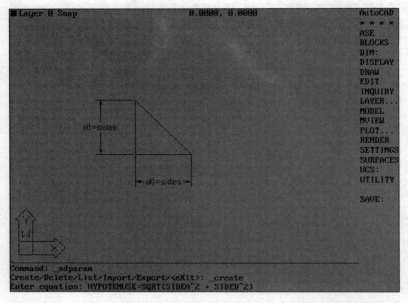

Figure 6.22 Use parameters to create dimensions based upon equations.

4. Make duplicates of the .PRM file and modify the parameter values in the file as required.

5. Open each drawing containing the model and import the parameter file.

Using script files you can even automate this process. This lets you create a hundred variations of a model from a single design.

To export the parameter settings to a .PRM file:

1. From the Designer Parameters menu, choose **Export** (Figure 6.23).
2. Enter the name of the parameter file you want to create.

To import a .PRM file:

1. From the Designer Parameters menu, choose **Import** (Figure 6.24).
2. Enter the name of the parameter file you want to import.
3. From the Designer menu, choose **Update.**

Editing Features

After you create features, Designer lets you alter them by changing the values associated with the dimensions that control them. You can replace a di-

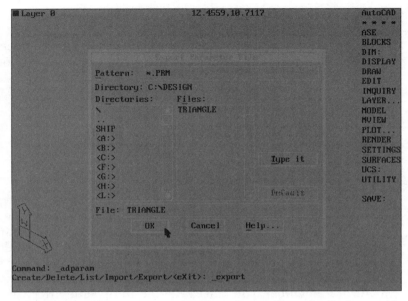

Figure 6.23 Export parameters to an ASCII file and edit them with a text editor.

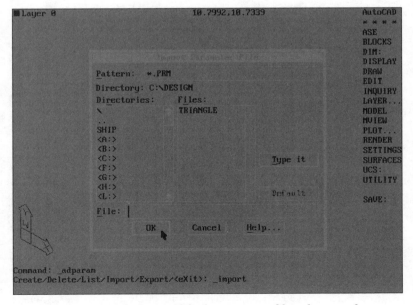

Figure 6.24 Importing modified parameter files changes the parameters that control your model.

mension value with a number or the name of another dimension or with a parametric dimension defined previously.

When you edit features, be sure to select the feature you want to edit in a view that shows the dimension you want to change; an isometric view, for example. You must be able to click on the dimension in order to change its value.

To edit a dimension:

1. From the Designer menu, choose **Edit Feature.**
2. Select the feature you want to edit.
3. Select the dimension you wish to change.
4. Enter a new value for the dimension (Figure 6.25).
5. From the Designer menu, choose **Update.**

It is possible to change the value of a dimension so that there is no solution to the parametric design. If this happens, use Undo to reverse the change to the dimension value. If you discover that your feature only has a single solution, you must re-create the profile used to define the feature. Remember, you can't redefine the profile after the feature has been created.

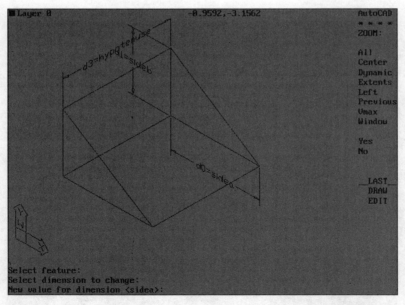

Figure 6.25 Select the dimension and enter a new value when prompted.

Using the Automated Drafting System

Once you create a parametric model using Designer, Designer can create a drawing based upon that model. In addition to simply letting you place views of your model in drawing mode, also called Paper Space, Designer lets you determine which views of the model will be shown, which dimensions are visible, the scale of the views, and whether hidden lines are visible.

Drawings created using the Automated Drafting System update when the model is changed, ensuring that the model and the drawing are always in sync. The first step in creating a drawing using the Automated Drafting System is to create a base view, which is then used to construct the other views. The base view allows you to select a side of the part with which Designer should align the X Y plane in Drawing Mode. After you define a base view, you can construct orthographic, isometric, detail, and cross-sectional views.

To create a base view:

1. From the Designer Drawing menu, choose **Create View**.
2. Select the Base option to specify that you want to create a base view (Figure 6.26).
3. Specify which Parts to show. In most cases, you will want to show all the parts in the drawing in the base view.
4. Specify the Scale of the base view. All orthographic views will have the same scale as the base view.
5. Specify if the view will show a Section of the part. You can elect to show a Full cross section or a Half cross section. Select **None** to display no cross section at all.
6. Specify how Hidden Lines should be handled. You can replace hidden lines with lines in a specific linetype; the hidden linetype, for example. You can also Blank hidden lines so they don't display at all, or you can select Do not calculate hidden lines, which will make a wireframe view of your part.
7. Specify a View Label if desired.
8. Select **OK** to exit.
9. Select the work plane or face aligned to the view you want to create by selecting two edges of your part or a work plane.
10. Type **R** to Rotate the part, if necessary. This lets you rotate the part on the X, Y plane to achieve the proper orientation.
11. Select a point to position the view on the drawing. You can select multiple points to move the view to its final position (Figure 6.27).

To create an orthographic view, you must first have created a parent view. In most cases a parent view is a base view of the part, but there are times when other views can serve as parent views. When you create an orthographic view you must select the parent view and then select the direc-

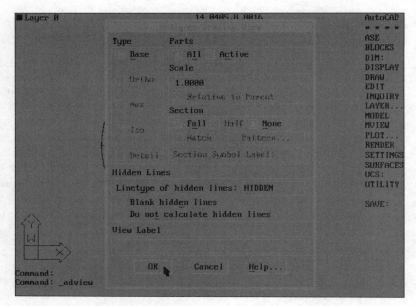

Figure 6.26 The Designer Drawing View dialog box lets you specify views you want to place in drawing mode.

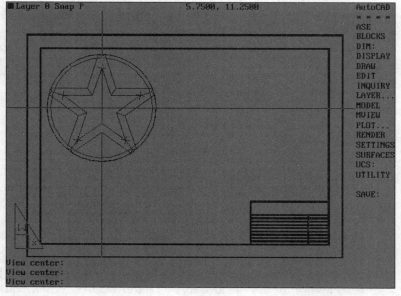

Figure 6.27 Place and reposition the base view by selecting a point in Paper Space.

tion from which the view should be projected. You can only select a point above, below, to the right, or to the left of the base view. To make this easier, Designer automatically turns Ortho on. The scale of the orthographic view will match the scale of the parent view. After Designer creates the orthographic view you may place that view anywhere in the drawing.

To create an orthographic view:

1. From the Designer Drawing menu, choose **Create View.**
2. Select **Ortho** to specify an orthographic view.
3. Specify if the view will show a Section of the part. You can create Full sections, Half sections, or select **None** to create an orthographic view that does not incorporate a section.
4. Specify how Designer should handle hidden lines. Hidden lines can be displayed in a unique linetype; Hidden, for example. Select **Blank** to hide hidden lines or Do not calculate hidden lines to make a wireframe view of the model.
5. Specify a view label if desired.
6. Select **OK** to exit the dialog box.
7. Select the parent of the new view. Usually this is the Base view.
8. Select a point to indicate where the orthographic view should be placed. You may only select a point to the left, right, above, or below the part.

After Designer creates the orthographic view, you can turn Ortho off and select a new location for the view (Figure 6.28).

Creating an isometric view is very similar to creating an orthographic view. In this case, however, you don't select a point directly above, below, to the right, or to the left of the base view. You must select a point that is diagonal to the parent view, which is to say to the upper right, lower right, lower left, or upper left of the parent view (Figure 6.29).

Detail views are enlarged views of the part that show small details and dimensions. Detail views don't have to be the same scale as the parent view, but they do have the same orientation as the parent view.

To create a detail view:

1. From the Designer Drawing menu, choose **Create View.**
2. Select **Detail** to specify a detail view.
3. Specify how Designer should handle hidden lines. Hidden lines can be displayed in a unique linetype; Hidden, for example. Select **Blank** to hide hidden lines or Do not calculate hidden lines to make a wireframe view of the model.
4. Specify a view label if desired.
5. Select **OK** to exit the dialog box.
6. Select a point in the parent view to serve as the center of the new detail view.

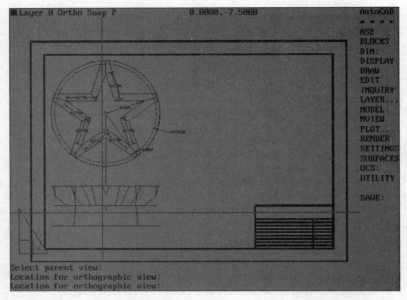

Figure 6.28   Orthographic views show the model from the left, right, front, or back.

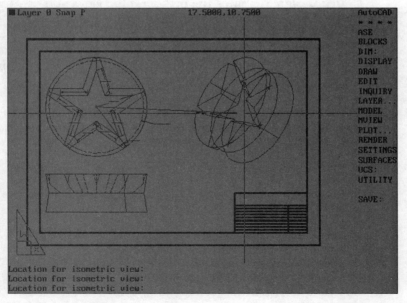

Figure 6.29   Isometric views show the model from the upper right, lower right, lower left, or upper left.

7. Select two points that define a window around the area of detail (Figure 6.30).
8. Select a point to locate the detail view.

Designer can also create cross-sectional views of a part. To determine the cutting plane on which the cross-sectional view will be based, you can create a work plane or select a point in the parent view. If you select the point option, the cutting plane passes through this point. If you select Full section, the cross-sectional view shows the entire cross section. If you select Half section, Designer creates two cutting planes, one parallel to the new view and one normal to it.

Remember that cross-sectional views update as the part changes. If you use the work plane option, make sure that you define the work plane such that it will always intersect the part at the desired point no matter how other features change. The work plane is the best to use when you want to generate cross sections at angles other than 0 or 90 degrees.

To create a cross-sectional view:

1. From the Designer Drawing menu, choose **Create View.**
2. Select the type of view you want to create. Designer only creates cross-sectional views on Base views, Orthographic views, and Auxiliary views.

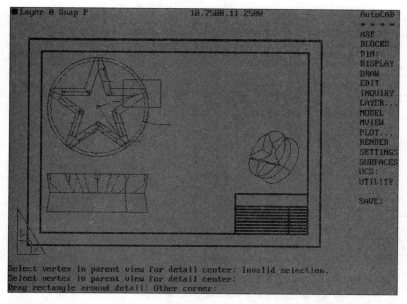

Figure 6.30   Select two points that define a window around the area of detail.

3. Specify Hatch if you want to have the cross section hatched to show where media exists.
4. Select the **Pattern...** button to specify a hatch pattern to be used in the cross section.
5. Specify a view label if desired.
6. Select **OK** to exit the dialog box.
7. Select the parent of the new view.
8. Select a point to indicate where the cross section view should be placed. Note that you can move the view after its initial placement (Figure 6.31).
9. Select a preexisting work plane in the parent view, or type **P** and select a point to show where the cross section should be taken (Figure 6.32).
10. Select a point in the parent view to indicate the depth of the cross section if necessary.
11. Type **F** to flip the cross section, or hit **Enter** to accept its orientation.

The Designer Drawing Dimension menu lets you move, freeze, or thaw dimensions in drawing views. The Move option moves dimensions within a view and will actually move dimensions between views. The freeze and thaw options control the display of dimensions in views.

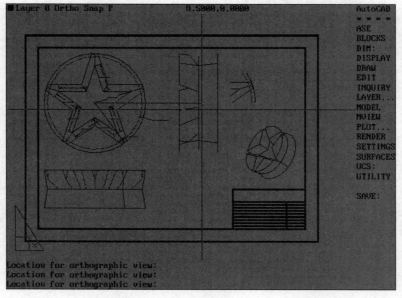

Figure 6.31 Position the cross section by selecting a point.

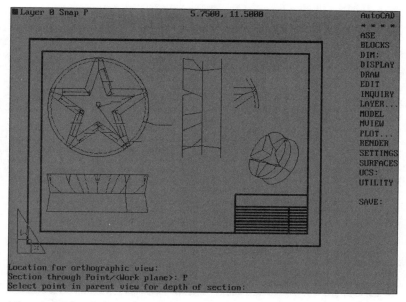

```
▪Layer 0 Snap P                    5.7500, 11.5000              AutoCAD
                                                                * * * *
                                                                ASE
                                                                BLOCKS
                                                                DIM:
                                                                DISPLAY
                                                                DRAW
                                                                EDIT
                                                                INQUIRY
                                                                LAYER...
                                                                MODEL
                                                                MVIEW
                                                                PLOT...
                                                                RENDER
                                                                SETTINGS
                                                                SURFACES
                                                                UCS:
                                                                UTILITY

                                                                SAVE:




Location for orthographic view:
Section through Point/<Work plane>: P
Select point in parent view for depth of section:
```

Figure 6.32   Select a point to indicate the cutting plane for the cross section.

Creating Features without Profiles

Some features, holes, fillets, and chamfers, do not require you to create a profile. These features are so well defined that Designer can create them with a very limited amount of information. For example, to create a hole, you need only define the hole within the Create Hole dialog box, and then position the hole on the feature.

Holes come in three varieties: drilled, counter bore, and counter sunk. You can specify the kind of hole you want to create, the depth of the hole, the radius of the hole, the radius of the counter bore or countersink, and the method used to place the hole from within a dialog box.

To create a hole:

1. From the Designer Features menu, choose **Hole** (Figure 6.33).
2. Select the type of hole you want to create. You can select Drilled, C'bore, C'sink to specify the hole type.
3. Specify the Drill Size. The diameter you enter here determines the diameter of the hole.
4. Specify C'Bore or C'Sunk size. If you specify a counter bored or counter sunk hole, you must also specify the depth and diameter of the sink or bore.

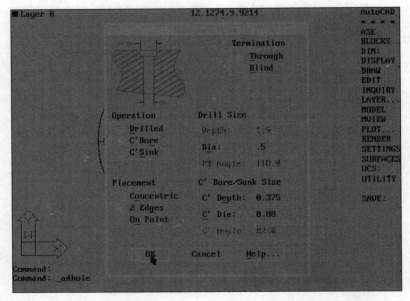

Figure 6.33   You don't need to create a profile or dimensions to create holes.

5. Select a termination option, Through or Blind. Blind specifies a predetermined depth for the hole, while Through ensures that the hole always passes through the part regardless of how thick the part becomes.
6. Specify the depth of the hole if necessary.
7. Select a placement option. Select Concentric if you want the hole to be concentric to a circle, 2 Edges if you want to place the hole based upon the distance from both edges, or On Point if you simply want to click to place a hole.
8. Select **OK** to exit the dialog box.
9. Place the hole. If you selected Concentric, you will have to select the edge of a circle or arc. If you selected 2 Edges you must select two edges and specify the distance of the hole from the two edges. If you selected On Point, you select the point you want to place the hole at by clicking on a preexisting work point or by entering coordinates.

Designer can create a rolling ball fillet that follows any edge of an active part. You can fillet multiple edges simultaneously, and if the selected edge or edges end at a point where the endpoints of two entities join and are tangent-continuous, Designer will automatically extend the fillet until it reaches a noncontinuous end. You cannot create fillets that change radius using Designer, but you can in AutoSurf.

To create a fillet:

1. From the Designer Features menu, choose **Fillet.**
2. Select the edges you want to fillet. Remember that you can select multiple edges if desired.
3. Enter the fillet radius.

Chamfering an edge is much like filleting an edge except that you don't specify radii, you specify chamfer distances. You can specify either one or two distances. If you specify Equal Distance, Designer chamfers two surfaces at an equal distance from the edge used to create the chamfer. If you select Two Distances, you can specify the distance the first surface is cut back from the selected edge, and the distance the second surface is cut back from the selected edge.

Summary

Designer can save you hundreds of hours at the CAD station. Creating intelligent parts based upon parametric features ensures that your designs always meet specifications established early in the design process. The automated drafting system keeps your drawings current with all changes made to the part, eliminating hours spent ensuring that plotted drawings reflect finished models.

But Designer's most powerful feature is its ability to assign parameters—variables defined by equations—to dimensions. By importing and exporting parameters from your drawings, you can create a family of parts in the time it takes to create a single parametric model.

CHAPTER 7

Introduction To AutoSurf

Surface Models For Numerical Control Applications.

If you have to create very complex models based upon digitized points, contour lines, or multi-planar three dimensional paths, you are likely to discover that AutoCAD's Advanced Modeling Extension and Designer cannot meet your needs. AutoSurf, Autodesk's most advanced modeling tool was specifically designed to create surface models of parts from just this type of information.

Unlike Designer, AutoSurf creates surface models rather than solid models. This means that you can't perform mass properties analysis on AutoSurf models, and you can generate cross sectional views. AutoSurf models are not parametric, which is to say that you can't redefine a model by changing a dimension and you can't create a family of parts drawings by importing a text file full of parameters.

On the other hand, AutoSurf's surface models are very accurate. Unlike AutoCAD's built in surfacing commands, AutoSurf surfaces can change based upon tolerance values. This is because AutoSurf models are not composed of faces. They are defined by non-rational uniform b-splines, or NURBs. This means that the accuracy of the model is practically infinite, determined only when you generate the tool paths for numerical control code.

Of course, creating accurate surface models doesn't automatically result in numerical control code. AutoMill, AutoSurf's companion product, generates tool paths based upon AutoSurf models. Post processors tailor these generic tool paths to create NC code for specific machines.

AutoSurf is an expensive application, far more expensive than AutoCAD equipped with Designer. And, as of the publication of this book, AutoSurf is not yet available for Release 13. Nevertheless, AutoSurf is Autodesk's most sophisticated three dimensional modeling tool, and the one which provides the most direct route from design to production.

In this chapter we provide an overview of AutoSurf's modeling capabilities. You learn how to create simple and advanced surfaces. You also learn how to edit surfaces, trim surfaces, offset surfaces, and blend surfaces. By the time you complete this chapter you should be able to tell if your work requires this sophisticated, surface modeling tool.

Simple Surfaces

AutoSurf generates a variety of primitive surfaces with very little input. You can create cones, cylinders, toroids, spheres and planes, and portions of these primitives, without creating any preliminary geometry. You can also create more complex surface primitives. You can define tubes that follow a three-dimensional path, define surfaces of revolution with a curve and an axis, and extrude surfaces with a curve an a path.

In most cases, you combine these simple surfaces to create more complex models. Unlike Designer and AutoCAD, which manipulate models using Boolean operations of union, subtraction, and intersection, AutoSurf uses more traditional operations, like trim and fillet, to combine simple surfaces into more complex surface models.

To create a partial torus:

1. From the AutoSurf Create Surface menu, choose **Torus.**
2. Type **??** to bring up the advanced options for this AutoSurf command (Figure 7.1).
3. Enter a start angle for the torus.
4. Enter an end angle for the torus.
5. Enter a center point for the torus.
6. Enter a diameter for the torus. This value represents the diameter of the torus measured from the center to the outermost edge.
7. Enter a radius for the tube of the torus. This value specifies the radius of the circle used to create the torus (Figure 7.2).

The steps required to create other primitives, like cones, cylinders, toroids, spheres and planes, are very similar to the steps outlined above. In

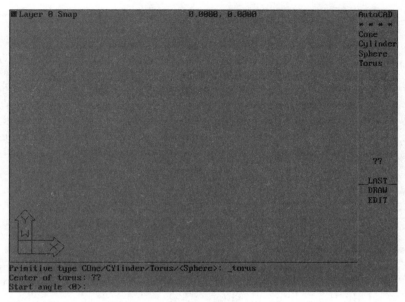

Figure 7.1 Type **??** at any AutoSurf prompt to see advanced options for the current command.

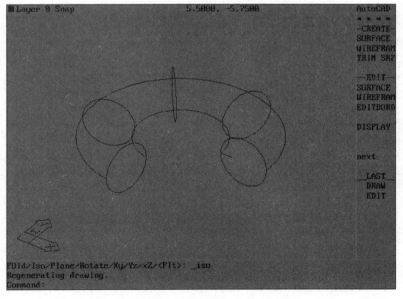

Figure 7.2 From the AutoSurf Display Views menu, choose Isometric to display an isometric view of your surface.

every case you can type **??** to see the advanced options for the command. In most cases you can create a partial primitive.

To create slightly more complex primitives you must define some geometry before launching the command. AutoSurf's revolved surfaces, ruled surfaces, and tubular surfaces need contours, paths, or axes defined prior to starting the command. Unlike Designer models, the geometry used to construct models using AutoSurf must be perfect. You can't redefine an AutoSurf model by changing this geometry later. This means you have to spend more time defining your initial geometry in AutoSurf, and you have to delete models and re-create them with new geometry if design specifications change during the course of a project.

To create a tubular surface:

1. From the Autosurf Create Surface menu, choose **Tubular.**
2. Select the line or polyline that defines the path for the tube (Figure 7.3).
3. Enter the diameter of the tube.
4. Enter **A** if you want Autosurf to give all the curves in the tube the same radius. Enter **M** if you want to define the radius for each bend in the tube separately (Figure 7.4).

   In addition to creating primitives and well-defined entities like tubes, you can create surfaces by extruding 2-D curves into the third dimension.

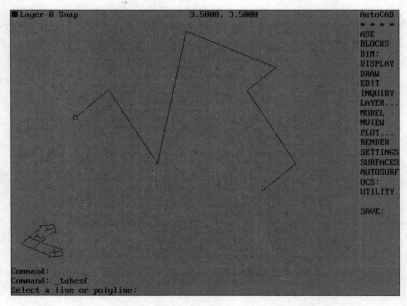

Figure 7.3 Use a 3-D polyline to create a path for the tube.

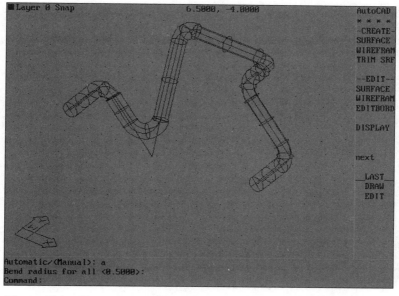

Figure 7.4 You can specify a radius for each bend in the tube, or assign all bends a single radius value.

This command, like the Designer commands you are already familiar with, lets you specify a draft angle. If the draft angle is less than 0 degrees, the extruded object will be narrower at the top than it is at the bottom.

To create a surface by extruding a line, arc, polyline, or spline:

1. From the AutoSurf Create Surface menu, choose **Extrude.**
2. Select the curve you want to extrude (Figure 7.5).
3. Select the method by which you want to specify the extrusion direction. You can select an entity that indicates the extrusion direction, extrude perpendicular to the V, extrude along the X, Y, or Z axis, or simply select a start point and an endpoint to define the extrusion direction.
4. Select the entity to be used to define the extrusion.
5. Enter a draft angle if desired. A positive angle widens the surface as the curve is extruded. A negative angle tapers the surfaces as the curve is extruded (Figure 7.6).

Note that the original components of the surface are retained in case you wish to make the model again. In general, you should try to keep these

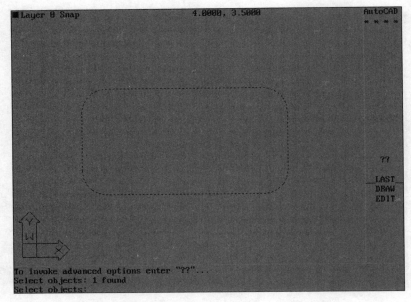

Figure 7.5 Entities you extrude can be open or closed.

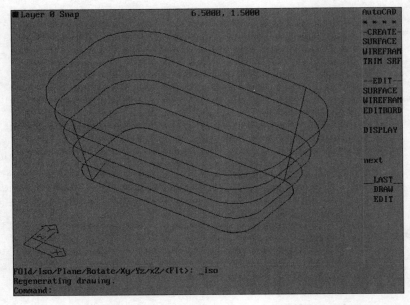

Figure 7.6 A positive draft angle widens the surface as the curve is extruded.

entities on a separate layer so they can be hidden and recalled if you have to change the model.

Displaying an AutoSurf Model

One of AutoSurf's most important features is that surfaces are defined without 3-D faces. If you want to generate a version of a model that you can hide or render, you issue a command that generates a special block containing the faces that represent the AutoSurf model.

While you are working with AutoSurf models, you rarely take the time to generate 3-D faces. Instead, you apply display lines to the surface of the model, which show the contour lines of a model. You can change the number of display lines, which is to say the visual resolution of a model, while you work.

When you first create a model, you may not be interested in seeing a very detailed representation since you are just blocking out the component. Later, as you refine edges and intersections, you may want to see the model represented with greater detail. So, in the beginning, you work with a small number of display lines on your model, and later in a project increase the number of flow lines.

Because AutoSurf does not limit a model's resolution, you can cut rough versions of a part throughout the design process, and generate high-resolution versions in the last stages of the project.

You can change the density of the display lines used to represent an AutoSurf model by changing the U and V values. U and V are arbitrary names used to refer to the two directions of a surface. It would be inappropriate to refer to the X and Y display lines of a surface model because X and Y refer to the orientation of a plane, and a surface may lie on any orientation on a plane. U and V lines refer specifically to the display lines that define the placement of faces on a surface.

To change the number of display lines used to represent surfaces:

1. From the AutoSurf menu, choose **Surface Display.**
2. Select the surface on which you want to display UV lines.
3. Select the desired display option. To display only UV lines, select the UV lines check box (Figure 7.7).
4. Type U and V values in the edit boxes to specify the number of UV lines shown on a surface (Figure 7.8).
5. Select **OK** to exit this dialog box.

You can follow this procedure at any time to display your surfaces with UV lines.

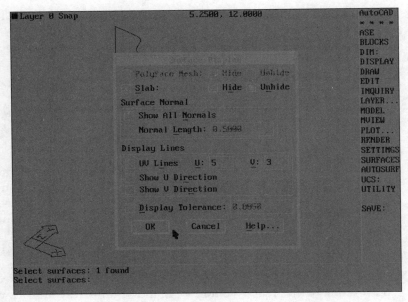

Figure 7.7 U and V are arbitrarily assigned names for the two axes of any surface.

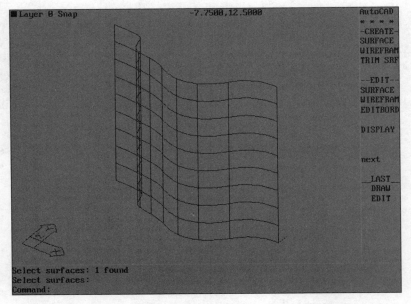

Figure 7.8 Increasing the U and V lines on a part does not increase file size.

Advanced Surfaces

In addition to primitive surfaces, AutoSurf lets you define a large number of very complex surfaces. These surfaces often take a series of lines or polylines as input, constructing a surface that passes near or through a number of points that vary in three dimensions.

AutoSurf can create surfaced objects by sweeping open or closed contours along paths. The paths in AutoSurf, unlike those used to create swept features in Designer, can vary in three dimensions and you can have more than one of them. AutoSurf refers to paths as rail curves, which can be defined by any line that passes through any sequence of X,Y,Z coordinates.

To create a swept surface:

1. From the AutoSurf Create Surface menu, choose **Swept.**
2. Select the curve that defines the cross section you want to sweep (Figure 7.9).
3. Type **??** to see the advance options for this command (Figure 7.10).
4. Select **Parallel** if you want to ensure that the cross sections will remain parallel to the original cross section. Select **Normal** if you want the cross section to remain perpendicular to the path at all points.
5. Select **Scale** if you want the cross section to increase or decrease on both the U and V axes as the cross section follows the path.
6. Select **Stretch** if you want the size of the cross section to change only in the direction that the rails converge or diverge.
7. Select **Direction** if you want to modify the direction the cross section turns as it follows the path.
8. Enter the Fit length. Any line of the curve that is shorter than this length will remain straight. Any line of the contour that is longer than this line will be curved.
9. Enter the Fit angle. Any angle smaller than the specified angle will have sharp corners; any angle wider than the specified angle will be smoothed.
10. Select the rail curve or curves you want to sweep the curve along (Figure 7.11).

In addition to creating surfaces based upon 2-D contours, you can also create a surface based upon a series of contour lines. This is useful if you have created a series of contours by sampling the X,Y,Z coordinates of an existing object. You can input these X,Y,Z coordinates to create the U lines, that is, the contour lines, and then use the following steps to turn the U lines into a part.

There are a number of tools that you can use to sample points on an object to construct accurate contour curves. Some tools are pen-like instruments. When you touch the tip of the instrument to the object, the X,Y,Z coordinates are calculated. A more sophisticated version of this tool

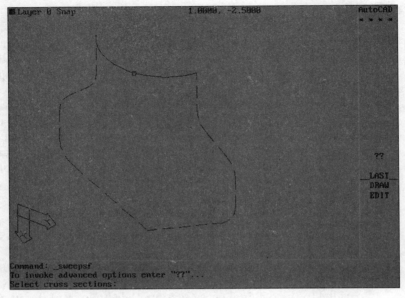

Figure 7.9 You can sweep open or closed curves.

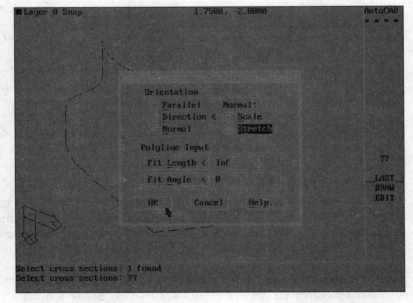

Figure 7.10 Advanced options for swept surfaces let you determine the orientation of cross sections to the path.

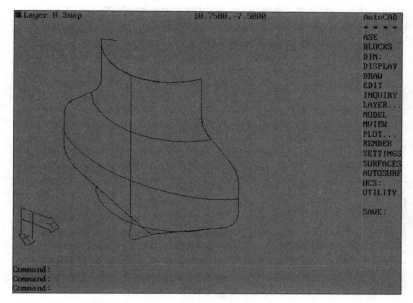

Figure 7.11 Multiple rail curves can stretch or scale a curve during a sweep operation.

samples X,Y,Z coordinates by laser. In both cases the X,Y,Z coordinates must be connected to create contour lines. To do this, use the 3-DPOLY command. Once you have connected the points, you can use them to create a surface.

To create a surface from U lines:

1. From the AutoSurf Create Surface menu, choose **Loft** (U lines) (Figure 7.12).
2. Type **??** at any prompt to change the fit length and fit angle values.
3. Select the U lines. You must do this in some order. You can select them from top to bottom, bottom to top, left to right, or right to left. The important thing is not to skip any lines during your selection.

If you digitize the contours of a part along two perpendicular axes, you can generate a more accurate representation of the part. In this case, the two sets of lines are called U lines and V lines, and you need to set AutoSurf's tolerance to match the maximum desired gap between U lines and V lines. Then, as the surface is constructed, AutoSurf will warn you if any gap between consecutive points on the U and V lines exceeds this measurement.

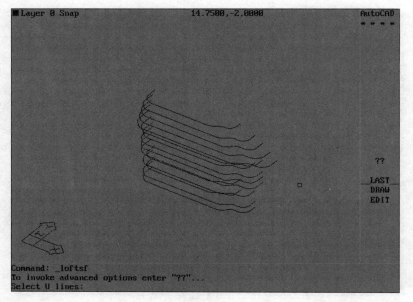

Figure 7.12   You can enter coordinates or use 3-D digitizers to create contour lines.

To create a surface from U and V lines:

1. From the AutoSurf Create Surface menu, choose **Mesh.**
2. Select the U lines. Remember to select them in order from top to bottom or left to right and without skipping any lines (Figure 7.13).
3. Select the V lines. Remember to select them in order and without skipping any lines.
4. Approve or disapprove the gap between U and/or V lines. If you elect to disapprove a gap, the command will be canceled (Figure 7.14).

   To create a smooth fillet or clean intersection between two surfaces, you create a third surface. The new surface is completely independent of the surfaces required to generate it, so it can be erased or modified as required.

   You can generate a blended surface between two or three existing surfaces. The blended surface will match the curvature of the last points of the two or three existing surfaces. This means that the blended surface will not create a sharp corner or discontinuous edge on the part.

   When you blend surfaces, remember to select the surfaces on the portions that you want to keep. The blended surface you generate will truncate intersecting surfaces retaining only the sides of the surfaces selected during the command.

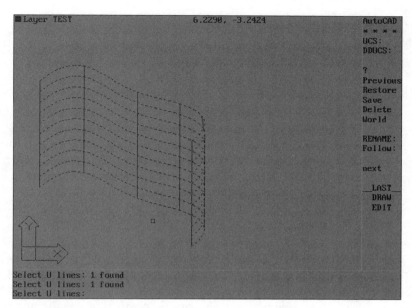

Figure 7.13   Using U lines and V lines to define a surface makes for a more accurate model.

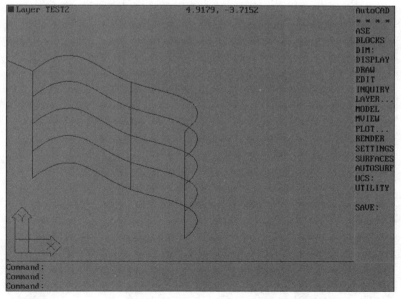

Figure 7.14   AutoSurf automatically compares the gap between the U and V lines to see if they exceed the tolerance established in the AutoSurf Preferences dialog box.

To create a blended surface:

1. From the AutoSurf Create Surface, choose **Blend.**
2. Select the first surface you want to blend (Figure 7.15).
3. Select the second surface you want to blend.
4. Select the third surface you want to blend, if necessary, or hit **Enter** to exit the command (Figure 7.16).

This command generates a new surface tangent to the existing surfaces. Advanced options for this command allow you to weight the new surface so it more closely matches the curvature of one of the selected surfaces.

You can also create a constant or variable radius fillet surface between two existing surfaces. Fillet surfaces, like blended surfaces, are independent surfaces that can be erased or modified without affecting the surfaces used to create them.

To create a rolling ball fillet with a variable radius:

1. From the Autosurf Create Surface menu, choose **Fillet** (Figure 7.17).
2. Select the first surface you want to fillet. Make sure you select the surface by selecting a point on the portion of the surface you want to keep.
3. Select the second surface you want to fillet. Select the surface by picking a point on the portion of the surface you want to keep.

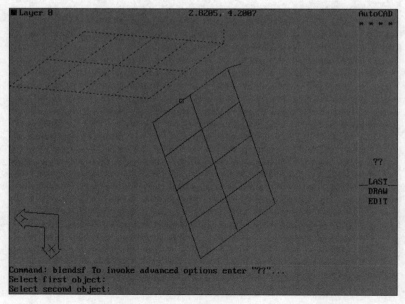

Figure 7.15　Select surfaces on edges you want to blend.

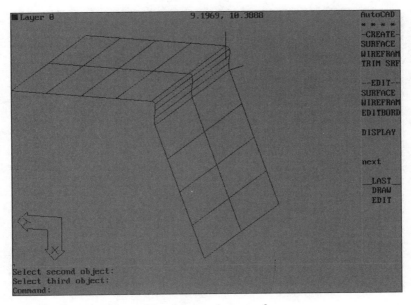

Figure 7.16 You can blend up to three surfaces.

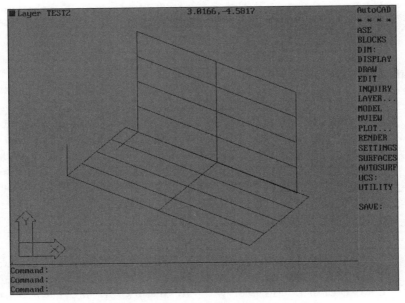

Figure 7.17 Surfaces you want to fillet must intersect.

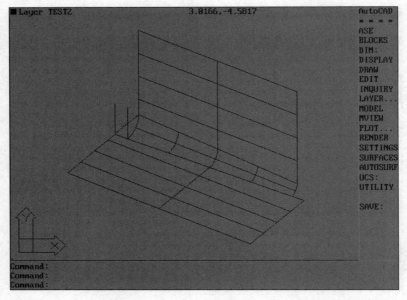

Figure 7.18   You can create constant or variable rolling ball fillets.

4. Enter the first radius value. This value specifies the starting radius of the rolling ball fillet.
5. Enter the second radius value. This value specifies the ending radius of the end of the rolling ball fillet (Figure 7.18).

Trimmed Surfaces

Sometimes you want to work with only a portion of a more complex surface. For example, most lenses are portions of spherical surfaces. To create a lens using AutoSurf, you must begin with a sphere and trim away the excess media. To create trimmed surfaces, you create a surface using the techniques outlined earlier in this chapter, then you project a contour onto that surface. The Trimmed Surface commands let you keep the portion of the surface that falls inside the projected contour, or the portion of the surface that falls outside the projected contour.

The surfaces at which you project contour lines are called slab surfaces. All the surfaces we have reviewed up until this point are slab surfaces. Once you project a contour onto the surfaces and hide the excess surface, you will have created a trimmed surface. From the Display Surfaces menu, choose Slab if you ever want to display the slab surface from which a trimmed surface was generated.

To create a trim surface:

1. From the AutoSurf Create Trim Surface Project menu, choose **Trim.**
2. Select the 2-D curve you want to project (Figure 7.19).
3. Select the surface to be trimmed. Remember that where you click on the surface determines which portion of the surface is retained after the trim operation.
4. Enter **D** to specify that the projected 2-D curve is projected normal to the current view. Hit **Enter** to specify that the 2-D curve is projected normal to the surface.
5. Enter **Y** to specify that the original objects should be retained after the trim operation is completed (Figure 7.20).

There are a number of ways you can project contours onto a surface. You can choose to project the contour so that it is normal to the surface, along the X, Y, or Z axis, or follows a line that specifies a direction. If you choose, you can project the contour so it remains parallel to the current view.

In addition to creating trimmed surfaces by projecting curves, you can also create trimmed surfaces by forcing surfaces to trim each other. This allows you to create a sharp intersection between two surfaces.

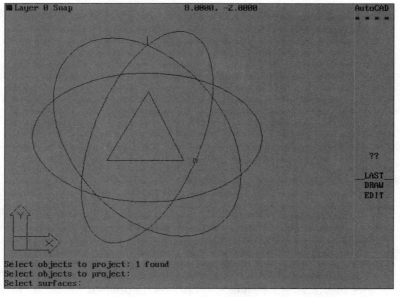

Figure 7.19 Use circles, arcs, polylines, or splines to trim a surface.

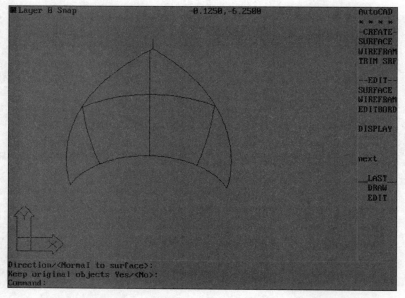

Figure 7.20 The surface that results from a trim surface operation depends upon the method selected to project the contour.

To force one surface to trim another:

1. From the AutoSurf Create Trim Surface Intersect menu, choose **Trim** (Figure 7.21).
2. Select the first surface on the portion of the surface that you want to retain.
3. Select the second surface on the portion of the surface you want to retain.

The advanced options for this command let you retain one or both surfaces after a trim operation. Use this feature when one surface must trim several surfaces in succession (Figure 7.22).

Modifying Surfaces

After you develop a model, or components of a model, using AutoSurf surfaces, you will probably need to edit it. For example, you may need to combine a number of small surfaces into a one or more large surfaces, or you may need to create a second copy of a surface for use in another operation.

When you edit surfaces, it is important to make normals of the surfaces are facing the right direction. The normal of the surface can be considered the top of the surface, and it is the portion that the cutting tool will

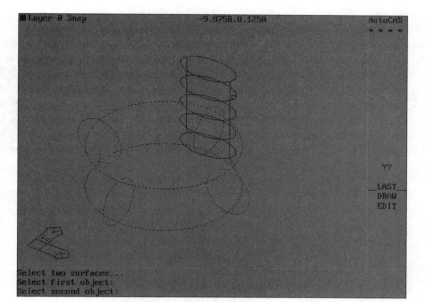

Figure 7.21 By default, the Trim Surface command trims both surfaces.

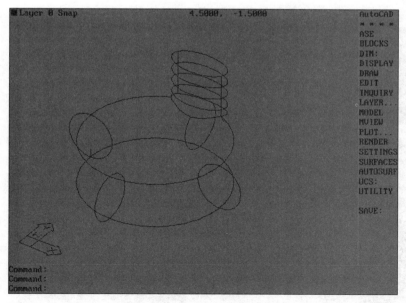

Figure 7.22 Use **??** to activate the advanced options for trim surface commands and you can retain unmodified surfaces for later use.

follow when you develop the NC code used to cut the part. Every surface has a normal line that indicates which side of the surface is the normal side.

If you fillet one surface to another such that their normals are facing opposite directions, the part will be unmillable because the cutting tool will cut the stock away to reveal the top, or normal, of one surface, but it won't be able to cut away the stock to reveal the normal of the other surface. In short, always make sure that the surface normal line is on the side of the surface that you want the cutting tool to touch. From the Surface Normals menu, choose Switch if you want to switch the normal on a surface.

To join two surfaces into a single surface:

1. From the AutoSurf Edit Surface menu, choose **Join** (Figure 7.23).
2. Select the first surface you want to join.
3. Select the second surface you want to join (Figure 7.24).

If you offset a surface, you create a smaller or larger version of an existing surface. Like AutoCAD's 2-D OFFSET command, you can use this operation over and over again to make scaled versions of components. Note, as you follow the instructions for offsetting a surface, advanced options let you retain the original surface or delete it if desired.

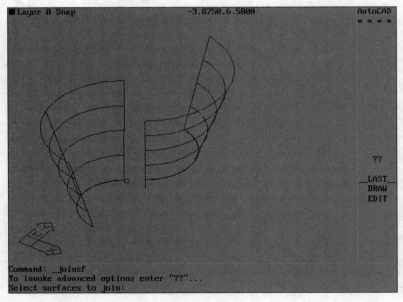

Figure 7.23 Surfaces you join together need not touch.

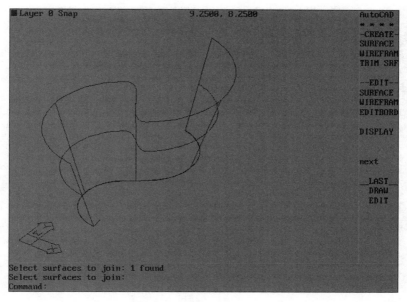

Figure 7.24 Joining two surfaces into a single surface closes gaps between surfaces.

To offset a surface:

1. From the AutoSurf Create Surface menu, choose **Offset** (Figure 7.25).
2. Select the surface you want to offset.
3. Enter the offset distance (Figure 7.26).

Sometimes a surface is too large to work with, or a portion of a surface needs to be refined. By breaking the surface into pieces, you can replace or modify one piece of the surface without affecting the rest of the model.

You can break surfaces along U and V lines, based upon percentages of the surface, or based upon points of discontinuity. A C0 discontinuity point is where a surface has a sharp corner or hard edge. A C1 discontinuity is a point where the curvature of the surface changes very abruptly. If you want to smooth out these sharp changes in a surface, break the surface at C0 or C1 discontinuity points then use a fillet surface or a blend surface to replace the rough edges.

To break a surface:

1. From the AutoSurf Edit Surface menu, choose **Break** (Figure 7.27).
2. Select the surface you want to break.
3. Type **U** to break the surface along the U lines; type **V** to break the

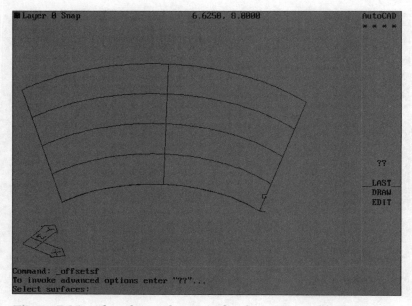

Figure 7.25 The advanced options for this command let you retain the original object after the offset operation.

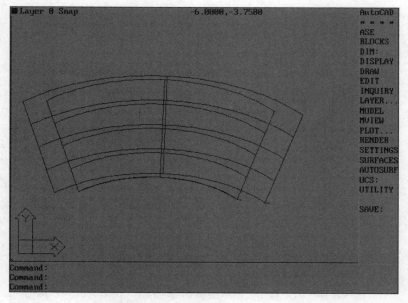

Figure 7.26 Use offset surfaces to define parts that must fit together after production.

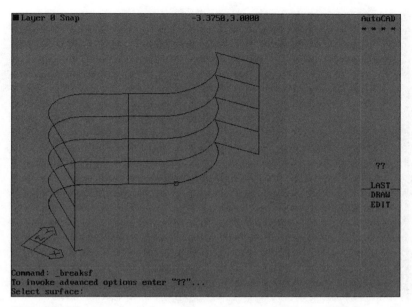

Figure 7.27 Break surfaces along UV lines or at points of discontinuity.

surface along the V lines. Type **C0** or **C1** to break the surface at points of discontinuity. Enter **UV** to break the surface along both U and V lines (Figure 7.28).

In addition to the editing operations outlined here, you can also edit surfaces by pulling on control points. This method can be quite useful when you need to make minor adjustments to a surface.

From AutoSurf to AutoMill

After you define surface models using AutoSurf, you use AutoMill to create numerical control code. AutoMill lets you specify tool cutting size, speed, in points, out points, and ramping angles. It also lets you specify additional control codes, specific to your company and your equipment, which it will automatically insert in the file. This lets you tell the machine to stop for tool changes or apply additional coolant.

With the information you provide, AutoMill generates rough and finishing paths, and exports this information to a generic NC file. Post processors available from Autodesk tailor this generic file for specific machines.

AutoMill and its post processors can use a single AutoSurf file to generate NC code for a variety of machines. This reduces the time required to

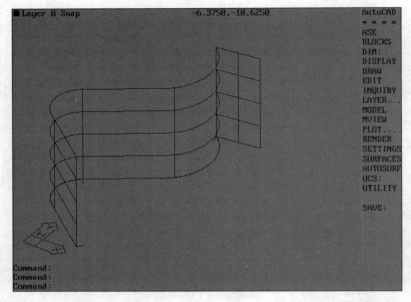

Figure 7.28 Broken surfaces display no gaps, but they do display more U and V lines.

reprogram machines between jobs, and may allow you to split production of a part between machines from a variety of manufacturers.

Summary

If you need to generate models from digitized points, contour lines, or multiplanar three-dimensional paths, then you should investigate Auto-Surf. Accurate, flexible, easy to use, AutoSurf is perfect for users who incorporate complex surfaces into their designs or for those who need to be able to move parts from one kind of machine to another without starting from scratch each time.

CHAPTER 8

Customizing AutoCAD

Unlike most CAD programs, AutoCAD has an open architecture. This means that you can customize almost every aspect of AutoCAD. AutoCAD lets you create your own commands, customize menus, add commands and symbols to the tablet, and modify the behavior of the mouse buttons. You can create keyboard shortcuts for AutoCAD's commands or your own. You even have access to linetypes, hatch patterns, font definitions, and the drawing database itself. In addition to what you can do yourself, you can use the work others have done to embellish your own work environment.

Some of the techniques for customizing AutoCAD require programming knowledge. AutoCAD has an internal programming language, AutoLISP. Additionally, it accepts compiled C-language programs through the AutoCAD Development System (ADS). There are even utilities available that permit BASIC programming language to integrate with AutoCAD.

In this section you will learn techniques for customizing the AutoCAD environment and creating useful commands that will help you in your daily work. You do not need to know programming languages such as C or AutoLISP, but several AutoLISP programming examples are included.

In these exercises, you will modify files. Never modify the only copy of a file. Always make a backup of the file before you make changes. Save the backup with a different extension or in a separate directory. Don't use the extension .BAK for your backup. Many text editors use and overwrite the .BAK extension, and so does AutoCAD.

Simple Menu Tricks That Save Time

The menu is a good place to start customizing. If you use the menus for launching commands, you already know that, sometimes, finding a command on the menu takes longer than typing the command directly from the keyboard. Menus have the advantage of listing the commands, so if you don't know the name of the command, use the menus.

Menus group commands in a logical fashion. Often, however, what is logical to the programmer who wrote the menus is not logical to you. As you work through these exercises, take a good look at the screen and pull-down menus. Think about what you would add or change.

Using the Screen Menu as a Macro Launcher

Earlier in this book, you learned that the screen menu responds to the keystrokes that you type. If you type the letter **D**, the DRAW menu highlights. To open the DRAW menu, press the **Insert** key. Unfortunately, to get to any other menus that begin with the letter D, you have to keep typing until you have typed enough letters to distinguish it from the DRAW menu.

You cannot differentiate some of the menu selections in this way because they contain spaces. Pressing the Spacebar is like pressing Enter at the command line. Three of the standard AutoCAD menu selections begin with the word DRAW. In an optimized menu macro launching system, each menu selection has a unique first letter or first two letters. Table 8.1 displays the original AutoCAD root menu and the proposed new root menu. With the new root menu, you type a maximum of two keys to launch any submenu. The Standard AutoCAD menu is defined in the file ACAD.MNU. To make the menu changes, modify a COPY of your ACAD.MNU file.

The file ACAD.MNU resides in the DOS\SUPPORT subdirectory of the AutoCAD directory. Before modifying your ACAD.MNU file, be sure to make a copy of it. You can do this from DOS with the COPY command.

To make a copy of the menu file *before* you change it:

1. In DOS, change directories to the DOS\SUPPORT subdirectory.
2. Copy the file by a different name; for example: COPY ACAD.MNU ACADORIG.MNU

Table 8.1   Original and New Root Menus

ORIGINAL	PROPOSED
AutoCAD	AutoCAD
* * * *	*****
FILE	FILE
ASSIST	ASSIST
VIEW	VIEW
DRAW	1DRAW
DRAW2	2DRAW
DRAW DIM	DIM
CONSTRCT	CONSTRCT
MODIFY	MODIFY
MOD DIM	EDIT DIM
DATA	DATA
OPTIONS	OPTIONS
TOOLS	TOOLS
HELP	HELP

Use a text editor that can save files in nondocument mode. The **DOS** text editor is a good choice. Start the text editor and open the file **ACAD.MNU**.

Renaming the Menu Items

Use the DOS editor's FIND utility to locate the line that begins with ***SCREEN. You should see the following:

```
***SCREEN
**S
[AutoCAD ]^C^C$S=s
[* * * * ]$S=OSNAP
[FILE ]$S=01_FILE
[ASSIST ]$S=02_ASSIST
[VIEW ]$S=03_VIEW
[DRAW ]$S=04_DRAW
[DRAW2 ]$S=05_DRAW2
[DRAW DIM]$S=06_DRAWDIM
[CONSTRCT]$S=07_CONSTRUCT
[MODIFY ]$S=08_MODIFY
```

```
[MOD DIM ]$S=09_MODDIM
[DATA ]$S=10_DATA
[OPTIONS ]$S=11_FORMAT
[TOOLS ]$S=12_TOOLS
[HELP ]$S=13_HELP
```

The menu labels for the screen menu are on the left and between the brackets [ ]. Don't change the text outside the brackets. You will learn what it means later. Menu labels have a maximum of eight characters, not counting the brackets.

To make the menu label changes:

1. Change the menu labels per Table 8.1.
2. Save the file.

To see the menu changes:

1. Begin AutoCAD. If your default prototype drawing uses the ACAD menu, you will see the changes immediately.
2. Type **MENU** at the command line if you don't see your changes. Select **ACAD** from the Menu files dialog box.

Try typing the first letter of a menu. When the menu is highlighted, press the **Insert** key to launch the menu. To begin the Ellipse command, you can type **D Insert, E Insert.**

> *Many submenus have the same problem as the Root menu. You can use the same technique to modify the submenus so a one- or two-key sequence selects an item from each submenu.*

Modifying the Screen Menu Object Snap Labels

The bottom half of the screen menu displays the object snaps. You can see all the object snaps if your screen resolution is 1024 × 768 or better. You can use the same technique to modify the object snap labels. Take a look at the original and proposed object snap menu labels in Table 8.2.

> *Use the ANSI.SYS device (described later in this section) to remap your Insert key to a more convenient location.*

Table 8.2   Original and Proposed Object Snap Menu Labels

ORIGINAL	PROPOSED
App Int	AApp Int
Center	CCenter
Endpoint	EEndpt
Insert	INsert
Intersec	IIntersc
Midpoint	MMidpt
Nearest	NEarest
Node	NNode
Perpend	PPerpend
Quadrant	QQuadrant
Quick	QUick
Tangent	TTangent
None	NOne
From	FRom

By making the proposed changes, you can easily launch the object snaps. To get an endpoint, type **EE Insert**.

Although there are better ways to generate keyboard macros, this technique is fast if you feel comfortable using the screen menu. It doesn't require a lot of programming or knowledge of any specific programming language.

Creating Custom Keyboard Macros

Keyboard macros are a very fast way to launch commands in AutoCAD. There are many ways to create keyboard macros in AutoCAD. In fact, Auto-CAD has many keyboard macros built into it. Type **L** at the command prompt and press **Enter** or the Spacebar. The L key is the keyboard macro for the LINE command.

Customizing the ACAD.PGP File

Simple keyboard macros are easy to create in the ACAD.PGP (ProGramming Parameters) file. The ACAD.PGP issues AutoCAD commands only.

You cannot use the ACAD.PGP to create macros that issue a command with an option. For example, you can create the macro Z for Zoom, but you can't create the macro ZP for Zoom Previous.

When you issue a keystroke and press **Enter**, AutoCAD looks for an AutoCAD command by that name first. If it doesn't find one, it looks in the ACAD.PGP. If it doesn't find it there, AutoCAD looks for an AutoLISP command that matches the keystroke. Command macros created in the ACAD.PGP take precedence over AutoLISP macros with the same name.

In addition to storing keyboard macro definitions, the ACAD.PGP also provides an interface with DOS commands. This means you can run other programs directly from AutoCAD. The ACAD.PGP file resides in the DOS\SUPPORT subdirectory of the AutoCAD directory. Make a copy of this file with the COPY command in DOS, as previously, or from within AutoCAD with the FILES command.

To make a copy of the ACAD.PGP file before you change it:

1. From the File pull-down menu, choose **Management, Utilities.**
2. Select **Copy File.**
3. Select the DOS\SUPPORT directory.
4. Select **ACAD.PGP** and **OK.**
5. Supply a new name for the destination file. ACADORIG.PGP is a good choice.
6. Select **OK** to create a copy of the file.

Use a text editor that can save files in nondocument mode. The DOS text editor will do this. Start the text editor and open the file ACAD.PGP.

External Command Format

The top portion of the ACAD.PGP file is the DOS interface to external commands. There are several DOS commands already in the ACAD.PGP. The first few lines begin with a semicolon (;). AutoCAD ignores everything after the semicolon. Programmers use semicolons to include comments that are not part of the program itself. The following is the external command portion of the ACAD.PGP. The first line describes the syntax for external commands.

```
; <Command name>,[<DOS request>],<Memory reserve>,[*]<Prompt>,<Return code>
CATALOG,DIR /W,     0,File specification: ,0
DEL,DEL,            0,File to delete: ,4
DIR,DIR,            0,File specification: ,0
EDIT,EDIT,          0,File to edit: ,4
SH,,                0,*OS Command: ,4
SHELL,,             0,*OS Command: ,4
TYPE,TYPE,          0,File to list: ,0
```

Commas separate the different positions of each line. AutoCAD counts each comma and expects certain information in each positions within the line. The first position in the line is the AutoCAD command that you will type. The second position is the DOS command that is issued. The third position is the memory reserve. If that position holds a zero, AutoCAD uses its available base memory to issue the command. The fourth position is the prompt you see when you run the command. The last position is the return code. The return code is either a zero (0) to return to the text screen, or a four (4) to return to the graphics screen.

In the first line, the AutoCAD command CATALOG issues the DOS command DIR /W which displays a directory in wide format. The File specification prompt allows you to specify which files the directory will display. For example, if you answer the File specification prompt with B*.DWG, the CATALOG command displays all the drawing files that begin with the letter B in a wide format. The zero at the end of the line tells the CATALOG command to remain in the text screen so you can see the file listing.

> *The ACAD.PGP command EDIT launches the DOS editor directly from AutoCAD. Use the EDIT command to edit the ACAD.PGP without exiting AutoCAD. When you reenter AutoCAD, use the REINIT command to reinitialize the ACAD.PGP.*

Creating Reference Screen Macros

One significant enhancement you can make is to use the TYPE command to display technical data. The following file is an example:

1/64	.015625	11/32	.34375	43/64	.671875
1/32	.03125	23/64	.35937	11/16	.6875
3/64	.046875	3/8	.375	45/64	.703125
1/16	.0625	25/64	.390625	23/32	.71875
5/64	.078125	13/32	.40625	47/64	.734375
3/32	.09375	27/64	.421875	3/4	.750
7/64	.109375	7/16	.4375	49/64	.765625
1/8	.125	29/64	.453125	25/32	.78125
9/64	.140625	15/32	.46875	51/64	.796875
5/32	.15625	31/64	.484375	13/16	.8125
11/64	.171875	1/2	.5	53/64	.828125
3/16	.1875	33/64	.515625	27/32	.84375
13/64	.203125	17/32	.53125	55/64	.859375
7/32	.21875	35/64	.546875	7/8	.875
15/64	.234375	9/16	.5625	57/64	.890625
1/4	.250	37/64	.578125	29/32	.90625
17/64	.265625	19/32	.59375	59/64	.921875

9/32	.28125	39/64	.609375	15/16	.9375
19/64	.296875	5/8	.625	61/64	.953125
5/16	.3125	41/64	.640625	31/32	.96875
21/64	.328125	21/32	.65625	63/64	.984375

This type of information is easily created with a text editor. You can create anything from drill charts to tables of formulas, and display them right on the text screen from within AutoCAD.

To create a reference screen for fractions/decimal equivalents:

1. Create the chart just shown, or some other text file in a text editor and save it by the file name FRACTION.REF.
2. Use your text editor to add the following line in your ACAD.PGP file.

```
FRAC,TYPE FRACTION.REF,0,,0
```

3. Save the ACAD.PGP file and enter AutoCAD.
4. Type **FRAC** to see the file.

As you can see, this simple macro can save time by putting information at your fingertips.

NOTE   To ensure that AutoCAD finds your reference screen each time, place reference screen files in a directory on AutoCAD's search path specified in the SET ACAD = environment variable in the batch file that begins AutoCAD. You can optionally supply the path right in the ACAD.PGP file. Example: FRAC,TYPE C:\MYDIR\FRACTION.REF,Ø, , Ø

Adding Command Aliases in the ACAD.PGP

The second portion of the ACAD.PGP file is the *command alias* section. You can use it create macros that issue AutoCAD commands. You can define your own command aliases by following the format below:

```
A,      *ARC
C,      *CIRCLE
CP,     *COPY
DV,     *DVIEW
E,      *ERASE
L,      *LINE
```

The first position represents the command alias. This is what you type to issue the command. The second position is the command, prefixed with an asterisk (*). Don't forget the comma and the asterisk.

To add the command alias O for Offset:

1. Add the following line to the ACAD.PGP in the command alias section:

    ```
    O,     *OFFSET
    ```

2. Save the file and return to AutoCAD.
3. Reinitialize the ACAD.PGP by typing **REINIT** at the Command prompt
4. Type **O**.

NOTE   Avoid using tab characters when creating these macros. AutoCAD uses spaces to separate the macro alias from the command. The spaces between the alias and the command are optional.

Don't disregard the notice in the ACAD.PGP file about overdoing it with command aliases. They do take up memory so think conservatively. Even better ways to create command aliases are described later in this section.

The ANSI.SYS Device

The ANSI.SYS device comes with your DOS software. It is used to reassign keys or change system colors. There is a limit to the number of keys you can remap, so choose wisely. Macros issued using the ANSI.SYS device look like commands typed at the keyboard. This is important because other types of macros require a Command prompt. By programming the ANSI.SYS, you can issue transparent commands or interactive object snaps easily.

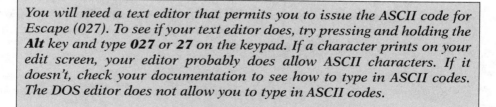

You will need a text editor that permits you to issue the ASCII code for Escape (027). To see if your text editor does, try pressing and holding the **Alt** *key and type* **027** *or* **27** *on the keypad. If a character prints on your edit screen, your editor probably does allow ASCII characters. If it doesn't, check your documentation to see how to type in ASCII codes. The DOS editor does not allow you to type in ASCII codes.*

The ANSI.SYS device installs in the CONFIG.SYS file, which loads certain devices as your computer boots up. You can use the TYPE command to see if your CONFIG.SYS file already contains the ANSI.SYS device. From the DOS prompt, type:

TYPE C:\CONFIG.SYS

From the AutoCAD Command prompt type:

TYPE

File specification:

C:\CONFIG.SYS

If you don't see a line that says DEVICE=ANSI.SYS, your system probably does not load it.

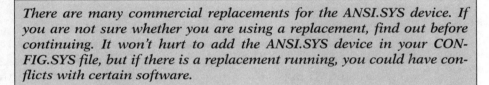

There are many commercial replacements for the ANSI.SYS device. If you are not sure whether you are using a replacement, find out before continuing. It won't hurt to add the ANSI.SYS device in your CONFIG.SYS file, but if there is a replacement running, you could have conflicts with certain software.

Make a copy of your CONFIG.SYS file before you change it.

Installing ANSI.SYS in the CONFIG.SYS

To use the ANSI.SYS device driver, place the following line anywhere in your computer's CONFIG.SYS file:

```
DEVICE=C:\DOS\ANSI.SYS
```

Changes to the CONFIG.SYS file do not become effective until the computer reboots. If you added this line to your CONFIG.SYS file, reboot your computer.

Programming with ANSI.SYS

Each key on the keyboard has a scan code. The ANSI.SYS device lets you intercept the key code and place text on that keystroke. Table 8.3 shows the scan codes and the keystrokes they represent. The alphabet key scan codes go from left to right across the keyboard. For example, the Alt-E keystroke has a key code of 18.

When you redefine your keyboard, be careful not to redefine keys that AutoCAD uses. These include: F1, F6 through F10, Insert, Enter, Backspace, and the Cursor keys.

Table 8.3   Scan Codes and the Keystrokes They Represent

SCAN CODE	KEYSTROKE
16-25	Alt-Q through Alt-P
30-38	Alt-A through Alt-L
44-50	Alt-Z through Alt-M
59-68	F1 through F10
84-93	Shift-F1 through Shift-F10
94-103	Ctrl-F1 through Ctrl-F10
104-113	Alt-F1 through Alt-F10
133-134	F11 through F12
135-136	Shift-F11 through Shift-F12
137-138	Ctrl-F11 through Ctrl-F12
139-140	Alt-F11 through Alt-F12
120-129	Alt 1 through Alt-0
3	Null (Equivalent to Ctrl-C in AutoCAD)
13	Enter
14	Backspace
15	Tab
71	Home
72	Cursor Up
73	Page Up
75	Cursor Left
77	Cursor Right
79	End
80	Cursor Down
81	Page Down
82	Insert
83	Delete

The process of creating ANSI macros is fairly simple. Don't get over-whelmed by the escape codes, ANSI device, ASCII characters, and scan codes. The basic command format for creating an ANSI macro is:

```
ESC[scan code;"Text";13p
```

ESC	The Escape code. This is a special character that you must produce with your text editor. Check your text editor's documentation to see how to produce this code.
[	Accompanies the escape character. Together, these two characters prepare the ANSI.SYS device for a key re-definition.
Scan code	The code for the key that you are redefining. The scan code may be prefixed with 0; indicating that the key is an extended ASCII key. Extended keys are Alt-key combinations, function keys and special keys like Page Up or Delete.
"Text"	The actual text that types at the command line when you press this key or key combination. If you want the keypress to cancel any previous commands, you can prefix the text with 3; which is the equivalent of pressing Ctrl-C. Don't use this if you want the command to be transparent.
13	The scan code for the Enter key. This is the equivalent of pressing Enter after issuing the command.
p	Terminates the key definition.

Creating Load and Unload Files

To create the file that defines the keys, use a text editor that can represent the escape character. Name the file LOAD.KEY.

To redefine the F3 key to display the Layer Control dialog box:

1. Enter the following code on the first line:

```
Esc[0;61;"'DDLMODES";13p
```

   0;61 is the F3 key. Be sure to put an apostrophe (') before the word DDLMODES so that it will be a transparent command.
2. Save the file.
3. Enter AutoCAD.

4. At the Command prompt, type

```
TYPE LOAD.KEY
```

5. Press **F3** to see the Layer Control dialog box.

To redefine the Alt-E key combination to issue the Endpoint modifier, reenter the LOAD.KEY file. Then:

1. Enter the following code on the first line:

```
Esc[0;18;"ENDP";13p
```

0;18 is the Alt-E key combination.
2. Save the file.
3. Enter AutoCAD.
4. At the Command prompt, type

```
TYPE LOAD.KEY
```

5. Draw some lines on the screen. During the LINE command, press **Alt-E** to get the Endpoint object snap modifier.

You can add many key definitions to the LOAD.KEY file. Good candidates are the object snaps and commonly used transparent dialog boxes because they are issued while another command is active.

Unloading the Key Definitions

The key definitions are independent of the program you are in. If you exit AutoCAD and press **Alt-E** at the DOS prompt, it still types ENDP at the DOS prompt. To clear the key definitions, you must create a file that returns the keys to their original definitions.

To create the UNLOAD.KEY file:

1. Create a new file named UNLOAD.KEY. You can save some typing by copying the LOAD.KEY file to UNLOAD.KEY.
2. To create the code that clears the definitions listed previously, enter the following lines:

```
Esc[0;61;0;61p
Esc[0;18;0;18p
```

3. Save the file.

4. Type the following command at the Command prompt:

```
TYPE
File to list: UNLOAD.KEY
```

In this example, each line actually defines a key. In this case, each key is simply defined to its original definition, which, essentially, undefines the key.

> *Place the TYPE LOAD.KEY and TYPE UNLOAD.KEY statements in the batch file that begins AutoCAD. TYPE LOAD.KEY should go before the line ACAD %1 %2. TYPE UNLOAD.KEY should go after the line ACAD %1 %2. Now, every time you begin AutoCAD, your key definitions will load. As you exit AutoCAD, the key definitions will unload.*

Programming in AutoLISP

AutoLISP is a programming language that is included with AutoCAD. AutoCAD evaluates AutoLISP programs and expressions internally, so you don't have to process or compile an AutoLISP program; you can simply write it and use it. In fact, you can issue AutoLISP expressions directly from the AutoCAD command line. Try this by typing the following at the Command prompt:

```
(* 5.74 25.4)
```

The expression you entered multiplies two numbers. The result, of course, is the value 5.74 expressed in millimeters.

Rules for AutoLISP Programs

As you write AutoLISP programs, you need to be aware of some basic rules. The following apply to all AutoLISP programs:

- For every open parenthesis there must be a close parenthesis.
- For every open quote, there must be a close quote.
- Numeric values may not begin with a decimal point. Use 0.500 instead of .500.
- AutoLISP file names should have the extension .LSP.

If you follow these rules, your AutoLISP programs should load properly. Whether they work properly, however, depends on many other factors.

How to Load AutoLISP Programs

The command for loading AutoLISP programs is actually an AutoLISP expression. It must follow the rules just given. To load an AutoLISP program, follow the command syntax below:

```
(LOAD "PROGRAM")
```

If you need to specify a path for the program, use front slashes (/) or double back slashes (\\) to specify the path. Never use a single back slash (\). The following are two examples:

```
(LOAD "C:/LISPDIR/PROGRAM")
(LOAD "C:\\LISPDIR\\PROGRAM")
```

Replace the word **PROGRAM** with the name of the program you want to run. Don't enter the extension .LSP as part of the name. AutoCAD knows you are loading an AutoLISP program.

If you forget one of the parenthesis, you will get an error which results in the prompt 1>. The number indicates how many parentheses are missing. Enter the appropriate number of close parentheses to return to the command prompt. If you forget a quotation mark, or begin a numeric value with a decimal point, you will get the error "Invalid dotted pair," and the program will not load until you correct the error.

Macro Templates in AutoLISP

Keyboard macros can speed up any operation in AutoCAD, and can be created in many ways using various techniques. AutoLISP macros are more powerful than ACAD.PGP macros because AutoLISP provides access to AutoCAD's system variables and command structures. AutoLISP macros can be very complex, but they don't have to be. One way to generate keyboard macros without too much AutoLISP programming is to use *macro templates*.

What Are Macro Templates?

Macro templates provide the basic structure for various types of macros. By using macro templates, you can create many powerful keyboard macros easily. Any program can serve as a template for another program. These macro templates are specifically designed to provide you with an easy way to create keyboard macros.

Creating Macro Templates

Below are three types of macro templates. *Command templates* create aliases for AutoCAD commands. This is another way of creating aliases similar to the ones you created in the ACAD.PGP. *Command + Option* templates issue a command with an option. These cannot be created in the ACAD.PGP. *Toggle templates* toggle system variables or commands that set system variables. To create AutoLISP macros, use your text editor, and place your macros in a new file called MACROS.LSP.

The Command Template

Command macros are aliases for AutoCAD commands; they are simple keyboard macros. The syntax for command templates is:

```
(defun C:KEYSTROKE( ) (command "COMMAND_NAME") )
```

The AutoLISP function DEFUN defines a function. The capital letter C: indicates that the function will serve as a command. KEYSTROKE is the key or keys that issue the command. The set of open and close parentheses ( ) is where local and global variables for the function are defined. In this case, there are none. The word Command tells AutoCAD that you are issuing an AutoCAD command. The COMMAND_NAME is the name of the command. For example:

```
(defun C:DL( ) (command "DIMLINEAR"))
```

Create the command macro just shown and save it to the file MACROS.LSP.

To try the DL macro:

1. Type **(LOAD "MACROS")** at the AutoCAD Command prompt.
2. Type **DL** and press **Enter** or the **Spacebar**.

The Command+Option Template

Command + Option macros are a fast way to issue commands and options. You can create several Command+Option macros to cover each command and option possibility. These macros are no more complicated than command macros. The Command+Option template syntax is:

```
(defun C:KEYSTROKE( ) (command "COMMAND_NAME" "OPTION") )
```

Good choices for Command+Option macros are Zoom Previous, Erase Last, Layer Set, and Fillet Crossing. The following example shows the Zoom Previous Command+Option macro:

```
(defun C:ZP( ) (command "ZOOM" "P"))
```

The Toggle Template

You can toggle many AutoCAD system variables. Toggles turn system variables on or off. Toggle macros test the system variable to determine its current setting and reverse the setting. The same toggle macro turns a system variable on if it is off or off if it is on.

Toggles perform a test to determine the current condition of the system variable. The AutoLISP function IF performs the test. Toggles require a little more programming than the examples just shown. Fortunately, with toggle templates, you can create many macros with the same template. The syntax for toggles is:

```
(defun C:KEYSTROKE( )
  (if (= (getvar "SYSTEM_VARIABLE") 0)
    (setvar "SYSTEM_VARIABLE" 1)
    (setvar "SYSTEM_VARIABLE" 0)
  )
)
```

For this toggle macro template, the IF function checks to see if the system variable value is 0. The GETVAR function *gets* the value of a system variable. The SETVAR function *sets* the value of a system variable. The following is an example that toggles the DIMUPT system variable.

```
(defun C:UPT( )
  (if (= (getvar "DIMUPT") 0)
    (setvar "DIMUPT" 1)
    (setvar "DIMUPT" 0)
  )
)
```

In plain English, here's what happens, line by line:

Define a command function UPT

IF the value of the system variable DIMUPT is 0,

Set the value to 1

Otherwise, set the value to 0

Parenthesis to finish the IF function

Parenthesis to finish the DEFUN function definition

You can place the entire function on a single line:

```
(defun C:UPT( ) (if (= (getvar "DIMUPT") 0) (setvar "DIMUPT" 1)(setvar
"DIMUPT" 0)))
```

By modifying the toggle template, you can toggle many system variables with a couple of keystrokes.

Using MSLIDE and VSLIDE to Display Graphical Reference Information

You can use AutoCAD's MSLIDE command to store graphic screens in slide format. A slide displays over the current drawing and doesn't disturb the drawing itself. You can use MSLIDE to capture graphical reference information and display it on your screen. For example, a representation of a weld symbol, showing the locations and specifications for the various information, displays on the screen to assist you in creating the exact type of weld you want.

You can use VSLIDE to display specification control drawings or drawings of parts that you have created in order to verify dimensions or other information.

To make a slide with the MSLIDE command:

1. Draw some graphics.
2. Issue the command MSLIDE and name the slide.

To view the slide with the VSLIDE command:

1. Issue the command VSLIDE.
2. Enter the name of the slide.

You can capture anything on your screen as a slide. Complex formulas, cutting tools, punch shapes, graphs, block libraries, and other graphics are good candidates for reference slides.

Summary

AutoCAD's open architecture lends itself to customizing. You can customize the screen menu and use it to launch commands. You can customize and rearrange the pull-down and cursor menus, and you can add or rearrange the button assignments. You can add your own commands to AutoCAD through the ACAD.PGP, ANSI.SYS, or AutoLISP interfaces. You can access Auto-CAD's help utility or create your own. You can even develop on-line reference information in the form of text screens or slides.

We have only touched the surface of what you can customize in Auto-CAD. Automation of repetitive tasks and instant access to information are the keys to increased productivity.

CHAPTER 9

CAD Resource Acquisition and Management

The fundamental task of the CAD manager is managing CAD resources. A company's CAD resources are usually directly related to their monetary resources, but a CAD manager can have a very positive financial effect on his or her company by properly managing CAD resources. Resource management falls into four broad categories: CAD hardware, software, training, and good information management.

A good CAD manager develops harmony between the hardware, software, and personnel. Additionally, the CAD manager usually has the added responsibility of satisfying upper-level management, which often puts the CAD manager in the position of justifying expenditures for the CAD department. The CAD manager's job is to make the best use of the available resources. Often, he or she must make some hard choices.

Hardware

CAD managers usually have the unenviable task of justifying hardware purchases to high-level management. They are also in the position of explaining to CAD operators why there is no budget for a faster computer or a better monitor. Many CAD operators during their interviews with a prospective employer, ask specifically about the hardware they will be using. Additionally, slow, outdated hardware often becomes a morale issue. A CAD manager must somehow satisfy both high-level management and the CAD department with hardware purchases.

Adequate hardware to run your CAD software is essential. If a designer or CAD operator has to wait longer than a few seconds for the computer to react, he or she has lost the train of thought. It's not recommended that you submit purchase requisitions based on that statement alone, but it is necessary to understand that a good job requires quick, responsive tools.

Selecting the Right CAD Station

Every year, finding the right CAD station gets harder and harder. First you have to pick an operating system. Will you use DOS? Will you use Windows? What about UNIX or Macintosh? Then you have to select third-party applications. Do you need Designer? What about AutoSurf? How about AME or those third-party applications that give you hundreds of nuts and bolts and other blocks? Can you make do with AutoCAD alone or will you be sacrificing too much productivity? And, if you have multiple users, you'll probably have to consider networking.

Your AutoCAD dealer can help you make some of these decisions, and so can a well-informed consultant. But it is nice to have some guidelines to follow when making your first purchases and when considering the advice you receive. The most important consideration in purchasing a CAD system should be to buy what will fit your environment best. Be sure to take into account the following factors when making your buying decisions:

- Choose the operating system and third-party applications that are already familiar to your CAD users or be sure to provide enough training to overcome the unfamiliar system. If you give a Macintosh user a DOS workstation to run AutoCAD on, he or she will need more support than if you gave him or her a Mac that ran AutoCAD. Sometimes the falloff in productivity is acceptable. Maybe your company has made a commitment to DOS, or your MIS department loathes Macintosh systems. Just remember that if you elect to give a user an unfamiliar operating system his or her productivity will fall somewhat while he or she becomes familiar with the new system.

- Choose a system for which you can find support. If your company has 70 UNIX workstations and 50 X Terminals, purchasing a single DOS workstation may mean no one will ever want to help you install software or access the files on the network. Similarly, if your dealer has never sold or supported a UNIX workstation, then purchasing a UNIX workstation to run AutoCAD may severely curtail the value of your on-site technical support contract.

- If you work for a company with an established policy regarding computer hardware and software, it is probably best to find a dealer who can provide a CAD solution that follows that policy. That way your AutoCAD users can take advantage of the support and peripherals available to the rest of the company.

- Choose a system for which you can find training. Remember a CAD station is only as good as its user. You are looking for a CAD system you can support and that your user can run. If you have a new user who needs training to run AutoCAD, he or she should also get training on how to use the operating system and utilities required to maintain the system as well. Three hours spent trying to copy a file onto a floppy disk or delete a .DWK file are three wasted hours. Make sure your dealer or ATC or consultant can provide all the training you and your users will need. Don't commit to any network or any operating system unless you can find training for it.

Selecting the right CAD station requires research not only into AutoCAD, but into the skills and experience of your users, your company computer policies, your local dealers, and the training facilities in your area. If you do a good job fitting your AutoCAD systems to your environment, you'll find CAD significantly improves your productivity. If you do a bad job, you'll find CAD can be an expensive mistake.

Graphics Cards and Monitors

CAD operators look at their monitors all day long. There is nothing more taxing than staring at a fuzzy monitor for long periods of time. Crisp and clean graphics reduce fatigue and promote productivity. When upgrading a monitor, avoid small monitors; 17″ monitors are relatively inexpensive and are a good value. Further, CAD monitors should have a dot pitch of .28mm or less; avoid those with a larger dot pitch. Also, be sure the monitor you select is capable of at least 1024 × 768 resolution, noninterlaced. Most new monitors are capable of 1280 × 1024 resolution.

Select a graphics card that complements the monitor. If your monitor is capable of 1280 × 1024 resolution, your graphics card must be able to produce that resolution, otherwise you will have to use a lower resolution. When considering a graphics card, be sure that it will produce the resolution you need in noninterlaced mode, with the number of colors you want. Most CAD graphics cards will deliver at least 1024 × 768, noninterlaced, with 16 or 256 colors. High-end graphics cards or *graphics accelerators* have special hardware and software capabilities. For graphics-intensive programs such as CAD or Windows, graphics accelerators enhance the processing of graphics information.

Printers and Plotters

In many engineering firms, plotting creates a bottleneck, even though plotting technology has come a long way in the last few years. If your plotter is the weak link in your office, there are a couple things to consider. Is your plotter used for check prints? If it is, there are some inexpensive large-format printers that can take some of the load off your plotter. Also, you can use laser printers to generate 8 1/2" × 11" check prints that are very legible, even for large-format drawings. You can spool or batch-plot your drawings so plotting can take place after hours. There are even software drivers that enhance printer output so that an inexpensive dot-matrix printer serves for check prints.

If it is time to upgrade your plotter, consider one of the new ink-jet plotters. Their speed is usually much faster than a pen plotter and the quality is excellent. They often have the added advantage of using roll-feed media that permits unattended plotting overnight. If you will be generating color renderings of your designs, there are many color ink-jet or thermal printers that produce very good results. (Printers and plotters are discussed in detail later in this chapter.)

AutoCAD provides drivers for dozens of printers and plotters, and you'll find that manufacturers of printers and plotters will give you even more. So when you search for a printer or a plotter, it isn't enough to see a driver for the device in the plotter configuration menu or to see it listed in the AutoCAD Installation and Performance Guide.

When you select a printer or a plotter a number of factors are important. First of all, you are looking for a device that you know will meet your requirements. More than one company has been surprised to discover that a certain plotter requires special paper or that their preprinted sheets won't work because the plotter needs wider margins than the paper provides.

To make sure that a suggested output device will meet your needs, try plotting one of your drawings using the device. Find out before you purchase the product exactly what you will have to do in order to plot a drawing. In some cases, you can rent a plotter for a short period of time. Some dealers will offer this as a service. You may also be able to take one of your CAD stations to the dealer's offices and pay to have it configured to work with the plotter being sold. Either way you'll get a chance to see the plotter connected to your system plotting your drawings.

Second, you are looking for an output device that you can get installed and maintained. If your dealer has to ship a plotter or printer away to be repaired, does he or she offer a temporary replacement until it comes back? If the manufacturer provides a warranty, find out if someone will come to your premises or if you have to ship the plotter. Does the manufacturer's warranty cover parts and labor, or just parts? You may elect not to purchase a plotter that offers a manufacturer's warranty that requires you to ship the plotter to the manufacturer and then pay a high hourly rate for the labor necessary to diagnose and fix the problem.

The more you spend for an output device, the more these issues should concern you. Many plotters cost more than economy cars and some cost more than luxury sedans. Take the time before you buy to be sure that your output solution will work when you take it back to the office. In the final analysis, your CAD station is only as good as its plotted drawings.

Upgrading Old Computers

Although you can still run AutoCAD on a 386-based computer, it probably isn't wise to do so. If you have even a marginal budget for hardware, consider upgrading the 386 machines in your CAD department. Hardware prices for 486 machines are very low, and Pentium system prices are also falling rapidly. If your CAD operators do any 3-D drafting, a 486 machine is the starting point. You may be able to find other places in your company for the 386 machines.

Be careful when upgrading your CAD systems. There are many things to consider. It is often tempting to upgrade only the weakest link in the system, but remember, everything works together. It doesn't make sense to upgrade to a fast motherboard when you are still using a slow hard drive. Computer technology is moving at such a rapid pace that by the time one part of the system is obsolete, chances are, the other parts are also well on their way. If you are on a limited budget, consider a chip upgrade to get another six months out of your current hardware.

AutoCAD will run with 8 megabytes of RAM. A V-8 will run on seven cylinders, too, but don't be misled by this minimum requirement. A good starting point is really 16 megabytes of RAM. Any less and you may encounter a considerable amount of disk paging which significantly slows down any CAD system and frustrates CAD operators. If you intend to use the CAD system for solid modeling, parametrics, or rendering, consider 32 megabytes.

Software

A CAD manager is ultimately responsible for the CAD software. This involves many issues including software licenses, software integration, installation and configuration, customizing, and third-party enhancements. Beyond installation and configuration, the CAD manager should have a thorough understanding of each software program that is on each CAD system.

AutoCAD Software

AutoCAD software can take many forms. Even assuming that each CAD system is running DOS, you could have AutoCAD for DOS, AutoCAD for Windows, or AutoCAD LT running. Additionally, Autodesk products that complement AutoCAD for mechanical applications include AutoSurf, AutoCAD Designer, AutoMill, AutoVision, AutoCAD Data Extension, and AutoCAD Workcenter. Other Autodesk products that don't run in AutoCAD but are used to generate data for AutoCAD include 3D Studio, Generic CADD, and AutoSketch.

Licenses

It is the CAD manager's responsibility to ensure that software licenses are in order. This means that for every station running AutoCAD, the company should have purchased a licensed copy of AutoCAD. Be sure to send in the registration cards. If any of your CAD stations are running old versions of the software, be sure to upgrade. The price of upgrading an old version of AutoCAD is negligible compared to the value of the latest software.

Third-Party Enhancements

Use third-party enhancements when they boost productivity. AutoCAD has a very rich selection of third-party programs and utilities that automate and simplify many AutoCAD tasks. Enhancements that are especially worth consideration are mechanical symbol libraries, drafting enhancements, plotting utilities, and management utilities.

Don't overlook shareware and freeware utilities. Many bulletin boards feature AutoCAD utilities. Especially worthy of mention is CompuServe's AutoCAD forum (GO ACAD). The libraries of this forum are loaded with useful utilities written by some of the world's best AutoCAD programmers.

Installation and Configuration

There are several installation and configuration issues facing the CAD manager. It is tempting to install and configure each CAD system in the same way, and whenever possible, this should be done. It saves time when the CAD manager has to troubleshoot a configuration problem. But in AutoCAD, customizing yields productivity. With this in mind, CAD operators should have the freedom to make their own configuration decisions. They should use custom menus, macros, AutoLISP programs, and third-party enhancements that boost their productivity.

Getting CAD operators to agree on a layer color scheme can be a formidable task. Each CAD operator should be free to decide which colors are easiest on his or her eyes. A simple script program that redefines layer colors can permit custom layer colors for individuals while maintaining drawing consistency within the office.

Often, CAD operators must share CAD systems. In such cases, use multiple batch files to begin AutoCAD, with individual configurations in separate directories. Each CAD operator should have his or her own working directory that contains custom menus, programs, and add-on software.

Getting Training and Technical Support

If there is one factor that contributes more than any other to the success of AutoCAD in an enterprise, it is training. With the appropriate training, almost any obstacle can be surmounted. If you've been well trained to use AutoCAD, you'll probably be able to figure out how to install a new printer or a mouse or a graphics card. If you have enough training in AutoCAD, you will know how to import a DXF file or an IGES file generated by another CAD package. With the right kind of training in AutoCAD, you can generate 3-D models, create rendered images and export them to desktop publishing applications, even create custom menus and AutoLISP routines that automate the most tedious and time-consuming aspects of your job. The key to success in Auto-CAD is training because the fastest equipment in the world won't speed up a user who doesn't know how to draw a line, create a layer, or plot a drawing.

If you are thinking of purchasing AutoCAD, or if you already have Au-toCAD and are having difficulty making the application work in your environment, you should probably consider taking some classes or working with a consultant to get training that will help you make better use of your AutoCAD time. There are a number of places you can go to get training in AutoCAD. A few of them are listed here:

- Autodesk maintains a list of Authorized Training Centers that offer courses in AutoCAD. These training centers must meet stringent requirements in order to be admitted to the ATC programs. They must be affiliated with an accredited educational institution like a trade school, junior college, college, or university. They must have a laboratory that meets relatively high performance standards, and they must offer regular courses in AutoCAD at a variety of levels.

- Autodesk dealers often provide training in third-party applications. Although dealer training is often more expensive than the training offered by ATCs, dealers usually offer classes that are hard to find elsewhere.

- Junior colleges, colleges, and universities sometimes offer courses in AutoCAD based around an academic schedule. For example, they might offer classes that meet every Tuesday and Thursday for 18 weeks. These classes take longer to complete than the professional courses offered by ATCS and dealers, but they also give you a chance to practice what you learn back at the office. Classes offered at traditional academic institutions usually cost less than the classes provided by dealers or ATCs.

Finding technical support for your AutoCAD installation may not be as simple as finding training. Some dealers offer technical support contracts with systems they sell, and many will offer contracts even for systems they don't sell. These contracts can be expensive, and you'll only get the level of support you want if the dealer's technical support representatives are familiar with your applications and the operating system and network you are running.

You may decide to turn to consultants for technical support. Consultants who specialize in supporting AutoCAD systems for specific industries or specific kinds of installations are available, but sometimes it is hard to find them. One place to look for a computer consultant may be your local AutoCAD user group. If you contact Autodesk, they will refer you to your local user group and you can attend the next meeting. You may meet your consultant at the meeting, or you may get a recommendation from someone attending the meeting.

Another good place to search for an AutoCAD consultant is the ACAD forum on CompuServe. If you have an account, simply log in, provide your password, and then type **GO ACAD**. In the What's New/Want Ads forum, you can post an ad that lists your requirements. If you post this advertisement a few times, you'll probably find a consultant with good qualifications that you can turn to for technical support.

Optimizing the Working Environment

So, you have one or more well-configured and supported CAD stations, a carefully selected output device and perhaps a network. You even have happy, well-trained users at each keyboard. Does this mean that your CAD station will deliver its peak performance? In general, the answer is yes. The factors that most affect the performance of your CAD station have to do with the skill level of your operators and the quality of your equipment.

On the other hand, there are studies that indicate that it will be easier to keep your users happy if their work environment is conducive to making computer work easier. This means nonglare screens, diffuse lighting, chairs that support the lower back, a desk at a height that doesn't strain the muscles of the wrist, and a company policy that encourages CAD operators to change tasks or take breaks when eyestrain sets in.

A number of professional organizations and unions offer guidelines on the furniture and alignment best suited to CAD operators. For example, it is generally agreed that operators should not have to look up to see the computer monitor as this increases neck strain and eyestrain. If you work with a company that has set policies or a union, make sure your system meets the specifications outlined for computer workstations.

If, however, you don't have any guidelines to work from or a union to take into account, start with the following:

- A very comfortable chair that provides back support. You or your employees will be spending hundreds of hours in this chair. They will not move much because CAD tends to be rather absorbing and requires a great deal of prolonged concentration.

- If your feet swell, or your chair is particularly high, make sure you invest in a foot rest. If you have been experiencing back pain, support for your feet may reduce that pain by allowing you to lean back against the chair instead of forward toward the desk.

- A large desk. You will need a surface on which to put your drawings while you make changes to them; a place for a digitizer or mouse to roam; and a place for your keyboard, a phone, a monitor, pencils, and pens. Some people convert drafting boards into large computer desks. The important thing is that the drafting board be adjustable to the height of a normal desk or that you buy a very tall and comfortable chair.

- Place your monitor so that you don't have to look up at it or turn your head to see it. It should be directly in front of your chair when you are working and a comfortable distance away. You can purchase monitor stands that will attach to your desk and allow you to drag the monitor to any position in space. This can be an excellent choice if desk space is at a premium in your office.

- Find a place for your keyboard that provides support for your wrists and does not require you to support the weight of your arms as you type. Some users find they like to work with the keyboard in their laps; others like to have their keyboards in a drawer or in a specially designed keyboard holder.

- Your mouse or digitizer should be placed where you can reach it without straining. Your wrist should be supported when you use the mouse or digitizer. In fact, although many users initially believe they will prefer using a stylus or pen-like pointer instead of a puck with their digitizer, in time most users find it very tiring to clench the hand into a fist and support the arm for eight hours a day. Unlike working at a drafting board, you never move your body to ease the strain on your arm.

- Diffuse lighting. Some computer users insist that light from a natural source is easier on their eyes than incandescent or fluorescent light. Others insist that daylight changes throughout the day and therefore makes it difficult to be sure there is an even light level at all times. In any case, you want to avoid having any hot spots or glare on your monitor, and you do not want to face a light source. Just like the aperture of a video camera, you'll find it hard to see something as dark as a computer screen if you are staring right at a light source.

- Finally, remember to take breaks. If you are used to working at a drafting board, your body has helped you to remember that you need to rest every once in a while. If you find that you've made several silly mistakes in AutoCAD in a short period of time; or you discover that you've just made one really massive error; or if your eyes, arm, wrist, or back hurt, take a break.

You aren't just being good to yourself. You are increasing your productivity. If you take a ten-minute break every hour and a half you'll actually increase your performance on the CAD station. You'll eliminate mistakes because you won't be too tired to think, and you'll save time because you'll be aware enough to use the best method to complete a task.

CAD File Management

Proper drawing management requires a conscious effort by the entire design team. CAD file management issues include the management of the drawing files, drawing backup and archiving, engineering changes, and drawing maintenance. Sensible file naming and part numbering schemes are an important part of drawing management. If you can't find a drawing that you need, you have lost the time it took to create it *and* the time it takes to re-create it.

Hard Disk Management

By paying some attention to the structure of your hard disk, you can store and retrieve drawing files easily. The goal is to organize your hard disk into subdivisions called subdirectories so that the information is easy to locate. Follow the techniques in this section for organizing drawing files, block libraries, AutoLISP programs, and other information whether related to AutoCAD or not. There are several approaches to setting up a hard disk. The first works well for engineering firms that have multiple clients.

Client/Project Directory Structure
One approach for setting up a hard disk directory structure is by client. If your firm works with many clients, this may be a good system. Each client has its own directory. If there are several projects for that client, each project may have its own subdirectory. Common drawings, formats, and such may reside in a common subdirectory or in the client directory.

Drawing Type Directory Structure

Another approach to structuring your directories is by drawing type. If you do several specific types of drawings, this approach is a good one. You can create directories for assemblies, detailed parts, schematics, parts lists, documents, and renderings. By using good file naming conventions, you can easily distinguish between one client's assemblies and another's.

Backing Up Your Drawings

A backup is a copy of your drawing. Computers sometimes corrupt files. Operators sometimes make mistakes, such as deleting or copying over a drawing. Even lightning strikes or static electricity can cause data loss. It is absolutely essential that you back up *everything* worth saving.

There are many ways to back up drawings. The easiest way is to save it with another name. This creates a copy of the drawing on your hard disk. Obviously, this method only works well as long as your hard disk is functional. Use this method of backup regularly during the design process and whenever you or others make significant changes to the design.

Another way to back up drawings is on diskette. Diskette backups are very easy to do and don't take much time on a drawing-by-drawing basis. Diskette backups have the advantage of not cluttering up your hard disk; additionally, you can store diskettes off site in case of a disaster.

Tape backup systems provide a fast and convenient way of backing up your data on a file-by-file basis or all at once. You can selectively back up modified files or certain directories, or your entire hard disk. Most tape backup systems can compress data as they store it. Tapes are small and easy to transport. This makes tape backups handy for off-site storage. A good practice is to back up your modified drawings each day and your entire hard disk each week. Rotate tapes between on-site and off-site locations.

Many companies use a network. If your company uses a networked environment, back up your drawings by copying them to the network drive. Then, each time the network is backed up, your drawings will be backed up. Be sure to let the network administrator know that your directories on the network should be backed up regularly.

Why You Need an AutoCAD Dealer

If you are relatively new to the use of computers in a mechanical engineering office, or if you have used other CAD applications but never AutoCAD, you probably have many unanswered questions. Should we run AutoCAD on DOS or Windows? Which network operating system best meets our requirements? Are there any third-party applications that will increase our productivity?

Finding answers to these questions can be time-consuming unless you have help. Since the systems you buy today will be with you for several years to come, and since any network operating system you select will profoundly influence the network operating system you will be using five years from today, you don't want to make any mistakes. Yet the issues behind these decisions are very complex. Will Microsoft Windows NT be a de facto standard in 1996? Is the current version of this product stable enough to support multiple AutoCAD users? Can Novell NetWare bridge the gap between Windows workstations and DOS workstations for the years to come?

To answer these questions, you will have to be part oracle and part system administrator. The decisions about operating systems and network configurations are complicated by the fact that AutoCAD is nothing like your standard spreadsheet or word processing application. Installation, configuration, and maintenance of AutoCAD stations require a knowledge of plotter configurations, digitizing tablets, and screen drivers. AutoCAD has its own peculiarities: the environment variables it requires, the memory managers it is compatible with, and the files it absolutely must be able to find.

In short, if you are unfamiliar with computer technology, or even more important, unfamiliar with AutoCAD, you will certainly need help making the right decisions for your firm. A good local AutoCAD dealer can give you that help. He or she can answer questions about printers and plotters, demonstrate third-party applications, and help you navigate AutoCAD's configuration routine. Many AutoCAD dealers have dozens of installations in their area, and they have sold and provided support for hundreds of AutoCAD stations. If you need to implement a CAD solution in your company, and you don't know where to turn, start with the AutoCAD dealers.

Choosing an AutoCAD Dealer

The first step in finding an AutoCAD dealer is to call Autodesk on (415) 507-5000. The dealer referral line can give you the names and phone numbers of AutoCAD dealers in your area. If you are outside the United States and don't know how to contact your nearest Autodesk subsidiary, call the number listed here. The dealer referral line can give you the phone number for your local Autodesk who can give you a list of dealers in your vicinity.

Once you know who your local AutoCAD dealers are, you can fax them an overview of your requirements. How many AutoCAD stations do you think you will need? Will you require a network? What functions should the network perform? Do you have any preferences in terms of operation system or network software? With this information, dealers should be able to prepare a demonstration of the AutoCAD solution they would like to propose. This solution may incoporate hardware, software, and third-party applications, perhaps even a network operating system and project management software. If you decide that you don't like aspects of their system, or if they recommend a solution or product that they can't show you right away, you may elect to have a second meeting with the dealer to iron out these issues.

After one or two meetings, you should request a proposal that describes the hardware, software, and services a dealer can provide, and gives a price for those items. If possible, you should request that every product or service in the proposal be associated with a specific price. This allows you to cut costs by removing items from the proposal.

Don't be surprised if the AutoCAD dealer charges you more for hardware or software than you would pay if you purchased the same products from your local discount computer store. In some cases the increased prices are not justified because the dealer doesn't offer any more support or service than a discount computer store. But most dealers do provide a number of services that are invaluable. Many dealers include delivery and installation of all software and hardware as part of the purchase price. Some provide telephone support for AutoCAD and third-party applications. The best dealers include delivery, installation, and telephone support with every sale, and keep well-qualified professionals on staff to keep those promises.

In choosing a dealer, be sure to do the following:

- During your preliminary meetings with the dealer, make time to review the dealer's premises. Is the room where your computer will be assembled busy? Is it well organized? How many technical support people are on staff? What are their names? Who will be delivering and installing your hardware and software? The answers to these questions will let you know if the dealer has the resources required to install your system and help you maintain it in the future. By learning the names of the support and installation staff, you will know who to call when you have a technical problem.

- Ask your dealer for four or more references from recent installations similar to yours. Be sure that these references had similar applications in mind when they purchased the product, a similiar number of users, and were using the same operating system and/or network software you plan to use. Contact these references and ask them how many stations they purchased, how long the installation took, and how well the solution provided by the dealer is working. You should also ask their opinion of other dealers in the area.

All AutoCAD dealers are not created equal. Some are better than others, and most specialize in a specific discipline. Ideally, the dealer you select will specialize in mechanical applications so he or she will understand your requirements and concerns.

Don't automatically take the lowest bid you receive assuming that you will get all the installation and technical support services you'll need. Conversely, don't take the highest bid you receive assuming that an expensive installation is a good installation. Double check the quality of the dealer with customers he or she has done business with in the past.

If you end up working with an AutoCAD dealer that is completely un-satisfactory, and you have documents to back up your assertion that the dealer did not do a good job, you can contact Autodesk. The staff there listen to well-founded complaints about their dealers and can sometimes help you resolve disputes.

CHAPTER 10

Networking Design to Production Work Groups

Overview of the Design Process

As most designers are aware, the design process is rarely a smooth flow from designer to drafter to production department. Designers create the first version of a part, but drafters may discover that the dimensions specified by the designer describe a part that can't exist in three dimensions. NC programmers and machinists may review a design from the drafting department only to learn that a part can't be milled as described. To create almost any component, a team of professionals must work together. This team, composed of designers, drafters, NC programmers, machinists, and project managers is often called a work group.

Traditionally, members of a work group have communicated with one another using paper drawings. Designers sketch a part based upon the specification, creating the first version of the drawing; drafters firm up the details and add dimensions and annotation. Later, NC programmers use the drawing to develop NC code which will drive the machines that cut the prototype. Project managers use the drawing to track the part as it moves through the design process.

Throughout the development process, problems and suggestions for the part are noted on the drawing or in documents that refer to the drawing. So when companies begin using AutoCAD in the drafting department, it isn't surprising that before long other departments are also using Auto-CAD to help facilitate their part of the design and production process. Designers may use AutoCAD to create solid models and perform mass properties analysis. The NC programmers in the manufacturing department may use third-party applications to develop NC code. Managers may track the time employees spend working on drawings and use the information to generate invoices. And all of these processes may revolve around a single AutoCAD drawing.

Of course, unfamiliar problems arise when the design process centers around an electronic drawing rather than a paper one. For example, destroying an electronic drawing is much easier than destroying a paper document. In fact, a single command entered at the keyboard by a novice user can wipe out a project full of drawings.

To allow members of a work group to use AutoCAD drawings as a communications medium, while still protecting vulnerable electronic data from accidental loss or intentional destruction, many companies combine their AutoCAD stations into a CAD network. Network security and backup protocols protect the drawings while also providing members of the work group quick access to drawings.

In this chapter we review factors you should consider before binding all the AutoCAD stations in your company into a network, and give you a quick overview of how your AutoCAD installations will be affected. At the end of this chapter you will learn how AutoCAD can help you manage your work group more efficiently.

When Should You Consider Networking?

Many firms implement CAD as a mechanism for creating drawings long before they consider networking. If CAD is used only by two operators in the drafting department, a network may be an expensive and unnecessary complication. But, as the number of departments using AutoCAD and the number of CAD users in your company grows, tracking electronic drawings becomes more difficult.

The kinds of problem you encounter in managing distributed CAD/CAM resources are quite different from those you run into when CAD is the sole responsibility of the drafting department. For example, instead of trying to find a single original drawing, you are suddenly confronted by dozens of drawings, some with the same name, all similar, and all modified within the last 24 hours. At worst, you wake up one day to discover that the shop has two versions of a part, based on two entirely different drawings, neither one of which is substantially correct.

There are a number of symptoms that indicate that a company should consider creating a CAD network for its work group. Although a network is not a panacea that will solve problems caused by poor organization or mismanagement, a network can help a good system administrator or project manager manage better. The employee overhead required for complying with naming conventions, security protocols, and accurate timesheets is slashed as the network takes over these mundane, albeit important, functions.

Network Quiz

If you answer yes to five or more of these questions, you should probably consider linking your workstations together with a network. The amount you spent on the network is likely to be offset by increases in productivity.

Are multiple departments accessing the same files?
Do drawings seem to get lost or damaged as they move from department to department?
Do you often end up with more than one version of a drawing?
Do departments maintain separate versions of a drawing?
Do you find it difficult to track multiple revisions of a drawing?
Do you have four or more AutoCAD users?
Do you find it difficult to keep track of the NC code associated with a part?
Do you find it difficult to track the time spent on a project for internal purposes like project management and estimation?
Do you spend more than 40 hours a month combining timesheets to construct invoices?
Do you find it difficult to back up your drawings more than once a week?
Do you find it difficult to archive completed project drawings for future reference?
Do your operators share peripherals like printers and plotters?

To decide if your company should consider a CAD network, review the following:

1. Are multiple departments accessing the same files? If drawings must be passed between departments as a project moves from design to production, tracking the drawings becomes very important. In the worst possible case, each department creates and maintains its own version of the drawing, duplicating work over and over again until the final part is produced. This method is not only time-consuming, but it is almost certain to introduce errors into the design process.

A network can allow you to maintain a single set of drawings for the entire company. There will never be any confusion about where the drawing resides, who has the latest version, or whether changes have been incorporated into the drawing. Many drawing management applications can track multiple revisions of a drawing, and some will also track NC programs, on-line change orders, proposals, and contracts. Such applications give most managers the control they need to organize projects and assign accountability.

2. Do you have four or more AutoCAD stations? If you have four or more AutoCAD stations at a single site, and you don't have a network, it's probably getting a bit difficult to ensure that drawings on all your machines are being protected against accidental loss.

Do you have a tape drive on each workstation? How do you ensure that each user backs up his or her station each day, or three times a week, or as often as your company guidelines suggest? Do you check to make sure that the tapes created actually contain the drawing files they should? If you haven't had to recover a file from tape recently, perhaps you should give it a try. Many people discover that they aren't as well protected as they thought. If you don't ensure that drawings are protected against loss, you must be aware that one or more failed stations, an act of sabotage by an unhappy employee, or theft of a workstation could represent a substantial financial loss to your firm.

By establishing a network where users can save their drawings in a single location, perhaps by project or organized into separate directories for each user, you make it possible for the company to back up all your drawings with a single tape drive on a regular basis. Even if your current, multistation backup procedures are working, you are still paying a premium in overhead as each operator laboriously performs the task of backing up his or her own system. You can cut the time dedicated to the process and increase productivity by automating this process.

3. Do you often end up with two versions of the same drawing? If your drafters or designers sometimes share projects, it isn't surprising that you occasionally end up with two versions of a drawing. One user misplaces a drawing, or names it incorrectly. A second user working on the same project has to make changes to the drawing and can't find it. He or she generates a new drawing.

At minimum, the hours required to create the second drawing represent a loss to the company. If both drawings end up in circulation, the cost can be much greater. It is not unheard of for two versions of a product to end up in manufacturing with the same name. In this case drafters, designers, programmers, and managers have all dedicated time to developing worthless drawings. A CAD network equipped with a drawing management application can enforce naming conventions and track drawings as they move from design to production.

4. Do you find it difficult to track the time spent on a projects? If you need to account for the time your CAD users spend working on drawings, perhaps because this time is billed to your clients or is billed internally, a network can help you maintain accurate records.

If you have five or six operators maintaining timesheets for each project and clerical help that turns those timesheets into documents from which an administrator or project manager constructs bills, you may be dedicating up to 20 percent of your CAD department's time to record keeping. A network can reduce this figure dramatically. When your users open a drawing, the network can automatically track the project, the drawing, and the time spent. These computer records can be imported into a database, spreadsheet, or word processor and be used to construct invoices.

These are not the only reasons to consider implementing a network. Even if you have only three CAD stations, it is hard to track more than a hundred drawings spread over three stations for any period of time. Sometimes companies invest in a CAD network just to reduce the administrative functions the members of a work group must engage in. After all, if your NC programmer is looking for the latest version of a design or your drafter is busy filling out timesheets and looking for change orders, neither employee is doing the work you had in mind when you hired him or her.

But be careful: a network won't solve every problem, and it can make some problems much worse. If inept or angry employees are erasing files on their own hard disks, don't implement an insecure network that lets them erase files on other stations as well.

Problems a Network Can't Solve

Although networks can help you track drawings, protect them against accidental loss, and help you manage human resources, they can't make up for poor organization or mismanagement. A network won't help you resolve these problems:

Inaccurate drawings	*Solve this problem with better training for your users.*
Sabotage	*A network can reduce the cost of sabotage, but not eliminate it completely. To eliminate sabotage, find the saboteur.*
Equipment failures	*Although a network can let you reroute a print job to a working plotter, it will do*

	nothing to help you maintain plotters or eliminate failures. In fact, since networks also need maintenance, you might end up with more problems than you started with. To resolve equipment problems, buy good equipment and maintain it well.
Slow system performance	*A network can actually slow AutoCAD performance, particularly if you plan to support a peer-to-peer network with no dedicated file server. In addition to running AutoCAD, stations will now have to run the network software and dedicate time to transferring files.*
Low morale	*Although a network can help reduce the repetition and frustration that contribute to low morale, it is not a cure for over-work or other causes of stress.*
Lost drawing files	*If you are losing drawing files because they have the wrong names, are placed in the wrong directory, weren't backed up, or are regularly overwritten with blank drawings by mistake (quite a common problem for new users), a network is not a cure for the problem. These problems, at least in small CAD departments, are caused by poor organization and lack of training.*

Before you invest in a network, identify exactly which problems you want to solve, and take time to determine exactly how a network can help. Its important to understand that a network can make many management and equipment problems much worse if it isn't implemented well.

Overview of Networking Alternatives

At its simplest, a network is nothing more than a mechanism that lets users on different workstations share files and output devices. Usually computers in a CAD network are connected to one another via a cable, although sometimes CAD stations on a network talk to one another over dedicated phone lines and high-speed modems.

Each station in a network must be equipped with a device that allows the station to send signals to other stations in the network. In the vast majority of cases, this means all the stations in your network require a network interface card. This board connects the computer to the network cable and handles communications between the workstation and the network. The network interface card selected for the workstations in a network depends upon the network software in use. Ethernet and Token Ring cards are the two most commonly installed types of network interface cards.

In addition to the network interface cards just outlined, all networks require a network operating system. Most network operating systems support dedicated and nondedicated file servers. They also allow you to transfer information from one machine to another or to a file server, establish printer queues, back up file servers from a single station, and implement network security protocols like login names and passwords.

Some popular network operating systems include Novell Netware, Personal Netware, Lantastic, NFS, Windows for Workgroups, and Windows NT. Choosing between these options requires an understanding of your company's current networking strategy and your objectives for future growth.

In many networks, one station in a network does nothing except handle file transfers and output devices. This station runs no software except the network operating system, and is called a dedicated file server. Network operating systems like Novell Netware often depend upon a dedicated file server that runs only the network operating system. In a network environment based around a dedicated file server, workstations run a very small application which keeps them in contact with the file server (Figure 10.1).

In some networks there is no dedicated file server, in which case, one or more stations in the network not only run applications like AutoCAD but also share the task of transferring files and managing output devices. Workstations that allow users to run applications while sharing files and managing output devices are called nondedicated file servers. Networks based upon nondedicated file servers are called peer-to-peer networks.

In a peer-to-peer network, every station serving as a nondedicated file server must run software that allows the station to serve files, address output device queues, and communicate with other stations in the network. This application is much larger than the application required by workstations in a network with a dedicated file server (Figure 10.2).

Choosing between Dedicated File Servers and Nondedicated File Servers

If you create a network designed around a dedicated file server, you must allocate one station to do nothing more than run the network operating system. This workstation will transfer files, maintain output queues, implement security protocols, and perform hundreds of other tasks. You cannot

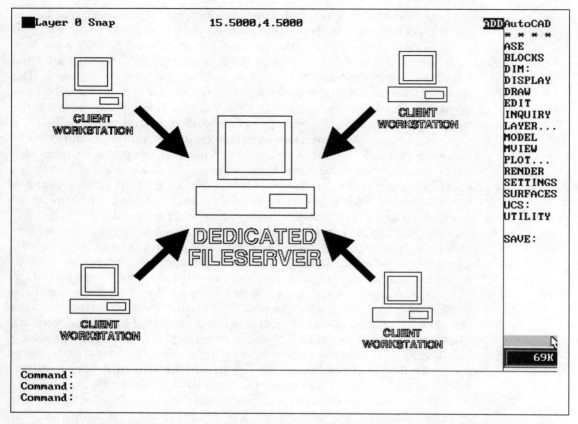

Figure 10.1 A dedicated file server runs the network operating system and handles all file transfers from machine to machine.

use this workstation to run AutoCAD or any other application. The other workstations in the network, called clients, run much smaller applications that allow them to transfer files to and from the file server.

If you create a peer-to-peer network designed around nondedicated file servers, the workstations in your network will share the task of transferring files, maintaining output queues, implementing security protocols, and performing other network administration tasks. In addition to performing these functions, each station will also be able to run AutoCAD. In a peer-to-peer network, all stations run the network operating system.

Some environments combine the two types of networks. Some workstations operate as nondedicated file servers and other workstations treat these workstations as dedicated file servers. In these environments, the nondedicated file servers have to run the complete network operating sys-

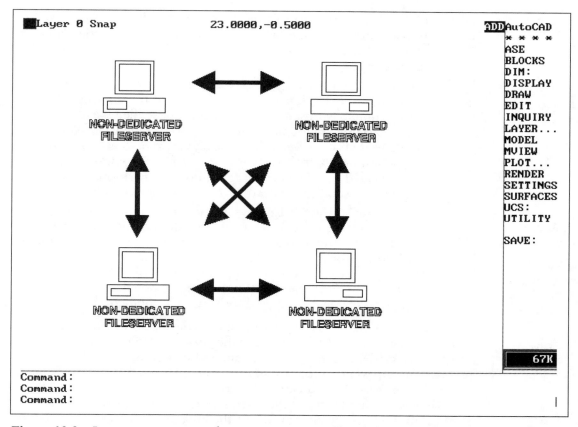

Figure 10.2 In peer-to-peer networks, every station is a file server and shares in the task of storing and transferring files.

tem while the client workstations run much smaller applications that allow them to transfer files to and from the file servers. This kind of network is often implemented by UNIX-based networks that support PCs as clients using NFS.

In selecting the networking alternative that will meet your needs best, keep the following general principles in mind.

- Any workstation selected to serve as both file server and CAD station needs to be equipped with enough RAM to be able to handle both operations. Running AutoCAD requires a minimum of 8mb of RAM, and if you are running AutoCAD under Windows, with third-party applications or you are working on drawing files over 2mb, you should consider 16mb of RAM a minimum value. Another 16mb of RAM is required to support most network operating systems, transfer large files, and handle print queues. An inadequate amount of RAM translates into slow AutoCAD performance, application failures, and slow file transfers.

- Any workstation selected to serve as a file server should be equipped with a 16-bit or 32-bit network interface card. Transferring files from workstation to workstation is greatly impeded when the transfer rate is slow. If you plan to implement a peer-to-peer network based upon nondedicated file servers, these file servers should also be equipped with 16-bit or 32-bit network interface cards. Slow transfer rates on nondedicated file servers translate into slow performance in AutoCAD and most other applications in use on the network.

- Workstations selected to serve as nondedicated file servers need hard disks large enough to accommodate the applications run on the file server, the network operating system, the files stored on the workstation for the network, and the swap space the network operating system requires for holding temporary files. You should consider 200mb hard disks a minimum for nondedicated file servers. Larger disks may be required for some environments.

Many organizations consider implementing a peer-to-peer network in an attempt to save money by avoiding the cost of a dedicated file server. As you can see by the general requirements outlined here, it may be more expensive to equip workstations to serve as nondedicated file servers than it is to simply purchase the dedicated file server.

One way around some of these requirements is to configure all stations as nondedicated file servers but to give the bulk of the file serving responsibilities to one or two well-equipped stations. Stations in the network that are not serving files or maintaining print queues but are running the network operating system don't need to meet all the requirements outlined previously. They can operate efficiently with somewhat smaller hard disks and less RAM because they are not engaged in bulk file storage or transfer operations.

If you do not equip your workstations and file servers adequately, your CAD network will be slow and suffer from numerous failures. If you are not already familiar with the hardware and software required to create a network, you should find an AutoCAD dealer or consultant who can help you make these important decisions. For more information on these topics, see Chapter 9.

Configuring AutoCAD in a Networked Environment

Once you tie your AutoCAD stations into your network, you will need to make some adjustments to your AutoCAD installations. There are two ways to install AutoCAD in a networked environment. Many people elect to install AutoCAD on each local workstation, and use the network only as a common file storage location, or to handle print queues. If you want to maintain an environment where the workstations can still keep working even if the file server fails, you should install AutoCAD on each workstation. You should also consider this methodology if you are running a number of third-party applications or you want to maintain separate menus or prototype drawings for each user. It is illegal for you to use this methodology if you don't have an AutoCAD license for each AutoCAD user on the network.

Some network administrators elect to install a single network version of AutoCAD on the file server. This allows a pool of AutoCAD users to share a number of licenses, which is useful when you don't want to purchase licenses for casual AutoCAD users. You should also consider this methodology if you need to support multiple users who will not always be sitting at the same workstation, or if you need to guarantee a uniform installation for the entire work group.

Both options require you to pay for multiple AutoCAD licenses. If you install AutoCAD locally, each workstation must have its own copy of AutoCAD, complete with a unique serial number and authorization code.

If you wish to support multiple AutoCAD users from a single installation of AutoCAD, you must acquire the network version of AutoCAD, and pay for the correct number of AutoCAD licenses, for which you will receive a network hardware lock and a multiuser authorization code. When you install AutoCAD on the file server, you must plug the hardware lock into the parallel port on the file server, and enter the number of licenses and the authorization code for those licenses during the configuration process. If you install a non-network version of AutoCAD on the file server, the first user who launches the application will be permitted to work. The second user will be told that the application is in use.

Note that the network version of AutoCAD currently supports only networks designed around Windows for Workgroups and Novell Netware. This means that only users on these networks can share licenses. Companies with other networks must purchase a single AutoCAD license for every user.

Installing AutoCAD on Workstations in a Networked Environment

If you elect to work with AutoCAD in a networked environment, you must make some adjustments to your installation. For example, you need to tell AutoCAD where to place its temporary files, where to find its prototype drawings, and how to place plot files in the network printer queues. Complete instructions for most of these operations can be found in the *AutoCAD Installation Guide* which comes with AutoCAD. In the following paragraphs we review the modifications most administrators make when configuring their workstations to work in a networked environment.

Initial Drawing Setup

You may want multiple AutoCAD users to share a common prototype drawing stored on the network. This lets you implement a common layering standard, make changes to the title block, and even automatically load a custom menu. Remember that menus loaded into a prototype drawing will automatically appear in every drawing based upon that prototype drawing.

When specifying the name of the prototype drawing, be sure to identify a drive or directory that all users have rights to. AutoCAD must be able to read the prototype drawing, and any menus or users won't be able to run the application. For best results, ensure that all CAD users have the same paths and drive names for the drawing files, prototype drawings, and menus stored on the network. This is especially important if your users will move from machine to machine in the network. If AutoCAD requires a prototype drawing from a directory that a user doesn't have access to, it will load without your prototype drawing.

You may want to create a support directory on the network and add that directory to the SET ACAD command in the AutoCAD batch file, or to the AUTOEXEC.BAT file.

To configure AutoCAD to look for a prototype drawing on a network drive:

1. Type **CONFIG** at the command prompt.
2. From the Configuration menu, choose **Operating Parameters.**
3. From the Operating Parameters menu, choose **Initial Drawing** setup.
4. Enter the full path to the drawing.
5. Type **Enter** to exit the Operations Parameters menu.
6. Type **Enter** again to exit the Configuration menu.
7. Type **Y** to save your configuration changes, **N** if you want to discard them.

Placement of Temporary Files

AutoCAD creates a number of files while it works. If you use AutoCAD on a network for any length of time, you will see files with the extension .$AC appearing everywhere you store drawing files. This is because AutoCAD usually creates temporary files in the directory where the drawing file is stored. If AutoCAD terminates normally, with the END or QUIT command for example, it then removes the temporary files. If AutoCAD fails, due to a power failure or corrupt file, the temporary files are not removed.

Although the temporary files will not corrupt other drawing files or prevent anyone from working on drawings in a network directory, they do take up space. If you allow temporary files to be created where drawings are stored, you will eventually end up with a great deal of hard disk space dedicated to files of no use. Searching through these files and deleting them can become a time-consuming job for a system administrator.

You can configure AutoCAD to place temporary files in a directory on the local hard disk rather than on the file server. You can then add a command to the AUTOEXEC.BAT that deletes the files in this directory each time the computer powers up.

To configure AutoCAD to place temporary files in a specific directory:

1. Type **CONFIG** at the command prompt.
2. From the Configuration menu, choose **Operating Parameters.**
3. From the Operating Parameters menu, choose **Placement** of temporary files.
4. Enter the drive name and directory where AutoCAD should store temporary files.
5. Type **Enter** to exit the Operating Parameters menu.
6. Type **Enter** again to exit the Configuration menu.
7. Type **Y** to save your configuration changes, **N** if you want to discard them.

You may also want to configure AutoCAD to store its swap files on the local hard disk rather than on the file server. If you are running AutoCAD locally on each node, this is automatic. If you are running a network version of AutoCAD you must refer to the detailed instructions in the *AutoCAD Installation Guide* to learn how to tell the network version of AutoCAD to redirect swap files to local directories on each workstation.

Network Node Name

To make it easier to identify plot files located on the file server, you can give each workstation a network node name. This not only ensures that each plot file has a unique name, it also makes it easier to identify plot files when you need to remove one or more from a queue.

To assign each workstation a network node name:

1. Type **CONFIG** at the command prompt.
2. From the Configuration menu, choose **Operating Parameters.**
3. From the Operating Parameters menu, choose **Network Node Name.**
4. Enter a unique name for the workstation. Note that this name must be three or fewer characters.
5. Type **Enter** to exit the Operations Parameters menu.
6. Type **Enter** again to exit the Configuration menu.
7. Type **Y** to save your configuration changes, **N** if you want to discard them.

Sending Plot Files to a Network Plotter

You can configure AutoCAD to plot to a network plotter in a number of ways. In all cases, the objective is the same: to place a plot file in a network printer queue so that the network operating system can send the file to the plotter. Before attempting any of the procedures outlined here, make sure your network and your plotter work together.

1. Ensure that your plotter is correctly configured and attached to the file server per the directions of the plotter manufacturer. It is important to use the correct cable and to make sure the network addresses the device on the correct port.

2. Use your network operating system to create a printer queue that addresses the network plotter.

3. Configure AutoCAD to address the desired plotter and plot a drawing to a file.

4. Place the plot file in the network printer queue that addresses the network plotter device.

Don't try to configure AutoCAD to automatically address plot files to the network plotter until the four steps outlined result in plotted drawings. If you can't plot a file in the network queue, no change to the AutoCAD configuration will result in plotted drawings. After the printer queue and plotter are working together reliably, you can automate the process by which plot files are placed in the queue.

Redirecting Plot Files Sent to a Local Port

Most network operating systems are now capable of redirecting output sent to a local parallel or serial port to a network print queue. Although the steps required to configure the local workstation network software to perform this redirection vary, the effect is substantially the same. Any data directed at that port ends up in the network printer queue.

Redirecting output sent to a local port is a very simple way to place plot files in a network queue, but there are some environments that should not use this mechanism. If your workstations will run applications other than AutoCAD, and if those applications must address local output devices, or direct output to other network printer queues, this method may not work for you. Sending the wrong kind of data to a plotter or a printer can sometimes disable the output device. Fixing the problem may require you to power the output device on and off, or perhaps even reconfigure it. In an environment where output device assignments change throughout the day, you shouldn't be surprised if data meant for one output device ends up at your plotter. If you want to use port redirection to address network printer queues, you must ensure that each time the user launches AutoCAD or any other application, the correct port redirection statements are made. If you don't have to redirect your ports to more than one output device, you are unlikely to face this problem.

To configure AutoCAD to create plot files and direct them at a port:

1. Type **CONFIG** at the command prompt.
2. Type **5** to configure your plotter.
3. Type **1** to add a plotter configuration.
4. Enter the number identifying your plotter on the plotter list.
5. Specify the output port. You may enter any valid COM or LPT port.
6. Respond to any device-specific prompts.
7. Type **Enter** to exit the Configuration menu.
8. Type **Y** to save your configuration changes, **N** if you want to discard them.
9. Configure the network software on the local workstation to redirect output to that port to the network printer queue.

You must repeat this sequence of steps for all the CAD workstations on the network.

Plotting to a Network Print Spool Directory

If you have too many applications or too many peripherals to manage your network queues by redirecting output files, you may elect to make AutoCAD direct plot files to a spool directory on the network. This is an excellent alternative for system administrators who can't be sure that the output sent to a given parallel or serial port should always go to the plotter. The instructions that follow tell you how to configure AutoCAD and your system's environment variables to plot files in a spool directory.

Before you follow these instructions, first create a directory on the network to which all AutoCAD users have rights. In addition, find out which of your network operating system's commands allows you to place a file in a printer queue from the OS prompt.

To have AutoCAD direct plot files to a spool directory and add those files to the print queue:

1. Edit your AUTOEXEC.BAT or ACADR13.BAT file using any ASCII text editor.
2. Set the environment variable SET ACADPLCMD = to your plot command using the %s variable in place of the file name. For example, on a Novell NetWare installation, you might enter **SET**

ACADPLCMD = NPRINT %s. The s must be lowercase, because this character will be replaced with the name of the plot file inserted in the spool directory. (Note that the *AutoCAD Installation Guide* lists other plot variables in addition to %s. Refer to this manual if you need to be able to add the name of the plotter, the plot queue, the login name for the user, or other information to the SET ACADPLCMD.)

3. Save and exit your text editor.
4. Launch AutoCAD in your customary fashion.
5. Type **CONFIG** at the command prompt.
6. From the Configuration menu, choose **Operating Parameters.**
7. From the Operating Parameters menu, choose **Plot** spooler directory.
8. Enter the name of the plot spooler directory on the network.
9. From the Operating Parameters menu, choose **Default** plot file name.
10. Enter **AUTOSPOOL** to tell AutoCAD that you want to plot to a file and have the file automatically entered in the print queue for the plotter.
11. Type **Enter** to exit the Operations Parameters menu.
12. Type **Enter** again to exit the Configuration menu.
13. Type **Y** to save your configuration changes, **N** if you want to discard them.
14. Remember to select Plot to file, when you want to plot to the network plotter. You can make this the default option for the plotter by reconfiguring the plotter.

AutoCAD will only allow you to support one output device in this fashion because it only recognizes one plot spooler command, ACADPLCMD.

Project Management in a Networked Environment

As we mentioned earlier, establishing a CAD network that ties together members of your work group will not automatically solve management problems. In fact, there are many management problems that a CAD network will exacerbate. For example, if you commonly misplace drawings in your office, sometimes ending up with two versions of the same drawing, sometimes losing them altogether, a network will give you hundreds of places to hide drawings from yourself. You will have to search through directory after directory, user after user, project after project to find each missing scrap of electronic data.

On the other hand, a network can give system administrators some very important management tools. You can protect the work of multiple CAD users against loss with a single backup operation. You can use the directory structure and access restrictions to organize drawings by project, and you can allow your operators to share prototype drawings, menus and applications. In the following paragraphs we give you some suggestions that can help you get your CAD network working for you rather than against you.

Protecting Drawings and Associated Documents

Establish a methodology that ensures that the work of each member of the work group is protected against accidental loss or intentional destruction. First, purchase and install a backup system for your network. In most cases, this will mean buying and installing a tape drive. If you have very large quantities of drawings to keep track of, if the data is extremely important, and if you want to be able to keep the archive indefinitely, you should look into a Write Once Read Many (WORM) optical drive. A WORM drive can store hundreds of megabytes on a single CD, the data cannot be overwritten, and the disks aren't subject to failure due to the loss of a magnetic field.

Once you have a backup methodology in place and you have tested it to make sure it works reliably, back up regularly. Backup mechanisms only work if you use them. Test your backup mechanism by trying to restore a file from a tape. Just because you can see a directory structure or files listed on a tape doesn't mean the data is intact. Try to load a file from the tape or other backup mechanism once a month.

Organizing Drawings and Associated Data

In order for a network backup procedure to be of any use, members of your work group must put their drawing files and associated data on the network in an organized fashion. The structure of the directories and file names used on the network is usually the one found in the archive, which is to say the tape or CD-ROM. If it is difficult to find a drawing on your network for a current project, imagine how hard it will be in a year to find the same drawing stored on a CD-ROM or tape.

In general, system administrators elect to place drawings and associated files on the network by project. In some cases, when users work independently most of the time, drawings can be organized in user directories. However you elect to organize your network and its directory structure, you must make certain that members of the work group are following your organizational standards. This means that your standards should be easy to understand and automated whenever possible. If you want users to store drawings in project directories, for example, implement a batch file or application that asks them to name a project before they launch AutoCAD.

The most important thing you can do to implement an organizational strategy for your network is to make it easy for your work group to do things the right way. If changing projects requires a user to exit AutoCAD, or if a naming convention requires a user to walk all over the office looking for approvals, then your users will naturally avoid following these procedures. If it is easy to change projects or find out the correct name to assign a new drawing, you'll find members of your team willing to cooperate.

Security

Because all your drawing files may be located on a single file server instead of a number of machines throughout your company, you need to implement security. It is possible to lose a great deal of data through acts of sabotage or through errors by inexperienced employees. Your most important security procedure is the implementation of a systematic backup methodology.

Security in a networked environment begins with the security of the file server(s). It doesn't do much good to password protect your network if someone steals a file server. Furthermore, even if someone doesn't steal a file server, just having access to it is enough to allow an experienced user to break into a system. So, if you are concerned about unauthorized access or sabotage of your data files, control access to the file servers.

The next step in protecting your network against unauthorized access is to control the workstations connected to the network. Many network operating systems allow you to prevent users from logging into the network outside business hours. Most let you lock out a user who enters the wrong password three or more times.

Almost all network operating system have at least one *super* user; this user name, which is ROOT on UNIX workstations and SUPERVISOR on Novell networks, has unlimited control over the network. Usually, you can log in at any station as the super user as long as you know the password. If you want to enforce strict security measures, most network operating systems will allow you to insist that the super user log in at only one workstation in the network. This means that knowing the super user password will not be enough to gain control of the network.

Another important security protocol is to assign user names and passwords to your users. Users should be required to change their passwords once every few weeks, and they must not be able to use the company name, the names of family members, or their phone numbers. They should pick passwords that are hard to guess; preferably long passwords that will be difficult to follow when typed in.

A final important component to any security strategy is to give users only the rights they need to do their job. A designer may not need to have access to the directories where NC programs are kept, and an NC programmer may not need to have access to the directory where sales contracts or design drawings are stored. If users don't need to have access to a directory, they shouldn't be given that access. To make implementation of this strategy easy, most network operating systems allow you to create groups of users. You might have a group called Designers. Any member of that group will have rights to the subdirectories and project directories assigned to the Design department. By adding a user to the Designers group, you automatically give him or her the same rights you have assigned to the rest of that group.

CAD Management Applications

CAD management applications can perform a number of services for a system administrator. These applications, which can be found in the *AutoCAD Resource Guide*, usually allow administrators to track drawings and other documents as they move from design to production. They enforce security and naming procedures, and they can even track information that system administrators can use to measure the progress of a project.

An overview of the kinds of services a CAD management application can provide is outlined here. For information on contacting dealers or consultants who can help you find or install a CAD management application, refer to Chapter 9.

- CAD management applications usually keep track of the users who log in to the management application, the files they open, and the time they spend in those files. This information is usually recorded in a text file which you can import into a database or spreadsheet application.

- Many CAD management applications also enhance network security features by letting you control access to drawings by assigning drawings to projects. This lets you authorize a user to work on all the drawings associated with a project, while preventing him or her from having access to drawings in other projects.

- Some CAD management applications track not only CAD drawings, but other documents as well. If you want to store your bids, change orders, letters, NC code, and other applications along with your drawings, consider these applications.

In addition to CAD management applications that keep track of drawings and enforce naming standards and security procedures, you may want to investigate other management tools. Dedicated project management applications can help you create accurate time tables for projects based upon input from your work group. These applications will let you identify the critical paths for a project, can show you how a slip in one date will affect project completion, and will even generate standard management charts if desired.

Electronic mail lets members of a work group communicate throughout the design process. Some applications let you send mail to a group with a single command, and will notify you as each member opens the document. Most products let you send copies of an email message to one or more parties, and many applications come with versions that can operate over modem so you can get your email without leaving home. Many products let you attach other files, like CAD drawings or electronic spreadsheets, to email documents. Used correctly, electronic mail can dramatically reduce the number of meetings required by a design team during a project. Electronic mail is a particularly useful tool for managing consultants and employees working remotely.

Group scheduling software can help you schedule meetings and announce project timetables. You can set meeting dates, block out vacation time and indicate schedule conflicts in most applications. If you give some applications a list of employees and a last acceptable date, they will list potential meeting times that all members have in common. Most applications have alarms that remind you of a meeting a specified period of time before an appointment.

Although these tools will not solve all management problems, they can help a good manager get more done. These tools reduce overhead by automating many common management tasks. They don't reduce the need for planning or communication but they do reduce the time it takes to perform these functions.

Summary

As we noted earlier in this chapter, networking will not solve problems in a work group caused by poor management or inadequate resources. A network is a tool that improves communication and enforces protocols and procedures. Make sure that you understand exactly how a new network will solve your company's problems before you make such an investment. A poorly implemented network is far worse than no network at all.

Index

▲ Notes

▲ Notes

▲ Notes

▲ Notes

▲ Notes

▲ Notes

▲ Notes

▲ Notes